WORKFORCE READINESS AND THE FUTURE OF WORK

Workforce readiness is an issue that is of great national and societal importance. For the United States and other countries to thrive in a globally interconnected environment of wide-ranging opportunities and threats, the need to develop and maintain a skilled and adaptable workforce is critical. National investments in job training and schools remain essential in stimulating businesses and employment agencies to collaborate productively with educators who provide both training and vocational guidance.

Workforce Readiness and the Future of Work argues that the large-scale multi-faceted efforts required to ensure a reliable and strong supply of talent and skill in the U.S. workforce should be addressed systematically, simultaneously, and systemically across disciplines of thought and levels of analysis. In a four-part framework, the authors cover the major areas of

- education in the K–12, vocational, postsecondary, and STEM arenas;
- economic and labor market considerations;
- employment, organizations, and the world of work;
- laws, policies, and budgets at the federal, state, local, and military levels.

With contributions from leading scholars, this volume informs high-priority workforce effectiveness issues of current and future concern and concrete research, practice, and policy directions to generate novel insights of a multilevel and system-wide nature.

Frederick L. Oswald is Professor and Herbert S. Autrey Chair in Social Sciences in the Department of Psychological Sciences at Rice University. His expertise, research, and grants focus on measuring individual differences (ability, knowledge, motivation, personality, interests) in organizational, educational, and military settings. He is the past president (2017–2018) of the Society for Industrial and Organizational Psychology (SIOP), a member of the Board of Human Systems Integration (BOHSI) of the National Academy of Science (2015–2021), and a fellow of the American Psychological Association, Association for Psychological Science, and SIOP. See http://workforce.rice.edu.

Tara S. Behrend is Associate Professor in the Department of Organizational Sciences and Communication at The George Washington University. Her work addresses career decision-making in STEM disciplines, and technology-based recruiting, selection, training, and skills development in organizations. She is the editor of *The Industrial-Organizational Psychologist*, Senior Research Fellow for the Massachusetts Institute for College and Career Readiness, a psychometrician for the American Council on Education, and a 2016 Cyber Initiative Fellow at the Center for Advanced Study in the Behavioral Sciences (CASBS) at Stanford University. See http://wave-lab.org.

Lori L. Foster is Professor in the Department of Psychology at North Carolina State University and the School of Commerce at the University of Cape Town. She served as a fellow with the Obama White House's Social and Behavioral Sciences Team (SBST, 2014–2016), and as a behavioral science advisor to the United Nations (2016). In her academic role, she oversees the 4D Lab, focused on research at the intersection of work, psychology, technology, and development. In the private sector, she is the Head of Behavioral Science at pymetrics. She is a fellow of the American Psychological Association, Association for Psychological Science, and SIOP. See http://4dlab.org.

SIOP Organizational Frontiers Series

Series Editor
Richard Klimoski, *George Mason University*

Editorial Board
Neal M. Ashkanasy, *University of Queensland*
Jill Ellingson, *University of Kansas*
Ruth Kanfer, *Georgia Institute of Technology*
Eden King, *George Mason University*
Fred Oswald, *Rice University*
Stephen Zaccaro, *George Mason University*
Deborah Rupp, *Purdue University*
Mo Wang, *University of Florida*
Gilad Chen, *University of Maryland*

Ferris/Johnson/Sedikides *(2018) The Self at Work*

Ellingson/Noe *(2017) Autonomous Learning in the Workplace*

Ashkanasy/Bennett/Martinko *(2016) Understanding the High Performance Workplace: The Line Between Motivation and Abuse*

King/Tonidandel/Cortina *(2014) Big Data at Work: The Data Science Revolution and Organizational Psychology*

Finkelstein/Truxillo/Fraccaroli/Kanfer *(2014) Facing the Challenges of a Multi-Age Workforce: A Use-Inspired Approach*

Coovert/Foster Thompson *(2013) The Psychology of Workplace Technology*

Highhouse/Dalal/Salas *(2013) Judgment and Decision Making at Work*

Cortina/Landis *(2013) Modern Research Methods for the Study of Behavior in Organizations*

Olson-Buchanan/Koppes Bryan/Foster Thompson *(2013) Using Industrial Organizational Psychology for the Greater Good: Helping Those Who Help Others*

Eby/Allen *(2012) Personal Relationships: The Effect on Employee Attitudes, Behavior, and Well-being*

Goldman/Shapiro *(2012) The Psychology of Negotiations in the 21st Century Workplace: New Challenges and New Solutions*

Ferris/Treadway *(2012) Politics in Organizations: Theory and Research Considerations.*

Jones *(2011) Nepotism in Organizations*

WORKFORCE READINESS AND THE FUTURE OF WORK

Edited by Frederick L. Oswald,
Tara S. Behrend, and Lori L. Foster

Routledge
Taylor & Francis Group

NEW YORK AND LONDON

First published 2019
by Routledge
52 Vanderbilt Avenue, New York, NY 10017

and by Routledge
2 Park Square, Milton Park, Abingdon, Oxon, OX14 4RN

Routledge is an imprint of the Taylor & Francis Group, an informa business

Library of Congress Cataloging-in-Publication Data
A catalog record for this title has been requested

ISBN: 978-0-8153-8140-2 (hbk)
ISBN: 978-0-8153-8141-9 (pbk)
ISBN: 978-1-351-21048-5 (ebk)

Typeset in Bembo
by codeMantra

CONTENTS

FOREWORD

At the time of this writing, thoughtful people from many professions are wrestling with how we as a society can better prepare our citizens for the world of work of the future. The issues involved are daunting. At its core, the challenge is to first be able envision the direction and strength of those forces that shape the nature of work itself, including emerging technology, government policy, and business competitive practices. One must then go on to reflect on and better understand aspects of society that can, will, and should be used to shape the way we go about preparing both current and the next generation of workers to be successful. As such, this volume by Oswald, Behrend, and Foster provides a very useful framework both for understanding the likely future demand for human talent and for teasing out some of the answers on how best to link such demand to the talent pipeline. In doing this, the volume makes clear that any set of solutions offered should be able to achieve and promote what the volume calls "decent work." They make it clear that industrial and organizational psychologists are in a good position to contribute to productive discussions on the part of key stakeholders −company leaders, educators, policymakers, and those involved in providing services to government and commerce. We already know a lot about the nature of work, the forces shaping it, and even much more on how to effectively develop and nurture work-relevant capabilities. Toward this end, the editors have done a great job organizing their volume around the big themes of education, employment, technology, and policy. Moreover, the chapters will also be of special value to those who want to take on research initiatives related to any of the critical issues covered. To put it simply, this volume should be very useful to those who want to increase their capacity to shape creative solutions that serve to align the supply of human talent with future workplace demands.

PREFACE

Frederick L. Oswald, Tara S. Behrend, and Lori L. Foster

Whether you are deciding which movie to watch on a Friday night, or deciding on a consequential medical treatment with your doctor, life is (among other wonderful things) a series of small and large investment decisions on the basis of inherently uncertain assessments about risk and reward. In the stock market, such uncertainty is hedged by diversified portfolios, such as through index funds, which consistently tend to outperform even the savviest financial analysts. How might such an investment analogy apply to the world of work? What is the equivalent of a diversified portfolio for (a) the investments that have been made by employers (recruiting, selection, and management decisions made by large-scale organizations, nonprofits, locally owned independents) and (b) the investments made by jobseekers (e.g., the prior decisions to attend college and choose a college major; older students who have been lifelong learners and seek to change careers)? Hopefully, these investments are more or less coordinated in the supply and demand arena of the employment setting, where employers often hope to find the best talent, to the benefit of the organization and, cumulatively, to the national economy; and job applicants often seek work that satisfies multiple criteria, such as decent pay, meaningful work, opportunities for skill and career advancement, and on-the-job autonomy. Ultimately, in order to find reasonable if not excellent matches between work supply and work demand, employers and applicants alike must navigate the increasingly choppy and ever-changing waters of education, training, the labor market, and technology, as well as state, national, and international regulations. As you might know firsthand, this proves to be a very challenging and complex problem and process for all parties concerned.

In some cases, policies and programs are being created to encourage workforce entrants to build up a diverse portfolio of experiences, skills, and networks of people, so that over time, they can better search, identify, and take advantage of opportunities that arise in an ever-changing employment context. As described in Chapter 2 of this volume (Renninger & Hidi), researchers are also examining how best to support students' development of their work-related interests and engagement, so that they ultimately seek out jobs and workplaces that will deliver higher levels of productivity, satisfaction, meaning for them.

In addition to students, employers are another key piece of the network to policies and programs, given that employers need to be engaged in civic and educational communities in order to most effectively contribute, learn from, and adapt to them. It is important to remember that employers are jockeying to reconfigure, innovate, and compete with one another in terms of available workforce talent (Chapter 5, Guzzo), just as much as the members of the talent pool themselves are competing with one another. But there are a wide range of strategies and tactics to consider when doing so.

The types of student/employee and employer engagement described above are important forms of *workforce readiness*. Workforce readiness is a complex notion that spans multiple levels, ranging from national, state, and local economies; to employment and educational policy; to neighborhoods, families, and individuals. To describe workforce readiness and the four major areas of our book, we offer Figure 0.1 to suggest that there is a dynamic relationship between the (a) education and (b) employment domains, such that each domain informs and influences the other. Further, these domains and their relationships are shaped and, in some cases, governed by (c) policies enacted from the top down and (d) technologies that are used "in the trenches" as they are implemented (sometimes disruptively so) from the bottom up.

Although Figure 0.1 is quite simple, it implies that workforce readiness is clearly a broad, dynamic, and challenging problem for employers, employees, jobseekers, and students alike. Understanding and ultimately improving workforce readiness clearly requires multiple areas of expertise, such as those

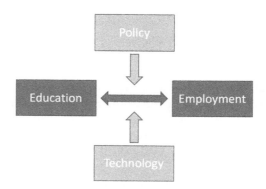

FIGURE 0.1 A Model of Workforce Readiness.

reflected by the authors and chapters of this book: for example, education, economics, federal policy, organizational psychology, veteran-to-civilian transitions, vocational psychology, and various forms of technological innovations that are relevant to all of the aforementioned domains. Indeed, this book was inspired by a multidisciplinary conference that we organized in June 2017, entitled "The Changing Workforce: Implications of Cyber Technologies," sponsored by the Stanford Cyber Initiative while one of the editors (Behrend) was on fellowship there. Many authors of this book participated in this conference, and they (like us) are excited about the opportunity to bring our complementary sets of expertise together. We are so grateful to the Cyber Initiative and to the Center for Advanced Study in the Behavioral Sciences (CASBS) for supporting this project.

As coeditors, we made deliberate attempts to ensure that the multidisciplinary volume on the topic that you currently hold in your hands would provide unique value to you. We explored and researched a wide range of relevant resources, for example, before developing the current book. For example, in terms of conferences, we identified Rice University's Humans, Machines, and the Future of Work Conference, held in December 2016, where you can still enjoy videos of the conference speakers at http://delange.rice.edu/conference_X/videos.html. In terms of websites, one can readily appreciate all the current and frequent data-driven reports being produced the Center on Education and the Workforce (CEW) at Georgetown University (see http://cew.georgetown.edu), as well as the Work Science Center at the Georgia Institute of Technology (see http://worksciencecenter.gatech.edu/). And in terms of books, one recent volume of relevance comes from a career and vocational counseling perspective: *The Handbook of Career and Workforce Development* (Solberg & Ali, 2017).

And in the media, hardly a day passes without a story on the nature and future of the workforce, in light of numerous ongoing economic and technological changes in the areas of employment and education. A case in point is found in the continuously expressed need for improving the quality, quantity, and equality in STEM (science, technology, engineering, and mathematics) education and the workforce (Chapter 4, Schneider & Young). As another example, the U.S. media have covered White House commitments, on the scale of tens of millions of dollars, to support factory jobs and industry-based apprenticeships that often struggle to find trained and qualified applicants (see https://www.dol.gov/apprenticeship/). Chapter 12 (Gaal) covers this important topic in further detail. And as a final more specific example, the *Harvard Business Review* highlighted the massive and critical need for AT&T's workforce of approximately 280,000 to self-manage their careers and constantly retrain themselves in light of constant changes in the technical demands of their jobs (Donovan & Benko, 2016). Many chapters of this book attempt to address the nature and impact of technologies as they affect education (Keevy et al., Chapter 13), the workforce (Lovric et al., Chapter 9; Akhtar et al., Chapter 10), and the economy (Holzer, Chapter 8).

Turning to the national and international setting, in 2015, the U.S. National Academy of Sciences commissioned a report on how child development, from birth to age eight, is a critical period for learning, health, and ultimately creating a vibrant workforce (see Institutes of Medicine & National Research Council, 2015, https://goo.gl/64msd9). Internationally, the World Bank has surveyed lower income working-age adults over four time periods of measurement, since 2011, to gauge the supply and demand of work-based skills: cognitive, socioemotional, and job-specific skills. These skills are in constant need for training and retaining over the adult lifespan, as one progresses through school (Chapter 3, Casillas et al.) and into the workforce (Chapter 11, Hilton). Understanding the nature—and changing nature—of occupations is a critical yet underresearched organizing perspective (Chapter 7, Dierdorff) for approaching both education and work in terms of the short- and long-term investments made by students and educators, and by employees and organizations.

As Douglass et al. point out in Chapter 1, the benefits of decent work extend far beyond the securement of a paycheck needed for survival. Psychological and societal benefits are also tied to work and workforce readiness. Throughout the development of this book, one of the editors (Foster) has been traveling extensively in the Middle East, Eastern Europe, and Africa, seeing firsthand the promise and potential of workforce readiness as well as the economic and social perils of talent shortages and underemployment. Throughout the world, large groups of people—including youth who are not in education, training, or employment—are getting left behind in today's changing world of work. Governments, nongovernmental organizations, international organizations, and corporations are stepping up their efforts to address this problem. For example, the United Nations Children's Fund (UNICEF) is working in partnership with the Government of Jordan, the International Labour Organization (ILO), civil society, and the private sector to connect disadvantaged youth to life skills training, volunteer opportunities, vocational training, and job mentoring. The idea is to equip young adults with the knowledge, skills, and experience needed to become more employable (https://www.youtube.com/watch?v=aIeMTXhbEs8). The United Nations Development Programme (UNDP) in Jordan has also put programs into place to support the employability and employment of marginalized youth and women in low-income communities—for example, by supporting those interested in starting a small business through skills and business development programs. Such programs are viewed as key to supporting sustainable livelihoods and also to countering terrorism and radicalization in a region threatened by violent extremism (http://www.jo.undp.org/content/jordan/en/home/projects/support-to-counter-terrorism--stabilization--and-counter--radica.html). A system-wide investment in skills development, identification, and translation efforts can result in large-scale individual and organizational benefits, whether it is internationally as described here, or in terms of U.S. military-to-civilian transitions as explained in Chapter 6 (Ainspan et al.).

In closing, we want to emphasize several points. First, investing in work-force readiness is essential for our future, in many key respects. The pursuit and engagement in meaningful and impactful work is critical to the prosperity and well-being of people, families, communities, and nations. When people lack the opportunity to engage in forms of education that ultimately develop themselves and the workforce, they may invest their time in other forms of be-haviors that are ultimately harmful to oneself and to society, out of desperation for other sources of psychological and financial support. Second, workforce readiness is a complex system of interdependencies and issues that are valuable to appreciate and address holistically. The current book benefits from the con-tributing authors' expertise in education, employment, technology, and policy. Third, in addressing these complexities, we strongly advocate that investments in the workforce and workplace can be very usefully informed by solid research designs, data based on those designs, and intelligent analyses that summarize those data and inform decision-making. This might be considered a scientific approach, requiring the expertise of academics from many disciplines, such as those represented in this book, collaborating with organizational, educa-tional, and government partners. Fourth, keeping all of all the previous points in mind, we recognize that we need optimists in the world in order to change it: Witness the many startup companies that develop workplace technologies, where with high risk and high optimism can come high reward—but hardly with guarantees. We also need pessimists in the world so that opportunity costs are minimized: To a pessimist, an investment in the new-and-improved future is too disruptive, too time-intensive, too risky, and too expensive. To a pes-simist, the immense investments of time and money startup companies might be better invested in incremental improvements to what is good-enough here-and-now. Optimists and pessimists are both wrong, and both right, in terms of how to invest in workforce readiness. We need them both in employment and educational circles, to create the sort of diversified portfolio of workforce readiness that we mentioned when opening up this chapter. Whether or not one decides to be an optimist or a pessimist in any given moment, we also urge all stakeholders not to shy away from being realists. Even knowing that there is no perfect approach to addressing or solving the complex problem of workforce readiness, anyone concerned about workforce readiness should nonetheless per-sist in the demand for good data that inform solid decision-making—assuming there is a real commitment to evaluating the workforce readiness goals that were pursued and promoted in the first place!

This book is a proud product of the diligent efforts of a collaborative team. We would like to thank all of the contributing authors, who were not only willing to share their expertise in their respective chapters; they spent time in sharing their chapters with one another prior to publication, to lend greater conceptual consistency to the book. We asked them to do something a lot different than the usual academic book chapter, in that they were tasked with speaking to a broad educated audience coming from many disciplinary backgrounds. Thanks to Christina Chronister at Taylor & Francis for her stalwart and expert support to move this book along from start to finish, with thanks to her colleagues as well, including Alex Howard and Kathryn Smale. Finally, big thanks to Rich Klimoski, Editor of the *SIOP Organizational Frontiers Book Series*, and his editorial board. Rich did not merely support our interest in developing the book; he then encouraged us to approach this project with greater creativity and possibility. We truly hope you enjoy the book and find it useful in your own thinking and work.

References

Donovan, J., & Benko, C. (2016, October). AT&T's talent overhaul: Can the firm really retrain hundreds of thousands of employees? *Harvard Business Review, 94*, 64–65.

Institute of Medicine and National Research Council. (2015). *Transforming the workforce for children birth through age 8: A unifying foundation.* Washington, DC: The National Academies Press.

Solberg, V. S. H., & Ali, S. R. (Eds.) (2017). *The handbook of career and workforce development: Research, practice, and policy.* New York, NY: Routledge.

CONTRIBUTORS

Nathan D. Ainspan, PhD, is a senior research psychologist in the Transition to Veterans Program Office at the U.S. Department of Defense (DoD). Throughout his 20-year research career, he has written, taught, and spoken about the psychological issues impacting transitioning service members, wounded service members, and the psychosocial benefits that employment can have on veterans and people with disabilities. He has edited four books in this arena. Nathan is an APA Fellow of Divisions 18 (Psychologists in the Public Service) and 19 (Military Psychology).

Reece Akhtar, PhD, is an organizational psychologist and analytics & innovation lead at RHR International, specializing in applied personality assessment and psychometrics. He uses novel sources of data and emerging technologies to create innovative executive assessment and development tools, and his main areas of research and consulting include talent analytics, digital signals of behavior, and organizational network analysis. He is a lecturer at University College London and New York University, and he has published scientific articles on personality and machine learning, talent management, and leadership.

Jamai Blivin is founder and CEO of Innovate+Educate, a nonprofit agency with an industry-led board, focused on education and workforce strategies to address the significant gaps between supply and demand in both education and workforce. Her work and expertise focus on the development and implementation of skills assessments that open up further employment pathways. Jamai serves on multiple national boards, including The Future at Work Coalition and the Urban Research Park Community Development Entity. She also sits on the City of Albuquerque Learning Council, City of Santa Fe Children's' Cabinet, and ACT State Leadership Board (New Mexico).

Abigail Carlton is a director of Social Impact at Indeed.com, where she leads Indeed's global efforts to help struggling job seekers overcome barriers and find quality jobs, harnessing our technology, data, expertise, and networks. She has worked to expand economic opportunity for low-income workers, families, and communities through 15+ years of professional and volunteer experience spanning the private and nonprofit sectors, government, and academia.

Alex Casillas, PhD, is a principal research psychologist in the Research Division of ACT, Inc., using design science and evidence-centered approaches to develop several behavioral assessments for predicting performance and persistence in both educational and workforce settings. One recent example is in leading a multidisciplinary research team in developing the ACT Holistic Framework, which articulates what effective behavior looks like from grades 3 through career. He has published dozens of articles and chapters in peer-reviewed outlets and has made presentations at national and international conferences.

Borhene Chakroun is the head of the section in charge of skills development at UNESCO-HQ. Borhene conducted a range of policy reviews and skills systems diagnosis in different contexts, and he has authored and coauthored various articles and books in the field of skills development. Much of his most recent work focuses on global trends in reforming skills and qualifications systems and global agenda for skills development in the context of the 2030 Sustainable Development Agenda.

Tomas Chamorro-Premuzic, PhD, is the Chief Talent Scientist at Manpower-Group, a Professor of Business Psychology at University College London and at Columbia University, and an associate at Harvard's Entrepreneurial Finance Lab.

Erich Dierdorff, PhD, is a professor of Management in the Driehaus College of Business at DePaul University. His work spans the broad areas of workforce strategy and human capital management, with research interests that include enhancing individual-level and team-level learning, as well as determining the most effective practices for work analysis, work design, work performance, and leadership effectiveness. In addition, he has contributed to numerous research efforts to examine, expand, and populate the U.S. Department of Labor's O★NET occupational database.

Richard P. Douglass, MS, is a 5th year counseling psychology doctoral student at the University of Florida. Currently, he is completing his doctoral internship at the University of Florida's Counseling and Wellness Center. His research examines how experiences of discrimination among marginalized groups are associated with vocational and well-being outcomes.

Ryan D. Duffy, PhD, is a professor of Counseling Psychology at the University of Florida. He is the author of over 100 journal articles and coauthored a book in 2012 entitled *Make Your Job a Calling*. He is currently an editorial board member on the *Journal of Counseling Psychology*, *Journal of Vocational Behavior*, and is editor of the *Journal of Career Assessment*.

Kemp Ellington, PhD, is an associate professor in the Department of Management of the Walker College of Business at Appalachian State University. His research interests include training and development and performance management, with particular interest in team training and multilevel influences on learning and behavior in the workplace.

Jessica W. England, MS, is a 4th year counseling psychology doctoral student at the University of Florida. Her research interests include exploring the impact of context and identity on career development and vocational outcomes.

John S. Gaal, EdD, is the Director of Training and Workforce Development for the St. Louis–Kansas City Carpenters Regional Council and Adjunct Professor at Webster University. As a labor representative, he currently serves on the St. Louis County Workforce Development Board, Missouri Workforce Development Board, International Foundation of Employee Benefit Plans' Board of Directors, and International Vocational Education and Training Association's Board of Directors (president-elect). Within the past decade, he completed terms of service on the U.S. DOL's Federal Advisory Committee on Apprenticeship, Association of Skilled and Technical Sciences' Board of Directors (president), and Association for Career and Technical Education's Board of Directors.

Nicholas P. Gensmer, BS, is a 2nd year counseling psychology doctoral at the University of Florida. His research interests focus on access to decent work for people of marginalized populations. He is also involved in research examining outcomes among a diverse array of minority populations in the realms of work, education, and calling.

Richard A. Guzzo, PhD, is a partner at Mercer, Inc. and co-leader of its Workforce Sciences Institute. His role includes practice and research. As a consultant, he provides data-based advice to for-profit and not-for-profit enterprises on a wide variety of issues, including strategic workforce planning. His current research interests include productivity and performance, workplace diversity, and social influences at work. He has published four books and dozens of articles and chapters. Prior to joining Mercer, he was Professor of Psychology at the University of Maryland (1989–97).

Suzanne E. Hidi, PhD, is an adjunct professor at the Ontario Institute for Studies in Education of the University of Toronto. Her early work focused on academic writing; this was followed by investigations of motivation in general and interest development in specific. Although her work has primarily focused on educational practice, she also considers the applications of these findings in the work place. Her current work addresses the integration of neuroscientific and psychological research in the area of human motivation, performance, and information search.

Margaret Hilton formerly served as a senior program officer of the National Academies of Sciences, Engineering, and Medicine. There, she worked with an expert committee to identify competencies needed for life and work in the 21st century along with educational approaches to develop those competencies. She facilitated another expert committee that identified competencies supporting success in higher education and examined how to assess those competencies. She received a Master of Regional Planning degree from the University of North Carolina at Chapel Hill and a Master of Education and Human Development from the George Washington University.

Harry J. Holzer, PhD, is the John McCourt SJ Professor of Public Policy at Georgetown, an institute fellow at the American Institutes for Research, and a senior fellow at Brookings. He is also a former chief economist at the U.S. Department of Labor and a professor of economics at Michigan State University. He received his Ph.D. in economics from Harvard University in 1983. His work focuses primarily on the low-wage labor market in the US, including topics such as labor market mismatch, employment difficulties of young and/ or less-educated men, welfare reform, affirmative action, community college programs for disadvantaged workers. and workforce development.

Ruth Kanfer, PhD, is Professor in the School of Psychology and Director of the Work Science Center (www.worksciencecenter.gatech.edu) at the Georgia Institute of Technology. She studies work motivation, engagement, and self-regulation in the context of skill learning, teams, job search, work transitions, and retirement. She has served on the National Academy of Sciences Science and Practice of Learning Committee that produced *How People Learn II.* Her current projects concern the effects of technology on work identity and engagement, future time perspective, and informal learning at work.

James Keevy is the Chief Executive Officer at JET Education Services, an independent public benefit organization located in Johannesburg, South Africa, founded in 1992. His responsibilities include working with government, the private sector, international development agencies, and educational institutions to improve the quality of education, as well as the relationship between education, skills development and the world of work. His diverse array of research regarding qualifications frameworks, the recognition of learning, and the professionalization, and migration of teachers has been published and presented internationally.

Lynne M. Kelley, PhD, is a personnel psychologist at the U.S. Navy 21st Century Sailor Office, where she is the leading research analyst, working to enhance research quality and provide insight for primary prevention initiatives and policy. As the former Chief of Evaluation and Assessment in the Transition to Veterans Program Office at the U.S. Department of Defense (DoD), she led two interagency working groups related to strategic planning and the assessment of military post-transition outcomes to enhance program evaluation and refinement for the DoD Transition Assistance Program.

Patrick C. Kyllonen, PhD, is a distinguished presidential appointee at Educational Testing Service (ETS). Patrick conducts innovative research involving college admissions and testing systems, workforce readiness assessment, international large-scale testing, and 21st century skills assessment (e.g., collaborative problem solving, situational judgment). He has been a frequent contributor of reports from the National Academy of Sciences, including the reports, *Education for Life and Work: Developing Transferable Knowledge and Skills in the 21st Century* (2012) and *Assessment of Intrapersonal and Interpersonal Competencies* (2017).

Darko Lovric is a principal with the consulting firm Incandescent, where he combines business and psychology to build bespoke execution strategies. He is particularly passionate about designing large-scale transformation efforts that lead to rapid and focused behavior change. Led by his belief that people problems are at the heart of many management challenges, Darko advises and partners with people analytics, psychology, and neuroscience ventures that can help shed light on how people think, act, and behave.

Mark McCoy is currently based in London where he is exploring the interactions between complex adaptive systems and human enterprise through applied research. Drawing on a blend of qualitative and quantitative approaches—from complexity science to adult developmental psychology—he supports leaders, startups, and institutions in the for-profit and nonprofit sectors in meaningfully engaging with complexity. Previously, Mark worked as a principal with the consulting firm Incandescent, with a primary focus on strategy development and execution for clients in the nonprofit sector.

Shanti Nayak is a principal with the consulting firm Incandescent. Her work is primarily focused on building strategies for systems change—ranging from the youth employment and workforce system, to the space of national service, to strengthening the capacity of the federal government. Her clients include philanthropic and nonprofit actors working as catalysts to effect change.

Karin A. Orvis, PhD, is the director of the Transition to Veterans Program Office at the U.S. Department of Defense (DoD). She has been instrumental in redesigning the DoD Transition Assistance Program, which ensures that service members are "career ready" and prepared to transition from military-to-civilian life upon separation from active duty. Her nearly 20 years of practitioner and scientific research experience spans the federal government, academia, and the private sector, with a focus on developing, implementing, and evaluating programs related to employee training, leader development, staffing, and organizational effectiveness.

Volker Rein, PhD, is working as senior research associate at the Federal Institute for Vocational Education and Training in Bonn, Germany. For a long time, he has been working on education and training systems in terms of policy, qualification transparency, and skills requirements in Germany, in Europe, and in the United States. In this field, his special focus in R&D is on the compatibility between occupational and academic education in terms of competence and proficiency. In this respect, he has carried out international in the United States and in Germany. He has published numerous articles on this topic, and he is member of several international education expert groups in the United States, in the EU and at UNESCO.

K. Ann, PhD, is the Dorwin P. Cartwright Professor of Social Theory and Social Action at Swarthmore College. She teaches in the Department of Educational Studies. Her research focuses on the development of interest, where interest is conceptualized and measured as both a psychological state and a motivational variable. Her research addresses the conditions that support interest to develop. Although her work has primarily focused on educational practice, she also addresses the applications of these findings in the work place.

Barbara Schneider, PhD, is the John A. Hannah Chair and University Distinguished Professor in the College of Education and Department of Sociology at Michigan State University. Her research focuses on understanding how the social contexts of schools and families influence the academic and social well-being of adolescents as they move into adulthood. She is a past president of the American Educational Research Association, and a fellow of the American Association for the Advancement of Science, National Academy of Education, American Educational Research Association, and the Finnish Academy of Science and Letters, one of its few international members.

Jason D. Way, PhD, is a senior research psychologist in the Center for Social, Emotional, and Academic Learning at ACT, Inc. in Iowa City, Iowa. He is the content owner of the ACT Behavioral Skills framework and the research lead for the ACT Engage family of assessments and the ACT Tessera Workforce assessment. His research interests are in the areas of personality and motivation and their relationships with academic and work criteria. He has published in outlets such as European Journal of Personality, Personality and Individual Differences, and Journal of College Student Retention, and has presented over 50 times at academic and professional conferences.

Dave Winsborough is the founder of Winsborough Limited and former Vice President of Innovation at Hogan Assessment Systems. Dave has particular expertise in modern methods of psychological measurement and profiles, talent management, leadership development, and high-performance teamwork. He conducts and publishes research in these areas, in addition to having published a recent book *Fusion: The psychology of teams* (2017).

Lindsey Young with multiple degrees in biology and education, is now working at Sparrow Hospital in Lansing, Michigan, as she prepares to apply to medical school. A recipient of multiple fellowships from Michigan State University and a contributor to Michigan Department of Education's M-STEP Science, her commitment to equity in health care and education remains a high priority.

1

THE PSYCHOLOGY OF WORKING AND WORKFORCE READINESS

How to Pursue Decent Work

Richard P. Douglass, Ryan D. Duffy, Jessica W. England, and Nicholas P. Gensmer

Traditional theories within vocational psychology have often prompted people to contemplate what types of jobs fit their personality and then attempt to secure such positions (e.g., Holland, 1959). Embedded in this approach is the idea that people can easily pursue any educational and occupational opportunities that match their desires. Unfortunately, most people are not able to freely choose the kinds of jobs they would like because of various reasons such as discrimination, economic constraints, and a lack of access to opportunities. Emerging frameworks within vocational psychology are beginning to acknowledge this issue by examining the factors that influence a person's choice of work. One such theory, the Psychology of Working Theory (PWT; Duffy, Blustein, Diemer, & Autin, 2016), attempts to reveal how people can pursue decent work, which is not necessarily work that a person is drawn to, but work that fulfills a person's basic needs and contributes to a greater sense of well-being. Duffy et al. contend that decent work is a fundamental right that should be available to all people. That is, people who want decent work should be able to attain it without first having to surmount numerous obstacles. This ideal is proposed to contribute not only to the well-being of individuals but also to the growth of society. This chapter explores the PWT and the central construct of decent work. In the following pages, we describe the concept of decent work, examine its antecedents and consequences, and, finally, explore the implications of the PWT and decent work for those either in the workforce or preparing to enter the workforce.

Conceptualizing Decent Work

Before discussing the implications and pursuit of decent work, we will first discuss what exactly comprises the construct. Building from the definition of decent work put forth by the International Labor Organization (ILO, 2008, 2012),

Duffy et al. (2016) conceptualize decent work as consisting of five unique factors: (a) access to adequate healthcare, (b) adequate compensation, (c) work hours that allow individuals to have free time and rest, (d) organizational values that are in line with personal and social values, and (e) work environments that promote interpersonal and physical safety. The presence of all five of these factors is thought to represent decent work, but it is possible to only experience some components. An employee, for example, may receive adequate health care and pay but work in an environment in which he or she feels unsafe. Another employee may also receive adequate compensation and health care while working in safe environment but not have time for rest. Although the examples above include some aspects of decent work, it may be helpful to consider what decent work looks like when all facets are present. Imagine going to a job every day where you felt safe interacting with colleagues and superiors; you feel able to voice any concerns you have. You work enough to make a fair wage with benefits that allow you to save for retirement and seek appropriate medical care. However, you don't feel overworked—you have enough time outside work to participate in hobbies and see family and friends. Lastly, you work somewhere that has the same value system as you, perhaps contributing a large amount of profits to charitable organizations. You may not necessarily love your job, but it helps you to satisfy your basic needs.

From this conceptualization, decent work concerns an employee's individual experience within the workforce. As such, Duffy et al. (2016) argued that it is ideal to measure decent work using both macro-level indicators (e.g., union density, unemployment ratios) and individual-level indicators (e.g., self-report measures). This view of decent work allows researchers to consider both the macro-level and contextual influences on individuals in the workforce. Regarding measurement, Duffy et al. (2017) developed the Decent Work Scale, which is a continuous measure designed to assess decent work among employed adults. This self-report measure can be used to help those currently in the workforce determine which aspects of decent work are present and provide an idea of what components might be missing. Example items of this measure include "I get good healthcare benefits from my job" and "I feel emotionally safe interacting with people at work." This measure, coupled with the presented conceptualization of decent work, suggests that it's best to not consider decent work as a dichotomy of "existing" or "not existing" but instead examine how decent a job might be. In this way, employees can assess the areas that are currently decent and evaluate how lacking areas might be improved.

What's So Good About Decent Work?

Although we have discussed what decent work is, we have yet to underscore why decent work matters. That's to say, what's so good about decent work? According to the PWT (Duffy et al., 2016), there's quite a bit of good to come from securing decent work in the way of satisfying one's needs and experiencing general and work-related well-being. For people preparing to enter the workforce—or those who are already employed—attaining decent work is an avenue through which individuals can experience a more fulfilling life, both in and out of the workplace.

Individual Benefits

The PWT theorizes that securing decent work is positively linked with satisfying survival needs, social connection needs, and self-determination needs. Satisfying these needs is then theorized to result in a greater sense of work fulfillment and overall well-being. It is through need satisfaction that decent work contributes to these positive outcomes. Survival needs are defined by having access to essential human needs such as food and shelter. Social connection needs are related to how an individual connects with society broadly. The need for social connection transcends the mere occurrence of interpersonal interactions at work and instead indicates positive and meaningful interactions within one's community and the feeling that they are contributing to society.

Regarding self-determination needs, one can turn to Self-Determination Theory (SDT; Ryan & Deci, 2000), which contrasts intrinsic with extrinsic motivation. Intrinsic motivation is an internal inclination toward exploration and mastery that is ignited by genuine personal interest and enjoyment. When an individual is intrinsically motivated toward a task, simply engaging in that task will be personally rewarding. Extrinsic motivation, on the other hand, involves completing a task chiefly for the achievement of some reward that is external to the task itself. For an individual who goes to work solely for a paycheck, the motivation to work is completely extrinsic. However, SDT outlines how extrinsically motivated work can still be self-fulfilling and more internally rewarding when certain needs are met, even if the work is not done out of pure personal enjoyment. These three psychological needs that encompass self-determination are feelings of autonomy, competence, and relatedness.

Autonomy refers to an individual's needs of flexibility and freedom at work. This does not imply complete independence or detachment from others at work, but rather a sense of choice and volition over one's actions in the workplace. Competence refers to an individual's perception that their skills are suited to job tasks. Feeling efficacious toward a task allows for greater internalization and feelings of mastery. Finally, relatedness is the feeling of being interpersonally connected with others. In the case of work, this includes not only a feeling of social belongingness but also a sense that one's work is seen as significant and valuable by others with whom that individual feels attachment toward (Ryan & Deci, 2000).

SDT classifies these three needs as basic psychological needs that are innate, essential, and universal to all people. When satisfied, self-determination needs contribute to a person's overall well-being by enhancing self-motivation and mental health. Insufficient fulfillment of these needs, however, is theorized to contribute to mental pathology and ill-being in the broader areas of one's life (Ryan & Deci, 2000). Thus, although some people may not necessarily find their work to be purely intrinsically fulfilling, one's job or career still offers a way to find meaning and purpose. Meeting self-determination needs in the workplace allows extrinsically motivated activities to be internalized and perceived as self-motivated, which is a profound benefit of decent work (Duffy et al., 2016).

Aside from resulting in greater need satisfaction, decent work is proposed to contribute to greater fulfillment at work and overall well-being. These domains are vast and encompass variables such as meaningful work, enjoyment of work, life satisfaction, and self-esteem (Duffy et al., 2016). The idea is that meeting basic survival needs, feeling connected with society, and experiencing self-determination at work pave the way for beneficial outcomes.

Other Benefits

Beyond benefits to individual employees, the widespread attainment of decent work has the potential to broadly impact communities and organizations. The adequate compensation and health care that is provided by decent work, for instance, can help to alleviate the negative effects of poverty and unemployment on the well-being of entire communities (Ali, 2013; Blustein, Kenny, Di Fabio, & Guichard, in press). In fact, when looking at high-conflict regions throughout the world, unemployment is often associated with civil unrest (ILO, 2018; Organization for Economic Co-operation and Development [OECD], 2015). In their review of the global expansion of decent work, Blustein et al. point to global economic development literature suggesting that work may help to foster a sense of security and meaning within individuals and societies (Bhawuk, Carr, Gloss, & Thompson, 2014; McWha-Hermann, Maynard, & O'Neill Berry, 2015). Also related to meaning, when individuals perceive their work to be meaningful—which is theorized to result from decent work—they are more likely to be engaged and productive at work, which is a major benefit to organizations (Grant, 2008). Thus, not only can decent work promote fulfillment and well-being, it can also create greater economic growth, leading to an increase in resources and creating more positions that meet the components of decent work (ILO, 2015). Better jobs provide more income to spend, which can be put into businesses, increasing the number of job positions available and raising pay and job conditions for employees. Further, through the increase in available job positions and the improvement of job conditions, providing decent work increases social equality and promotes social justice across *groups* of individuals.

In sum, the benefits of securing decent work extend beyond the individual and can impact society as a whole. Blustein et al. (in press) highlight the potential for scholarship surrounding decent work to inform social justice initiatives that help to improve the economic and psychological well-being for individuals *and* society. Although decent work is viewed as a human right by the ILO (2008), it is clear that providing employees with decent work can help to reduce community health and wealth disparities and promote economic growth.

The Psychology of Working Theory

Now that we've discussed what decent work is and why it's good, it's important to understand the factors influencing the process of securing decent work.

Past Theories

In an ideal world, a person would reflect on their personal preferences and pick a job that allowed them to enjoy their work while making a decent living. The two most popular theoretical models in the career development literature—Holland's Theory of Career Choice (Holland, 1959; Nauta, 2010) and Social Cognitive Career Theory (SCCT; Lent, Brown, & Hackett, 1994)—primarily focus on personal preferences as drivers of decision-making. In Holland's theory, the dominant focus is on the determination of an individual's interests in six main vocational domains (i.e., realistic, investigative, artistic, social, enterprising, and conventional) and how these interests match with a particular work environment, otherwise known as person-environment fit. The greater the fit, the more a person is thought to be satisfied with his or her work. SCCT extended Holland's theory by incorporating self-efficacy (an individual's performance beliefs around particular behaviors) and outcome expectations (beliefs about what will occur in the future, or outcomes, of performing behaviors) as key drivers in the development of interests, which ultimately are hypothesized to lead to choice goals and actions (Lent et al., 1994; Sheu et al., 2010). The SCCT does conceptually incorporate background contextual influences in its larger model, but this variable has received relatively little empirical research in comparison to self-efficacy, outcome expectations, and interests.

Research supporting each of these theories is robust, particularly as it relates to the role interests play in career choice selection (Nauta, 2010; Sheu et al., 2010). However, the vast majority of research on these theories has been conducted with college students, which is intuitive, because these theories concern predictors of choice, and students are a population where an array of career choices is available and highly salient. However, for the vast majority of adults, other factors apart from self-efficacy, outcome expectations, and interests play critical roles in their career trajectory. The PWT (Duffy et al., 2016) is focused on this population, individuals who do not come from high levels of privilege or status and are making career decisions in the real world (Blustein, 2006, 2013). As such, the PWT positions contextual factors related to economic and social issues as the primary drivers of securing decent work.

The Role of Context

According to the PWT, individuals are agents in their life and are also subject to a number of outside forces. From birth, individuals are agents in their life yet are also obviously subject to a number of outside forces. Within the PWT, two variables are considered to be key contextual influences on a person's life: experiences of marginalization and economic constraints. The PWT acknowledges that people experience marginalization for a variety of reasons, including but not limited to race, ethnicity, sexual orientation, gender identity, and ability status. In fact, people often experience multiple forms of marginalization based on the intersection of multiple non-majority identities (Cole, 2009). Additionally, people who experience frequent forms of marginalization are also inclined to experience economic constraints, or limitations surrounding economic resources. In tandem, these variables are theorized to directly impede an individual's pursuit of decent work through an overarching lack of access to opportunity.

The ways in which marginalization and economic constraints directly impact decent work can be seen across various marginalized groups within the United States. Racial and ethnic minorities, for example, still receive significantly fewer job callbacks when compared with White individuals (Quillian, Pager, Hexal, & Midtbøen, 2017). Specifically, Quillian et al. found that Whites currently field about 15% more callbacks compared with Latinas/os and 36% more callbacks than African Americans. Similarly related, over the past 18 years within the United States, African American men have experienced between 11% and 15% greater unemployment rates than White men (Hout, 2017). These disparities in relation to employment opportunities among racial and ethnic minorities in the United States are likely related to the long-standing elevated rates of poverty among this group in comparison to White Americans (Burton, Mattingly, Pedroza, & Welsh, 2017). Disparities in employment have translated to disparities in median accumulated family wealth in the United States as well, as African American and Hispanic families have been found to have only eight and ten cents of wealth, respectively, per one dollar of wealth among White families (Shapiro, 2017). Although this research only speaks to the trends and experiences of racial and ethnic minorities within the United States, it is demonstrative of the concomitant effects that marginalization and economic constraints can have on the pursuit of decent work among traditionally marginalized people.

Indirect Effects on Decent Work

In addition to the direct negative influences that marginalization and economic constraints have on the attainment of decent work, they are also proposed to have indirect influences through the mediating variables of work volition and career adaptability. What this suggests is that marginalization and economic constraints result in lower work volition and career adaptability, which in turn hinders the pursuit of decent work. Duffy, Diemer, Perry, Laurenzi, and Torrey (2012) defined work volition as a person's perceived capacity to make occupational choices despite constraints, and career adaptability regards the resources a person possesses to cope with the frequently changing tasks related to vocational development (Savickas, 2002). Both work volition and career adaptability are considered to be malleable constructs that are shaped by the events within a person's life. Thus, within the PWT, experiences of marginalization and economic constraints are theorized to contribute to individuals feeling less able to make occupational choices and less adaptable to the world of work, which ultimately constrains access to decent work. Indeed, numerous studies have documented the positive roles of work volition and career adaptability among students and adults in relation to positive vocational outcomes (Douglass & Duffy, 2015; Duffy, Autin, & Douglass, 2016; Duffy, England, Douglass, Autin, & Allan, 2017). Additionally, preliminary research operating from the PWT framework has been mostly consistent with these theorized associations, finding that greater marginalization and economic constraints are directly—and indirectly as a result of work volition—related to a reduced capacity to secure decent work (Douglass, Velez, Conlin, Duffy, & England, 2017; Duffy, et al., in press). These findings have been seen among samples of employed LGB people and racial and ethnic minorities. Regarding longitudinal research, two independent studies over the course of six months provided support for the causal chain between economic constraints, work volition, and career adaptability among students and adults (Autin, Douglass, Duffy, England, & Allan, 2017; Duffy, Autin, England, Douglass, & Gensmer, 2018). Although research in this area is still in its infancy, these findings provide general support for the pursuit of decent work as outlined by the PWT.

When considering these definitions, it's easy to see how attaining decent work may be difficult for some individuals. Imagine attempting to enter the workforce as a person from an underrepresented group with limited economic resources. Despite your best efforts to secure work that provides you with adequate compensation, fair working conditions, and values that align with your own, you are prevented from success by experiences of marginalization and limited economic resources. This contributes to feeling less adaptable and lowers your overall sense of choice. Eventually, you're forced to engage in precarious work, which is defined as a job that is part-time, provides no promise of future employment, and is often low-paying (Standing, 2010). This type of employment may prevent you from fully satisfying your needs, which inhibits your overall sense of fulfillment and well-being.

Although the PWT doesn't contend that the above example occurs for every employee or jobseeker with some form of constraints, it is a reality that many face (Blustein et al., in press; Burton et al., 2017; Hout, 2017; Peterson, Snipp, & Cheung, 2017; Quillian et al., 2017). However, Duffy and colleagues highlighted four factors that may buffer against the negative effects of marginalization and economic constraints. The first factor is having a proactive personality, or the feeling that one can be an active agent within their environment. People with proactive personalities feel that they can create change around them, and they thus engage in the world rather than withdraw from it. Second, social support may help people overcome adversity experienced in their pursuit of decent work. Such support may come in the form of emotional support and material resources through friends, family, or significant others in life. Third is critical consciousness, which regards an individual's reflection of inequalities within society and is typically accompanied by action to affect such inequalities. Lastly, beyond the individual level, economic conditions—in the form of macro-level conditions such as unemployment rate and access to training—may influence the pursuit of decent work. Overall, individuals preparing to enter the workforce that have greater levels of proactive personality, social support, critical consciousness, and favorable economic conditions may be more able to secure decent work. The entirety of the PWT model discussed within this chapter can be seen in Figure 1.1.

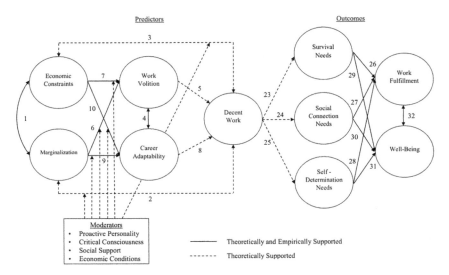

FIGURE 1.1 Theoretical model of the Psychology of Working Theory. From Duffy et al. (2016). American Psychological Association. Reprinted with permission.

Pursuing Decent Work

The last section of this chapter is concerned with strategies that may promote the attainment of decent work. We have discussed predictors and outcomes of decent work, but it is important to examine how individuals preparing to enter the workforce may attain decent work as well as individuals who may be looking to change career paths. Although the pursuit of decent work is a complex process with a host of influential factors, we will attempt to analyze approaches that can help to maximize the chances of finding and securing decent work.

Individual Concerns

At the individual level, it may be helpful to envision what decent work looks like based on one's circumstances. Although decent work is comprised of the same five components for all individuals, specific circumstances are going to shape what qualifies as decent work. Recall that the five components of decent work are adequate pay, proper health care, time for rest, safe working conditions, and organizational values that match individual values. Fulfilling these components will look different based on individual needs. For example, it is possible that individuals who are working to financially support a family may value adequate pay and healthcare benefits more than healthy individuals who only support themselves and may conceptualize decent work in their situation as having higher pay and better healthcare benefits. Further, individuals who prioritize work–life balance may put more value in securing work hours that allow for free time and rest as well as finding a workplace with organizational values that align with their personal and social values. It is crucial to consider the unique needs individuals have depending on their life circumstances, as well as what they may need to prioritize in order to attain decent work. Thus, prior to entering the workforce, people may benefit from asking questions such as "How much do I need to be compensated to meet my needs?" and "What values are important to me?" Such questions highlight the individual needs that must be considered. Adequate compensation in the form of salary, medical benefits, and paid time off will be different for a late-20s single woman when compared with a 39-year-old married woman with two children expecting a third child. Similarly, it may be difficult for some individuals to work at an organization that has a conservative political agenda that contrast with their personal beliefs. By asking such questions before beginning to search for a job, jobseekers can better gauge where they may experience decent work and better prepare for what to ask hiring committees when they are negotiating for potential positions. Similarly, those who are already in an employment position can evaluate their current job conditions and take the steps necessary in order to secure decent work. One way to go about doing this would be to use the Decent Work Scale self-report measure developed by Duffy, Allan, and colleagues (2017) referenced earlier in the chapter. Having the knowledge of what constitutes decent work based on individual needs is vital to securing decent conditions as we pursue work.

In addition to evaluating how individual needs and life circumstances may impact the pursuit of decent work, Duffy et al. (2016) put forth specific factors that might improve opportunities for attaining decent work even in the face of adversity. First, having proactive personality characteristics may also be critical in finding decent work. Personality characteristics have consistently been linked to positive work outcomes (e.g., Rottinghaus & Miller, 2013), and proactive personality characteristics in particular appear more malleable compared to other personality constructs. Having proactive personality characteristics, or tending to make decisions and act to change your life circumstances (Li, Liang, & Crant, 2010), has been associated with greater proactive actions at the workplace and higher work motivation (Fuller & Marler, 2008) as well as increased job search motivation and behaviors in individuals who are unemployed (Brown, Cober, Kane, Levy, & Shalhoop, 2006; Zacher, 2013). Further, proactive personality characteristics have been found to correlate with greater organizational citizenship, work engagement, increased subjective and objective career success, job performance, and overall well-being (Bakker, Tims, & Derks, 2012; Fuller & Marler, 2008; Li et al., 2010). It is also important to note that proactive personality characteristics have been associated with job crafting behaviors, in which individuals actively work to modify their jobs through changes in work tasks, content, relationships, and assigned meanings to aspects of their work (Berg, Wrzesniewski, & Dutton, 2010; Parker & Ohly, 2008; Wrzesniewski & Dutton, 2001). Through job crafting, individuals can increase their job resources (i.e., structural and relational) and job challenges, which in turn increases work engagement and performance (Bakker et al., 2012). Importantly, this ability to modify one's environment may be especially influential in individuals who have less resources, opportunity, and choice in their pursuit of decent work. Taking the initiative to change your work environment seems to be important in improving job conditions, work motivation and engagement, success and performance, and overall well-being.

Another useful strategy when preparing to enter the workforce is to cultivate a sense of critical consciousness. This often involves engaging in a critical reflection of any social inequalities that may be impacting individuals' lives and can also include taking actions to help remedy these issues (Freire, 1993). In this sense, an individual may reflect on the potential obstacles that they may encounter while pursuing decent work. Further, through this critical reflection, individuals can brainstorm and problem-solve how they may strive to overcome these obstacles and achieve their vocational goals. This is especially impactful in oppressed groups of individuals who may be forced to overcome barriers that other majority groups do not encounter, such as stigma, prejudice, and discrimination. Other factors that may occur at the macro level are policy considerations, such as visa restrictions or a lack of antidiscrimination laws (macro-level concerns will be further discussed below). Critical consciousness has been consistently correlated with positive developmental outcomes in adolescents who have experienced marginalization and has been found to increase agency by lessening the harmful effects of marginalization and economic constraints on individuals' career development (e.g., Diemer & Blustein, 2006). Longitudinally, higher vocational expectations as well as securing employment that has higher pay and higher status in adulthood have been shown to result from higher critical consciousness in marginalized adolescents over a period of 10 years (Diemer, 2009). By understanding how outside influences may affect the job search process, individuals may also be less likely to experience a diminished sense of work volition and career adaptability, which are both important explanatory variables in the connection between experiences of marginalization and economic constraints and attaining decent work (Duffy et al., 2016). Ideally, an individual would be able to engage in this exploration individually as well as with the help of members within their social support network. Having family or friends that can provide a sense of encouragement and support throughout the job search process may also help to reduce the effects of potential barriers.

Of importance, social support acts as another central variable in the attainment of decent work. Relationships help contribute to our knowledge about careers and aid in our problem-solving surrounding career development while also acting as a support throughout the process (Blustein, 2011). Social support from friends and peers, family members or significant others, and other community members is important in helping individuals to cope with and move on from the stress and trauma associated with vocational experiences, predicting academic and career success (Lent, Brown, & Hackett, 1994). Further, support associated with career contexts is also important and is associated with greater self-efficacy (Wright, Perrone-McGovern, Boo, & White, 2014), outcome expectations (Lent et al., 2015), and lower perceived career obstacles (Raque-Bogdan, Klingaman, Martin, & Lucas, 2013). Across several different marginalized populations (e.g., Fisher, Gushue, & Cerrone, 2011; Garriott, Flores, & Martens, 2013; Navarro, Flores, Lee, & Gonzalez, 2014), social support has consistently predicted beneficial outcomes in academic achievement as well as work outcomes. Increasing the social support that individuals experience at home as well as in work contexts can provide the guidance and support needed to succeed in securing decent work.

Macro-level Concerns

It is also necessary to acknowledge that the events that occur during the process of seeking decent work are not always controllable by the jobseeker. Developing the aforementioned pieces in this last section is not the only step—several influences at the macro level will affect the ability to secure decent work. Economic conditions, including the unemployment rate, minimum wage, and training and promotional opportunities (ILO, 2008, 2012), may inhibit the job opportunities that are available in any given area. Although individuals can attempt to track job trends and unemployment rates within their area, it may be necessary to relocate in order to find decent work. Another macro-level factor relates to the employment laws in place in a given area. Certain marginalized groups, such as gender and sexual minorities, may find that they live in a region where they are not afforded state- or federal-level employment protections. Working in such regions may make securing decent work—particularly the component related to interpersonally and physically safe working environments—more difficult for those entering the workforce. Conversely, some areas may consist of businesses that utilize affirmative action hiring practices, which places a specific emphasis on recruiting and retaining employees from underrepresented groups. By considering such factors—which are often beyond individual control—people can maximize their chances of finding decent work.

Of note, the burden of pursuing decent work must not fall solely on individuals, especially when considering the presented macro-level concerns. Scientists and politicians must help to advocate for socially just policies and laws that might be currently restricting access to decent work among minority groups. Additionally, organizations must be providing decent work in order for people to attain it. As highlighted earlier in this chapter, organizations—at least within the United States—still appear to evidence discrimination at the hiring level. Organizational leaders and hiring managers must be informed of potential implicit and explicit biases that may influence hiring strategies and develop tactics for ensuring the equal consideration of all candidates (Dobbin, 2009). Similar to the job crafting strategies discussed as it applies to individual employees, employers can implement their own take on crafting, encouraging employees to take a more autonomous and proactive approach to their work. Such approaches are likely to also help employees feel more supported within their work environments. It is our hopes that a combination of these strategies employed at both the individual and systems level can help individuals in their pursuit of decent work. We believe this aspirational standard for all employment will help to create more secure and beneficial lives for individuals and society.

References

Ali, S. R. (2013). Poverty, social class, and working. In D. L. Blustein (Ed.), *The Oxford handbook of the psychology of working* (pp. 127–140). New York, NY: Oxford University Press. doi:10.1093/oxfordhb/9780199758791.001.0001

Autin, K. L., Douglass, R. P., Duffy, R. D., England, J. W., & Allan, B. A. (2017). Subjective social status, work volition, and career adaptability: A longitudinal study. *Journal of Vocational Behavior, 99*, 1–10. doi:10.1016/j.jvb.2016.11.007

Bakker, A. B., Tims, M., & Derks, D. (2012). Proactive personality and job performance: The role of job crafting and work engagement. *Human Relations, 65,* 1359–1378. doi:10.1177/0018726712453471

Berg, J. M., Wrzesniewski, A., & Dutton, J. E. (2010). Perceiving and responding to challenges in job crafting at different ranks: When proactivity requires adaptivity. *Journal of Organizational Behavior, 31,* 158–186. doi:10.1002/job.645

Bhawuk, D. P., Carr, S. C., Gloss, A. E., & Thompson, L. F. (2014). Poverty reduction through positive work cycles: Exploring the role of information about work, culture and diversity, and organizational justice. In United Nations Development Programme (UNDP) (Ed.), *Barriers to and opportunities for poverty reduction: Prospects for private sector-led interventions* (pp. 63–94). Istanbul, Turkey: Istanbul Centre for Private Sector in Development.

Blustein, D. L. (2006). *The psychology of working: A new perspective for career development, counseling, and public policy.* New York, NY: Routledge.

Blustein, D. L. (2011). A relational theory of working. *Journal of Vocational Behavior, 79,* 1–17. doi:10.1016/j.jvb.2010.10.004

Blustein, D. L. (2013). The psychology of working: A new perspective for a new era. In D. L. Blustein (Ed.), *Oxford handbooks online.* Retrieved from http://www.oxfordhand books.com/view/http://dx.doi.org/10.1093/oxfordhb /9780199758791.001.0001/ xfordhb-9780199758791-e-001

Blustein, D. L., Kenny, M. E., Di Fabio, A., & Guichard, J. (in press). Expanding the impact of the psychology of working: Engaging psychology in the struggle for decent work and human rights. *Journal of Career Assessment.* doi:10.1177/1069072718 774002

Brown, D. J., Cober, R. T., Kane, K., Levy, P. E., & Shalhoop, J. (2006). Proactive personality and the successful job search: A field investigation with college graduates. *Journal of Applied Psychology, 91,* 717–726. doi:10.1037/0021-9010.91.3.717

Burton, L. M., Mattingly, M., Pedroza, J., & Welsh, W. (2017). Poverty. State of the union: The poverty and inequality report (Stanford Center on Poverty and Inequality, Palo Alto, CA), special issue, *Pathways Magazine.*

Cole, E. R. (2009). Intersectionality and research in psychology. *American Psychologist, 64,* 170–180. doi:10.1037/a0014564

Diemer, M. A. (2009). Pathways to occupational attainment among poor youth of color: The role of sociopolitical development. *The Counseling Psychologist, 37,* 6–35. doi:10.1177/0011000007309858

Diemer, M. A., & Blustein, D. L. (2006). Critical consciousness and career development among urban youth. *Journal of Vocational Behavior, 68,* 220–232. doi:10.1016/j. jvb.2005.07.001

Dobbin, F. (2009). *Inventing equal opportunity.* Princeton, NJ: Princeton University Press.

Douglass, R. P., & Duffy, R. D. (2015). Calling and career adaptability among undergraduate students. *Journal of Vocational Behavior, 86,* 58–65. doi:10.1016/j. jvb.2014.11.003

Douglass, R. P., Velez, B. L., Conlin, S. E., Duffy, R. D., & England, J. W. (2017). Examining the Psychology of Working Theory: Decent work among sexual minorities. *Journal of Counseling Psychology, 64,* 550–559. doi:10.1037/cou0000212

Duffy, R. D., Allan, B. A., England, J. W., Blustein, D. L., Autin, K. L., Douglass, R. P., ... Santos, E. J. R. (2017). The development and initial validation of the Decent Work Scale. *Journal of Counseling Psychology, 64,* 206–221. doi:10.1037/cou0000191

Duffy, R. D., Autin, K. L., & Douglass, R. P. (2016). Examining how aspects of vocational privilege relate to living a calling. *Journal of Positive Psychology, 11,* 416–427. doi:10.1080/17439760.2015.1092570

Duffy, R. D., Autin, K. L., England, J. W., Douglass, R. P., & Gensmer, N. (2018). Examining the effects of contextual variables on living a calling over time. *Journal of Vocational Behavior.* doi:10.1016/j.jvb.2018.04.003

Duffy, R. D., Blustein, D. L., Diemer, M. A., & Autin, K. L. (2016). The psychology of working theory. *Journal of Counseling Psychology, 63,* 127–148. doi:10.1037/0003–066X.55.1.34

Duffy, R. D., Diemer, M. A., Perry, J. C., Laurenzi, C., & Torrey, C. L. (2012). The construction and initial validation of the Work Volition Scale. *Journal of Vocational Behavior, 80,* 400–411. doi:10.1016/j.jvb.2011.04.002

Duffy, R. D., England, J. W., Douglass, R. P., Autin, K. A., & Allan, B. A. (2017). Perceiving a calling and well-being: Motivation and access to opportunity as moderators. *Journal of Vocational Behavior, 98,* 127–137. doi:10.1016/j.jvb.2016.11.003

Duffy, R. D., Velez, B. L., England, J. W., Autin, K. L., Douglass, R. P., Allan, B. A., & Blustein, D. L. (in press). An examination of the Psychology of Working Theory with racially and ethnically diverse employed adults. *Journal of Counseling Psychology.*

Fisher, L. D., Gushue, G. V., & Cerrone, M. T. (2011). The influences of career support and sexual identity on sexual minority women's career aspirations. *The Career Development Quarterly, 59,* 441–454. doi:10.1002/j.2161-0045.2011.tb00970.x

Freire, P. (1993). *Pedagogy of the oppressed.* New York, NY: Continuum.

Fuller, J. B., & Marler, L. E. (2008, August). *Change-driven by nature: A meta-analytic review of the proactive personality literature.* Paper presented at the meeting of the Academy of Management, Anaheim, CA.

Garriott, P. O., Flores, L. Y., & Martens, M. P. (2013). Predicting the math/science career goals of low-income prospective first-generation college students. *Journal of Counseling Psychology, 60,* 200–209. doi:10.1037/a0032074

Grant, A. M. (2008). The significance of task significance: Job performance effects, relational mechanisms, and boundary conditions. *Journal of Applied Psychology, 93,* 108–124. doi:10.1037/0021-9010.93.1.108

Holland, J. L. (1959). A theory of vocational choice. *Journal of Counseling Psychology, 6,* 35–45. doi:10.1037/h0040767

Hout, M. (2017). Employment. State of the union: The poverty and inequality report (Stanford Center on Poverty and Inequality, Palo Alto, CA), *Pathways Magazine* [special issue].

International Labor Organization. (2008). *Work of work report 2008: Income inequalities in the age of financial globalization.* Retrieved from http://www.ilo.org/wcmsp5/groups/public /@dgreports/@dcomm/@publ/documents/publication/wcms_100354.pdf

International Labor Organization. (2012). *Decent work indicators: Concepts and definitions.* Retrieved from http://www.ilo.org/wcmsp5/groups/public/---dgreports/--integration /documents/publication/wcms_229374.pdf

International Labor Organization. (2015). *Decent work and the 2030 Agenda for sustainable development.* Retrieved from http://www.ilo.org/wcmsp5/groups/public/---dgreports/---dcomm/documents/publication/wcms_436923.pdf

International Labor Organization. (2018). *World employment social outlook: Trends 2018.* Geneva, Switzerland: International Labor Office.

Lent, R. W., Brown, S. D., & Hackett, G. (1994). Toward a unifying social cognitive theory of career and academic interest, choice, and performance. *Journal of Vocational Behavior, 45,* 79–122. doi:10.1006/jvbe.1994.1027

Lent, R. W., Miller, M. J., Smith, P. E., Watford, B. A., Hui, K., & Lim, R. H. (2015). Social cognitive model of adjustment to engineering majors: Longitudinal test across gender and race/ethnicity. *Journal of Vocational Behavior, 86,* 77–85. doi:10.1016/j.jvb.2014.11.004

Li, N., Liang, J., & Crant, J. M. (2010). The role of proactive personality in job satisfaction and organizational citizenship behavior: A relational perspective. *Journal of Applied Psychology, 95,* 395–404. doi:10.1037/a0018079

McWha-Hermann, I., Maynard, D. C., & O'Neill Berry, M. (Eds.) (2015). *Humanitarian work psychology and the Global Development Agenda: Case studies and interventions.* New York, NY: Routledge. doi:10.4324/9781315682419

Nauta, M. M. (2010). The development, evolution, and status of Holland's theory of vocational personalities: Reflections and future directions for counseling psychology. *Journal of Counseling Psychology, 57,* 11–22. doi:10.1037/a0018213

Navarro, R. L., Flores, L. Y., Lee, H. S., & Gonzalez, R. (2014). Testing a longitudinal social cognitive model of intended persistence with engineering students across gender and race/ethnicity. *Journal of Vocational Behavior, 85,* 146–155. doi:10.1016/j.jvb.2014.05.007

Organization for Economic Co-operation and Development [OECD]. (2015). *Securing livelihoods for all: Foresight for action. Development Centre Studies.* Paris, France: Author. doi:10.1787/9789264231894-en

Parker, S. K., & Ohly, S. (2008). Designing motivating jobs. In R. Kanfer, G. Chen, & R. D. Pritchard (Eds.), *Work motivation: Past, present, and future* (pp. 105–131). New York, NY: Routledge.

Peterson, C., Snipp, M. C., & Cheung, S. Y. (2017). Earnings. State of the union: The poverty and inequality report (Stanford Center on Poverty and Inequality, Palo Alto, CA), *Pathways Magazine* [special issue].

Quillian, L., Pager, D., Hexel, O., & Midtbøen, A. H. (2017). Meta-analysis of field experiments shows no change in racial discrimination in hiring over time. *Proceedings of the National Academy of Sciences of the United States of America, 114,* 10870–10875. doi:10.1073/pnas.1706255114

Raque-Bogdan, T. L., Klingaman, E. A., Martin, H. M., & Lucas, M. S. (2013). Career-related parent support and career barriers: An investigation of contextual variables. *The Career Development Quarterly, 61,* 339–353. doi:10.1002/j.2161-0045.2013.00060.x

Rottinghaus, P. J., & Miller, A. D. (2013). Convergence of personality frameworks within vocational psychology. In W. B. Walsh, M. L. Savickas, & P. J. Hartung (Eds.), *Handbook of vocational psychology* (4th ed., pp. 105–131). New York, NY: Routledge Press.

Ryan, R. M., & Deci, E. L. (2000). Self-determination theory and the facilitation of intrinsic motivation, social development, and well-being. *American Psychologist, 55,* 68–78. doi:10.1037/0003-066X.55.1.68

Savickas, M. L. (2002). Career construction: A developmental theory of vocational behavior. In D. Brown & Associates (Eds.), *Career choice and development* (4th ed., pp. 149–205). San Francisco, CA: Jossey Bass.

Shapiro, T. (2017). Wealth. State of the union: The poverty and inequality report (Stanford Center on Poverty and Inequality, Palo Alto, CA), *Pathways Magazine* [special issue].

Sheu, H.-B., Lent, R. W., Brown, S. D., Miller, M. J., Hennessy, K. D., & Duffy, R. D. (2010). Testing the choice model of social cognitive career theory across Holland themes: A meta-analytic path analysis. *Journal of Vocational Behavior, 76,* 252–264. doi:10.1016/j.jvb.2009.10.015

Standing, G. (2010). *Work after globalization: Building occupational citizenship.* Cheltenham, UK: Edward Elgar.

Wright, S. L., Perrone-McGovern, K. M., Boo, J. N., & White, A. V. (2014). Influential factors in academic and career self-efficacy: Attachment, supports, and career barriers. *Journal of Counseling and Development, 92,* 36–46. doi:10.1002/j.1556-6676.2014.00128.x

Wrzesniewski, A., & Dutton, J. E. (2001). Crafting a job: Revisioning employees as active crafters of their work. *Academy of Management Review, 26,* 179–201. doi:10.5465/amr.2001.4378011

Zacher, H. (2013). Older job seekers' job search intensity: The interplay of proactive personality, age and occupational future time perspective. *Ageing & Society, 33,* 1139–1166. doi:10.1017/S0144686X12000451

PART I
Education

2

SUPPORTING THE DEVELOPMENT OF INTEREST IN THE WORKPLACE

K. Ann and Suzanne E. Hidi

Work is an omnipresent factor in most people's lives, so it is reasonable to ask why do people remain in their jobs? Research on motivation and learning indicates that people stay in all types of jobs when they find meaning and reward in what they are doing. According to Kaye, Jordan-Evans, and Career Systems International (2014), with one possible exception, the six "stay factors" that account for why people remain in their jobs seem to have interest as an underlying component. In order of influence (based on responses from 8,454 participants), the stay factors included: exciting, challenging, or meaningful work (62.9%); supportive management/good boss (40.6%); being recognized, valued, respected (39%); career growth, learning, and development (32%); and a flexible work environment (22%). The exception was fair pay (19%); however, pay may seem to be fairer when the other five factors are in place.

The most influential stay factor "exciting, challenging, or meaningful work" characterizes the kind of work that is considered to be interesting. The second factor, "supportive management/good boss," describes conditions that enable interest to develop. The third factor, "being recognized, valued, respected," points to the development of feelings of self-efficacy, which are coordinated with the development of interest. The fourth factor, "career growth, learning and development," describes the presence of ongoing opportunities to develop job-related knowledge, which is essential to the development of both interest and future goals. The fifth factor, "a flexible work environment," describes a structural feature of workplace design that allows a person flexibility in how long, where, and when they work, and may promote the development of interests at work. It is noteworthy that Kaye et al. (2014) found that the six factors were important, regardless of gender, age, position, job function, company size, and geography.

Interests and their measurement have had an important place in both education and business settings. The same measures—for instance, the seminal Strong Interest Inventory (1943)—have been used in educational counseling to help students choose a field of study and in business for personnel selection. The tacit assumption underlying these measures has been that interests are relatively stable and unchangeable individual attributes, or traits (Rounds & Su, 2014; Su, 2019). However, research conducted by ourselves and by a number of other (mainly educational) researchers has presented a very different picture (e.g., Harackiewicz, Smith, & Priniski, 2016; O'Keefe & Harackiewicz, 2017; Renninger, Nieswandt, & Hidi, 2015). Studies of interest provide evidence that interests follow a developmental course and are educable.

A key difference between our developmental approach and studies of vocational interest involves our focus on the adjustment of the fit between the person and the environment. If there is no fit, only a developmental approach can inform how a fit might be established (e.g., Renninger & Hidi, 2019, in press). Because it tends to conceptualize interest as a trait, or set abilities, research on vocational interest does not point to ways in which it might be bolstered or supported to develop (see Renninger & Hidi, 2019, in press; Rounds & Su, 2014; Su, 2019). That interest may be supported to develop has major implications for both education and employment.

In this chapter, we consider how the development of interest can benefit both workforce readiness and job performance. *Readiness* is defined here as the likelihood that persons entering the workforce are prepared to meaningfully engage in the challenges of their workplace. Such engagement requires the ability and willingness to learn, explore, and identify work-relevant strategies. In turn, the strategies that are enabled by readiness allow workers to address relevant technical and social problems that are posed at work, identify organizational and teamwork efficiencies, and define *performance*.[1]

Although there are a number of aspects of effective workplace functioning, the most important one for our consideration is that individuals may have to engage in activities over time, even if they are not interested in them. If their interest can be supported so that it can develop, it is likely to become its own intrinsic reward (e.g., Gottlieb, Oudeyer, Lopes, & Baranes, 2013). In other words, over time interest may be expected to beneficially affect performance, and external rewards would not be essential. If interest has yet to develop, or its development is not likely, then understanding how an employee, a manager, or an organization can use incentives and reward processes also becomes critical for supporting engagement.

Based on how the content of work is related to the individuals' activities, there are at least two broad types of workplace settings. One setting involves *continuous knowledge acquisition* and may be called *mindful*. It requires the type of mental engagement from an individual that benefits from additional information search and also from ideas that continue to expand a person's knowledge base in ways that result in improved job performance.[2] The other category we call *repetitious*. Repetitious jobs do not typically require continuous (information-based) knowledge acquisition, although improvements in performance can be expected when motivation increases. In fact, these two different settings are likely to require different interventions to motivate unmotivated workers.

It is important to recognize that the development of employees' interest can be a benefit for both the employee and the employer. Often, the employer or organization does not recognize how important an employee's interest can be, and may mistakenly assume that interest cannot be developed. The literature on interest development, and on rewards and incentives, provides information about how workforce readiness and performance can be promoted.

In the following sections, we describe findings from studies of interest development, undertaken both in and out of school, and consider their implications for the workplace. We explain how interest can be supported to develop, even if prior experience would suggest otherwise. For purposes of illustration, we describe the case of an architect who clearly has an interest in architecture yet needs to develop a new interest in sales and become more involved in the business side of the firm. We consider the implications of findings from studies of reward and incentives when work is experienced as repetitious versus mindful. We conclude by explaining the importance of interest, reward, and self-related processing for workplace readiness, as well as the likelihood that workers will choose to stay in their jobs, be motivated to learn efficiently, and make meaningful contributions to the workplace.

Interest Development

Conceptualized as a variable that develops, interest refers to the psychological state of a person during involvement with some content (e.g., sales activities associated with the design work of an architect in a company), *and also* to the likelihood that the person will continue to want to reengage with that content over time and enjoy the challenges that continued engagement provides (Hidi & Renninger, 2006; Renninger & Hidi, 2016). In our Four-Phase Model of Interest Development (Hidi & Renninger, 2006), we drew on the existing research literature to describe interest as developing through four phases: triggered situational, maintained situational, emerging individual, and well-developed individual interest (see Table 2.1). The model explains that knowledge can develop without interest, but interest development is always accompanied by the expansion of knowledge and deepening value.

To summarize, the first phase of interest development, *triggered situational interest*, describes the initial triggering of attention by environmental features that are, for example, novel, have some personal relevance and/or capture imagination, and promote information search. These features may be observed by the individuals themselves, but attention to them may be encouraged by

TABLE 2.1 The Four Phases of Interest Development (Hidi & Renninger, 2006): Definitions and Learner Characteristics.

| | Phases of Interest Development | | | |
| | Less Developed (Earlier) | | More Developed (Later) | |
	Phase 1: Triggered Situational Interest	Phase 2: Maintained Situational Interest	Phase 3: Emerging Individual Interest	Phase 4: Well-Developed Individual Interest
• Definition	• Psychological state resulting from short-term changes in cognitive and affective processing associated with a particular class of content	• Psychological state that involves focused attention to a particular class of content that reoccurs and/or persists over time	• Psychological state *and* the beginning of relatively enduring predisposition to seek reengagement with a particular class of content over time	• Psychological state *and* a relatively enduring predisposition to reengage a particular class of content over time
• Learner Characteristics	• Attends to content, if only fleetingly • May or may not be reflectively aware of the experience • May need support to engage from others and through instructional design • May experience either positive or negative feelings	• Reengages content that previously triggered attention • Is developing knowledge of the content • Is developing a sense of the content's value • Is likely to be supported by others to find connections to content based on existing skills, knowledge, and/or prior experience • Is likely to have positive feelings	• Is likely to independently reengage content • Has stored knowledge and stored value • Is reflective about the content • Is focused on their own questions • Has positive feelings	• Independently reengages content • Has stored knowledge and value • Is reflective about the content • Is likely to recognize others' contributions to the discipline • Self-regulates easily to reframe questions and seek answers • Appreciates and may actively seek feedback • Can persevere through frustration and challenge in order to meet goals • Has positive feelings

Reprinted with permission from K. A. Renninger and S. E. Hidi, (2016). *The power of interest for motivation and engagement.* NY: Routledge.

other people. For example, educators might intervene by inserting novelty or surprise into lab assignments, demonstrations, or exhibits (Nieswandt & Horwitz, 2015), and employ reflective feedback to focus attention either on why engagement is useful (Hulleman & Harackiewicz, 2009) or on specific elements of problem-solving (Renninger et al., 2014). For an interest to be triggered, the level of an individuals' content-related knowledge has only to be adequate for processing incoming information; their feelings may be either positive or negative.[3]

Once an interest is triggered, it may or may not then develop into a *maintained situational interest*. Individuals' triggered situational interest is typically maintained when they are supported to think about the content of their interest. This can be promoted by their interactions with other people and/or by tasks (e.g., assignments) or activities (e.g., board meetings). The time and opportunity to work together with other people to solve or work on real problems that have not yet been solved, or have multiple possible solutions, has been shown to maintain interest (e.g., Azevedo, 2006; Mitchell, 1993; Renninger et al., 2014; Swarat, Ortony, & Revelle, 2012). As with a triggered situational interest, the design of tasks can be adjusted to focus attention on content. Triggers for interest can help individuals to focus on (direct attention to) specific aspects of a task or an activity. For example, triggers for interest can point a person to the utility or relevance of engaging with particular content (e.g., Gaspard et al., 2015; Hulleman & Harackiewicz, 2009), help a person discover personal connections between the content and themselves (Bernacki & Walkington, 2018; Hidi, Renninger, & Northoff, 2017), or cause a person to pay more attention to content by introducing novel information (Anderson, Shirey, Wilson, & Fielding, 1987; Hidi & Baird, 1986; Palmer, 2004).

When the content of the problem is something individuals have experience with and can connect to, this self-related information can facilitate maintained interest and continued work (Hidi, Renninger, & Northoff, 2019). Repeated opportunity to reengage meaningfully with content appears critical, as it enables a person to develop their knowledge and desire to search for content-related information (Renninger & Hidi, 2019). When a person has a maintained situational interest, then his or her feelings tend to be positive. Their content knowledge is increasing, and as they come to understand the content more fully, their value for it begins to develop as well. They can benefit from encouragement to continue engagement.

There is now substantial evidence that interest develops through phases (e.g., Jansen, Lüdtke, & Schroeders, 2016; Knogler, Harackiewicz, Gegenfurtner, & Lewalter, 2015; Lipstein & Renninger, 2007; Michaelis & Nathan, 2016; Nolen, 2007; Wang & Adescope, 2016). When people develop interest, they are likely to search for relevant information, pursue a deeper understanding of that information, have or develop value for that content, and be willing to persevere in the interest development process, even when faced with difficulty (see review,

Renninger & Hidi, 2016). They are also likely to be engaged in meaningful learning (e.g., Jansen et al., 2016), and they are attentive and effortful in doing so. They set, pursue, and realize goals (e.g., Harackiewicz, Durik, Barron, Linnenbrink, & Tauer, 2008), and they develop and effectively employ learning strategies (e.g., Jansen et al., 2016; Nolen, 2007).

In any situation, there can be multiple potential triggers for interest (e.g., opportunities to work independently, opportunities to work in a group, novel information, challenge, personal relevance; Renninger, Bachrach, & Hidi, 2019). Individuals may notice and appreciate some of these triggers of interest, but other triggers may go unnoticed. Learners in later phases of interest are also able to self-trigger ongoing engagement because as triggers push them to consider new ways to make connections to what they know, they identify additional content that leads them to learn and reflect (see Renninger & Hidi, 2019).

Importantly, all people can be supported to develop at least some interest, and the key is that they probably need support to do so, whether this support comes from other people (e.g., Bergin, 2016), and/or the design or conditions of the learning environment (e.g., Crouch, Wisittanawat, Cai, & Renninger, 2018; Renninger et al., 2014). Such supports are most likely to be effective if they make the experience of continued engagement feel doable and worthwhile and thus can provide the basis for the development of interest.

For example, if the architect who has little initial interest in sales is provided with accessible and useful information about how to engage in selling the designs she develops, and/or receives acknowledgment of her developing capacity to sell, she might develop her interest. An accompanying salary boost might be expected to encourage her continued reengagement in selling, and as she develops her knowledge and value for sales, she might become successful as a salesperson. The practice of selling could thus become a developed interest, as she works to figure out how the selling she is doing can be managed even more productively.

Advances in neuroscience provide evidence that all persons are hardwired to develop interest in some content; this means that the potential to be interested is universal. More specifically, neuroscience has established that the information search that is one of the outcomes of the triggering, or activation of interest is associated with the reward circuitry in the brain (e.g., Gottlieb, Oudeyer, & Baranes, 2013; Gruber, Gelman, & Ranganath, 2014; Panksepp, 1998). This means that once interest is triggered and maintained, engaging the content of interest becomes its own reward. That interest has a physiological basis further suggests that when people have little or maybe no interest in a particular content area or environment, they may benefit from various forms of support to make connections between what they already know and new content. This type of scaffolding can make engaging new content feel worthwhile and rewarding, in turn triggering interest and its development.

Because we are physiologically wired to experience interest, a person does not have to learn to be interested in an activity, situation, or idea. A person does not need to learn to have a situational interest triggered, but instead may need support to develop individual interest from such triggering. Once interest is triggered, the related information search will serve as an intrinsic reward that activates the reward circuitry and thus supports further engagement. For example, the architect who recognizes the essential relation of sales to her design and becomes interested in sales, may then search for ways to improve her sales tactics, a search she would find rewarding on its own merits.

Reward and Self-Related Information Processing

Using a 2 × 3 between-subjects design, Kosfeld, Neckermann, and Yang (2016) examined how monetary incentives, symbolic incentives of recognition (such as a smiley button), and the meaningfulness of a task affect workers' performance. In the low-meaning condition, workers were told that their data will only be used for a quality check and that "those data will most likely never be used" (p. 2), whereas in the high-meaning condition, workers were told that their work was important for a research project. The results showed that both monetary incentive and meaningfulness of the task had positive and independent effects on performance. In contrast, recognition incentives only increased performance when workers received the low-meaning instructions, suggesting that recognition incentives can provide meaning only to a meaningless task as they may have a compensatory effect.

Kosfeld et al.'s (2016) study has implications for understanding how unmotivated learners can be supported to be motivated. That is, if the interest of unmotivated learners does not seem to develop, they may benefit from financial incentives and from help to recognize the importance of their work. In order to explain the facilitative effects of monetary compensation and meaning, we need to consider what is understood about both reward and self-related information processing. In doing so, we are able to suggest ways in which workforce readiness and performance can be improved.

Reward

The reward circuitry of the brain includes cortical and subcortical regions and is fueled by dopamine. It is activated either by the anticipation or the receipt of reward and has been shown to motivate approach and consummatory behavior. It has both affective and cognitive benefits, such as the increases in performance following monetary reward as demonstrated in the Kosfeld et al. (2016) experiment, as well as increases in attention and learning (see Della Libera & Chelezzi, 2009; Hidi, 2016; Lee & Shomstein, 2014).

Early neuroscientific research studies focused on the benefits of activating the reward circuitry using extrinsic reward; more recent investigations have clarified that intrinsic reward, such as searching for information, activates the same areas of the reward circuitry as extrinsic reward (e.g., Gottlieb et al., 2013; Gruber et al., 2014; Kang, Hsu, Krajbich, Loewenstein, McClure, et al., 2009) and has similar benefits for outcomes.[4] These findings indicate that the relation between information search and the activation of the reward circuitry is central to explaining the powerful and beneficial effects of interest on performance and learning (Ainley & Hidi, 2014; Renninger & Hidi, 2016).

Thus, although it has been demonstrated that both intrinsic and extrinsic rewards can provide similar support for motivation, research now clarifies that the functional role of intrinsic and extrinsic rewards differs depending on the phase of a person's interest development. That is, extrinsic reward seems to be more essential in the earlier phases when a person may require support to trigger and maintain interest (Hidi & Renninger, 2006). In the later phases, seeking information becomes intrinsically rewarding and is likely to lead to self-generation of further engagement.

Hundreds of studies have questioned the benefits of reward and suggested that they undermine intrinsic motivation (e.g., Deci, 1971; see Ryan & Deci, 2017), although researchers now agree that reward does not undermine behavior when no motivation for an activity exists (e.g., Hidi, 2016; Marsden, Ma, Deci, Ryan, & Chiu, 2014; Ryan & Deci, 2017).[5] Findings indicate that undermining intrinsic motivation only occurs in limited situations, such as giving tangible reward for activity that is driven by interest, and subsequently withdrawing the reward. Interestingly, the unexplained withdrawing of reward has been related to psychological pain and found to result in modification of activation in the brain (see Flaherty, 1996; Papini, Fuchs, & Torres, 2015).

Our consideration of reward focuses on the role it can play for individuals who are not intrinsically motivated, and we suggest that extrinsic reward is important in such cases. Yet, there is also an unresolved question about how intrinsically motivated individuals who are engaged in long-term activities maintain their motivation without external rewards/incentives.

Self-Related Information Processing

We suggest that Kosfeld et al.'s (2016) high-meaning condition may have led participants to associate tasks with themselves, as they were given information that their work was important. In other words, emphasizing the importance of the task in that study was likely to result in self-related processing. Other studies report that the neural processing of reward is associated with self-related information, as researchers have demonstrated that there exists a neural overlap of reward and self-relatedness in brain activation (e.g., Carter, McInnes, Huettel, & Adcock, 2009; de Greck et al., 2008; Ersner-Hershfield, Wimmer, & Knutson, 2009).

Over several decades, both psychological and neuroscientific research has shown the uniqueness of self-related information processing. Psychologists have shown its benefits for basic functions like perception, emotions, and reward, as well as for higher order functions like memory (Adcock, Thangavel, Whitfield-Gabrieli, Knutson, & Gabrieli, 2006; Murayama & Kitagami, 2013). Neuroscientists using functional magnetic resonance imaging also have found that the neural correlates of encoding information in the brain are different when it is related to oneself (Hu et al., 2016; Northoff et al., 2006; van der Meer, Costafreda, Aleman, & David, 2010), that is, special patterns of brain activation (higher neural activity) are involved in the neural processing of the self (see Hidi et al., 2019; Northoff, 2016).

We note that research findings have pointed not only to the association of interest to reward, but also to self-related information processing. For example, in a study of abstinent alcoholics and pathological gamblers who showed "normalization" of reward-related activity in the reward system, deGreck et al. (2009, 2010) found that the depletion of self-related activity reduced, interest. In other words, diminished self-related activity in the reward regions appears to be an index of diminished interest in behavior. More generally, the studies suggest that without a relation to the self, stimuli may remain "indifferent" for the subject and not trigger interest.

In the section that follows, we suggest that utility-value interventions are an instance of self-related information processing (see Hidi et al., 2017, 2019), because they involve a person making links between the content and self. Utility-value interventions consist of relatively simple tasks (e.g., written reflection) that require participants to make personal connections between their lives and academic content (e.g., Gaspard et al., 2015; Hulleman & Harackiewicz, 2009).

Utility-Value Interventions

Utility-value interventions are relatively simple, low-cost, and effective educational practices that have been found to increase interest and improve performance. Interestingly, these interventions have been found to benefit certain disadvantaged groups (e.g., underrepresented minorities, women) more than others, leading researchers to wonder why this is the case (Harackiewicz et al., 2016). Hulleman and Harackiewicz (2009) note that their study of utility-value interventions was foreshadowed by Oyserman, Terry, and Bybee's (2006) nine-week after-school "possible selves intervention" that was undertaken with African American middle school students. In Oyserman et al.'s study, participants were asked to imagine themselves as successful adults and to connect these images to current school involvements. The students who received the intervention showed many positive outcomes by the end of the year. They had more concerns about doing well in school, had better attendance records, and were judged to have more balanced perceptions of their possible selves. The Oyserman et al.'s study also suggests that the beneficial outcomes were related to the students' making personal connections to school activity.

Hulleman, Kosovich, Barron, and Daniel (2017) suggest that an explanation for the success of the utility-value intervention is its targeting of psychological mechanisms such as thinking frequently about connections between experience and information to be acquired. In Hidi et al. (2019), we proposed a modification of this explanation, by suggesting that "the pervasiveness of the self throughout the whole array of psychological functions may be especially relevant for understanding the impact of utility value interventions" (p. 24). In other words, these functions are recruited when the basis of interest is permeated and driven by the self-relatedness of information. Once self-related information processing triggers interest, material that could otherwise feel meaningless is understood to be both self-related and interesting.

As a result, it is not surprising that the students who are most likely to benefit most from utility-value interventions are those who are not originally interested in or involved with the content and thus are at risk in terms of academic success. The reward circuitry of individuals who experience self-involvement and/or interest in their tasks is likely to already have been activated, rendering the utility-value intervention unnecessary and thus ineffective.

To the best of our knowledge, utility-value interventions have not been adopted for use in the workplace. However, given that this type of intervention has been especially successful for supporting students with low-performance expectations, it seems likely that it could prove to be effective with low performing or unmotivated workers. The explanation of the success of utility-value interventions is that they lead a person to make links to content. In so doing, they activate the reward circuitry, trigger and maintain interest, and benefit learning.

It is plausible that individuals who do not benefit from utility-value interventions have already made connections to the content (e.g., selling in the architecture firm). It is also possible that as Kosfield et al.'s study points out, the meaningfulness of what individuals are asked to work with needs further consideration.

As findings from Crouch et al. (2018) demonstrate, individuals with more developed interest may respond differently to triggers than those who have less developed interest. Adapted to provide workplace examples, they suggest that persons in the architectural firm who have more interest in selling may not need to be helped to understand why selling is useful; rather, their interest would be further developed if they were supported to continue to stretch what they know about selling. In fact, because their interest has already been triggered, they voluntarily engage in seeking information and find it rewarding to do so. The meaningfulness of the work a person does has implications for whether interest needs to be supported to develop. As the findings about why people stay in their jobs in the Kaye et al. (2014) suggested, there are a number of factors and the most influential of these seem to point to employees' interest.

Concluding Thoughts

In this chapter, we have argued that in order to optimize workforce readiness and performance, support for interest to be triggered and developed is critical. We have also pointed to two different types of workplace settings, mindful and repetitious. We note that the development of interest can be supported in each, although support to develop interest may be easier in mindful contexts as these can involve individuals in meaning-making. The benefit to developing interest is that it is a reward experience; individuals with interest will independently reengage in ways that can be generative and productive for them and for the company or organization with whom they work. It is also possible for those in what might appear to be repetitious jobs to develop an interest in their jobs; when they do, this is rewarding for them, and ensures both productivity and the likelihood that they will want to continue in their job. For example, the elevator operator or the cashier who develop an interest in the people with whom they work and through this find meaning, are not interested in their repetitious jobs, per se, but rather in associated aspects of their job in which they have developed an interest.

Regardless of whether a type of job is mindful or repetitious, reward may be a necessary motivator at least initially for those who do not find meaning in their jobs. When an individual does not have interest, reward is needed to support engagement. As self-related information processing is interest enhancing, it appears that linking content to the self may be a useful starting point in efforts to support unmotivated workers' readiness and performance. Activation of the reward circuitry not only energizes but also enhances attention, memory, and its effects tend to be long lasting. Such activation has been associated with both the delivery of reward and reward expectations.

In summary, people are hardwired to develop interest, meaning that it is possible to support the interest of all people to develop. In the earlier phases of interest development, providing support that triggers interest,[6] creates personal connections to content, promotes utility, introduces novel content, and, can enable the person to make connections to content that become rewarding as their interest begins to develop. As engagement with content becomes rewarding, continued information search can be expected to follow. At this point, a person, like our architect, is able to self-trigger by identifying problems that need to be solved and seeking resources and opportunities to address them.

When the triggering of attention leads to repeated information search, the reward circuitry is activated, and individuals begin making connections to content that lead them to question and seek further information. Without such connections, they are not likely to be in a position to develop enough knowledge, corresponding value, and feeling to sustain meaningful engagement.

All individuals, whether they are students or workers, need to make meaningful connections to content. These connections provide a basis for continued work.

The findings from study of reward and self-related information processing provide good evidence that if a person is supported to make personally relevant (self-related), meaningful connections to content, this activates the part of the brain where the self and reward overlap, setting up the potential for all individuals' interest to develop. Leveraging the development of interest has benefits for all individuals, not only students. When interest is supported to develop and deepen, workers are likely to stay in their jobs, be motivated to learn, have improved efficiency, and make meaningful contributions to the workplace.

Acknowledgments

We thank the editors of this volume for their thoughtful suggestions on earlier iterations of this chapter. Editorial assistance provided by Richelle Robinson and Melissa Running is most appreciated. Research support from the Swarthmore College Faculty Research Fund is also gratefully acknowledged.

Notes

1 Our focus in this chapter on the developmental aspects of strategy use in the workplace provides background information that complements Casillas, Kyllonen, and Way's (this volume) discussion of the use of formative assessments to track soft skills (e.g., persistence) as indicators of workforce readiness.
2 This conceptualization focuses on how the content of work relates to the person and could be considered an additional category of "decent work," as discussed by Douglas, Duffy, England, and Gensmer (this volume).
3 Even though interest tends to be associated with positive feelings, negative feelings can also trigger interest which results in focused attention (Hidi & Harackiewicz, 2000; Iran-Nejad, 1987). In order to enable an interest in some content to develop, however, negative feelings have to subside. Supporting a person to experience positive affect can serve to attenuate their negative feelings.
4 Reeve and Lee (2016) suggest that in addition to the commonly activated areas of intrinsic and extrinsic reward in the brain, there are uniquely activated areas of each.
5 Generally, educational and social psychologists tended to focus on the negative aspects of reward, whereas neuroscientists, economists, and business professionals have been more concerned with evaluating the positive outcomes. For example, Anselme and Robinson (2019) report that uncertainty about the delivery of rewards has motivational properties that they refer to as Incentive Hope.
6 There are also limitations of context, genetic, and physical makeup that may temper how such interest unfolds (see Renninger & Hidi, 2016).

References

Adcock, R. A., Thangavel, A., Whitfield-Gabrieli, S., Knutson, B., & Gabrieli, J. D. E. (2006). Reward-motivated learning: Mesolimbic activation precedes memory formation. *Neuron, 50*, 507–517.

Ainley, M., & Hidi, S. (2014). Interest and enjoyment. In R. Pekrun & L. Linnenbrink-Garcia (Eds.), *International handbook of emotions in education* (pp. 205–227). New York, NY: Routledge.

Anderson, R. C., Shirey, L. L., Wilson, P. T., & Fielding, L. G. (1987). Interestingness of children's reading material. In R. E. Snow & M. J. Farr (Eds.), *Aptitude, learning, and instruction*, Cognitive and Affective Process Analyses (Vol. III, pp. 287–299). Hillsdale, NJ: Erlbaum.

Anselme, P. & Robinson, M, J. F. (2019). Incentive motivation: The missing piece between learning and behavior. In K. A. Renninger & S. E. Hidi (Eds.), *The Cambridge handbook of motivation and learning* (pp. 163–182). Cambridge, UK: Cambridge University Press.

Azevedo, F. S. (2006). Personal excursions: Investigating the dynamics of student engagement. *International Journal of Computers for Mathematical Learning, 11*(1), 57–98. doi:10.1007/s10758-006-0007-6

Bergin, D. A. (2016). Social influences on interest. *Educational Psychologist, 51*(1), 7–22. doi:10.1080/00461520.2015.1133306

Bernacki, M. L., & Walkington, C. (2018). The role of situational interest in personalized learning. *Journal of Educational Psychology.* doi:10.1037/edu0000250

Carter, R. M., Maccines, J. J., Huettel, S. A., & Adock, R. A. (2009). Activation in the VTA and nucleus accumbens increases in anticipation of both gains and losses. *Frontiers in Behavioral Neuroscience, 3*(21). doi:10.3389/neuro.08.021.2009

Crouch, C., Wisittanawat, P., Cai, M., & Renninger, K. A. (2018). Life science students' attitudes, interest, and performance in introductory physics for life science (IPLS): An exploratory study. *Physical Review Physics Education Research, 14*(1). doi:10.1103/PhysRevPhysEducRes.14.010111

Deci, E. L. (1971). Effects of externally mediated reward on intrinsic motivation. *Journal of Personality and Social Psychology, 18*(1), 105–115. doi:10.1037/h0030644

de Greck, M., Enzi, B., Prösch, U., Gantman, A., Tempelmann. C., & Northoff, G. (2010). Decreased neuronal activity in reward circuitry of pathological gamblers during processing of personal relevant stimuli. *Human Brain Mapping, 31*(11), 1802–1812. doi:10.1002/hbm.20981

de Greck, M., Rotte, M., Paus, R., Moritz, D., Thiemann, R., Proesch, U., & Northoff, G. (2008). Is our self based on reward? Self-relatedness recruits neural activity in the reward system. *Neuroimage, 39*(4), 2066–2075. doi:10.1016/j.neuroimage.2007.11.006

de Greck, M., Supady, A., Thiemann, R., Tempelmann, C., Bogerts, B., Forschner, L., & Northoff, G. (2009). Decreased neural activity in reward circuitry during personal reference in abstinent alcoholics—A fMRI study. *Human Brain Mapping, 30*(5), 1691–1704. doi:10.1002/hbm.20634

Della Libera, C., & Chelezzi, L. (2009). Learning to attend and to ignore is a matter of gains and losses. *Psychological Science, 20*, 778–789. doi:10.1111/j.1467-9280.2009.02360.x

Ersner-Hershfield, H., Wimmer, G. E., & Knutson, B. (2009). Saving for the future self: Neural measures of future self-continuity predict temporal discounting. *Social Cognitive and Affective Neuroscience, 4*(1), 85–92. doi:10.1093/scan/nsn042

Flaherty, C. F. (1996). Incentive relativity. In J. Gray (General Ed.), *Problems in the behavioural sciences* (Vol. 15). Cambridge, UK: Cambridge University Press.

Gaspard, H., Dicke, A. L., Flunger, B., Brisson, B. M., Häfner, I., Nagengast, B., & Trautwein, U. (2015). Fostering adolescents' value beliefs for mathematics with a relevance intervention in the classroom. *Developmental Psychology, 51*(9), 1226–1240. doi:10.1037/dev0000028

Gottlieb, J., Oudeyer, P.-Y., Lopes, M., & Baranes, A. (2013). Information seeking, curiosity and attention: Computational and neural mechanisms. *Trends in Cognitive Sciences, 17*(11), 585–593. doi:10.1016/j.tics.2013.09.001

Gruber, M. J., Gelman, B. D., & Ranganath, C. (2014). States of curiosity modulate hippocampus-dependent learning via the dopaminergic circuit. *Neuron, 84*(2), 486–496. doi:10.1016/j.neuron.2014.08.060

Harackiewicz, J. M., Canning, E., Priniski, S. J., & Tibbetts, Y. (2016, April). Why is writing about value so powerful? In K. A. Renninger (Chair), *The roles of interest and value in promoting learning.* Symposium conducted at the meetings of the American Educational Research Association, Washington, DC.

Harackiewicz, J. M., Durik, A. M., Barron, K. E., Linnenbrink, L., & Tauer, J. M. (2008). The role of achievement goals in the development of interest: Reciprocal relations between achievement goals, interest, and performance. *Journal of Educational Psychology, 100*(1), 105–122. doi:10.1037/0022-0663.100.1.105

Harackiewicz, J. M., Smith, J. L., & Priniski, S. J. (2016). Interest matters: The importance of promoting interest in education. *Policy Insights from the Behavioral and Brain Sciences, 3*(2), 220–227. doi:10.1177/2372732216655542

Hidi, S. (2016). Revisiting the role of reward in motivation and learning: Implications of neuroscientific research. *Educational Psychology Review, 28*(1), 61–93. doi:10.1007/s10648-015-9307-5

Hidi, S., & Baird, W. (1986). Interestingness: A neglected variable in discourse processing. *Cognitive Science, 10*(2), 179–194. doi:10.1207/s15516709cog1002_3

Hidi, S., & Harackiewicz, J. M. (2000). Motivating the academically unmotivated: A critical issue for the 21st century. *Review of Educational Research, 70*(2), 151–179. doi:10.2307/1170660

Hidi, S., & Renninger, K. A. (2006). The four-phase model of interest development. *Educational Psychologist, 41*(2), 111–127. doi:10.1207/s15326985ep4102_4

Hidi, S. E., Renninger, K, A., & Northoff, G. (2017). The development of interest and self-related processing. In F. Guay, H. W. Marsh, D. M. McInerney, & R. G. Craven (Eds.), *International advances in self research, Volume 6: SELF – Driving positive psychology and well-being* (pp. 51–70). Charlotte, NC: Information Age Press.

Hidi, S. E., Renninger, K. A., & Northoff, G. (2019). The educational benefits of self-related information processing. In K. A. Renninger & S. E. Hidi (Eds.), *The Cambridge Handbook of motivation and learning* (pp. 15–34). Cambridge, UK: Cambridge University Press.

Hu, C., Di, X., Eickhoff, S. B., Zhang, M., Peng, K., Guo, H., & Sui, J. (2016). Distinct and common aspects of physical and psychological self-representation in the brain: A meta-analysis of self-bias in facial and self-referential judgements. *Neuroscience & Biobehavioral Reviews, 61*, 197–207. doi:10.1016/j.neubiorev.2015.12.003

Hulleman, C., & Harackiewicz, J. (2009). Promoting interest and performance in high school science classes. *Science, 326*(5698), 1410–1412. doi:10.1126/science.1177067

Hulleman, C. S., Kosovich, J. J., Barron, K. E., & Daniel, D. B. (2017). Making connections: Replicating and extending the utility value intervention in the classroom. *Journal of Educational Psychology, 109*(3). doi:10.1037/edu0000146

Iran-Nejad, A. (1987). Cognitive and affective causes of interest and liking. *Journal of Educational Psychology, 79*(2), 120–130. doi:10.1037/0022-0663.79.2.120

Jansen, M., Lüdtke, O., & Schroeders, U. (2016). Evidence for a positive relationship between interest and achievement: Examining between-person and within-person variation in five domains. *Contemporary Educational Psychology, 46*, 116–127. doi:10.1016/j.cedpsych.2016.05.004

Kang, M. J., Hsu, M., Krajbich, I. M., Loewenstein, G., McClure, S. M., Wang, J. T., & Camerer, C. F. (2009). The wick in the candle of learning: Epistemic curiosity activates reward circuitry and enhances memory. *Psychological Science, 20,* 963–973. doi:10.1111/j.1467-9280.2009.02402.x

Kaye, B., Jordan-Evans, S., & Career Systems International. (2014). *What keeps you: A white paper about engaging and retaining talent.* Retrieved from www.keepem.com/pdf/WKY_2014_pdf

Knogler, M., Harackiewicz, J. M., Gegenfurtner, A., Lewalter, D. (2015). How situational is situational interest? Investigating the longitudinal structure of situational interest. *Contemporary Educational Psychology, 43,* 39–50. doi:10.1016/j.cedpsych.2015.08.004

Kosfeld, M., Neckermann, S., & Yang, X. (2016). The effects of financial and recognition incentives across work contexts: The role of meaning. *Economic Inquiry, 55*(1), 1-11. doi:10.111/ecin.12350

Lee, J., & Shomstein, S. (2014). Reward-based transfer from bottom-up and top-down search tasks. *Psychological Science, 25*(2), 466–475. doi:10.1177/0956797613509284

Lipstein, R., & Renninger, K. A. (2007). "Putting things into words": 12-15-year-old students' interest for writing. In P. Boscolo & S. Hidi (Eds.), *Motivation and writing: Research and school practice* (pp. 113–140). New York, NY: Kluwer Academic/Plenum.

Marsden, K. E., Ma, W. J., Deci, E. L., Ryan, R. M., & Chiu, P. A. (2014). Diminished neural responses predict enhanced intrinsic motivation and sensitivity to external incentive. *Cognitive, Affective, and Behavioral Neuroscience, 15*(2), 276–286.

Michaelis, J. E., & Nathan, M. J. (2016, June). *Observing and measuring interest development among high school students in an out-of-school robotics competition* (ASEE Paper ID #16242). Paper presentation to the American Society of Engineering Education ASEE 2016, New Orleans, LA: ASEE

Mitchell, M. (1993). Situational interest: Its multifaceted structure in the secondary school mathematics classroom. *Journal of Educational Psychology, 85*(3), 424–436. doi:10.1037/0022-0663.85.3.424

Murayama, K., & Kitagami, S. (2013). Consolidation power of extrinsic rewards: Reward cues enhance long-term memory for irrelevant past events. *Journal of Experimental Psychology, 143*(1), 15–20. doi: 10.1037/a0031992

Nieswandt, M., & Horowitz, G. (2015). Undergraduate students' interest in chemistry: The roles of task and choice. In K. A. Renninger, M. Nieswandt, & S. Hidi (Eds.), *Interest in mathematics and science learning* (pp. 225–242). Washington, DC: American Educational Research Association.

Nolen, S. B. (2007). The role of literate communities in the development of children's interest in writing. In G. Rijlaarsdam (Series Ed.), S. Hidi, & P. Boscolo (Vol. Ed.), *Studies in writing: Vol. 19. Writing and motivation* (1st ed., pp. 241–255). Oxford, UK: Elsevier. doi:10.1108/s1572-6304(2006)0000019015

Northoff, G. (2016). Is the self a higher-order or fundamental function of the brain? The "basis model of self-specificity" and its encoding by the brain's spontaneous activity. *Cognitive Neuroscience, 7*(1–4), 203–222. doi:10.1080/17588928.2015.1111868

Northoff, G., Heinzel, A., de Greck, M. D., Bermpohl, F., Dobrowolny, H., & Panksepp, J. (2006). Self-referential processing in our brain—A meta-analysis of imaging studies on the self. *NeuroImage, 31*(1), 440–457. doi:10.1016/j.neuroimage.2005.12.002

O'Keefe, P. A., & Harackiewecz, J. M. (2017). *The science of interest.* New York, NY: Springer.

Oyserman, D., Bybee, D., & Terry, K. (2006). Possible selves and academic outcomes: How and when possible selves impel action. *Journal of Personality and Social Psychology, 91*(1), 188–204. doi:10.1037/0022-3514.91.1.188

Palmer, D. (2004). Situational interest and the attitudes towards science of primary education teachers. *International Journal of Science Education, 27*(7), 895–908. doi:10.1080/0950069032000177262

Palmer, D. H., Dixon, J., & Archer, J. (2016). Identifying underlying causes of situational interest in a science course for preservice elementary teachers. *Science Education, 100*(6), 1039–1061. doi:10.1002/sce.21244

Panksepp, J. (1998). *Affective neuroscience: The foundations of human and animal emotion.* New York, NY: Oxford.

Papini, M. R., Fuchs, P. N., & Torres, C. (2015). Behavioral neuroscience and psychological pain. *Neuroscience and Biobehavioral Reviews, 48*, 53–69.

Reeve, J. & Lee, W. (2016). Neuroscientific contributions to motivation in education. In K. R. Wentzel & D. B. Miele (Eds.), *Handbook of motivation at school* (2nd ed., pp. 424–439). New York: Routledge.

Renninger, K. A., Austin, L., Bachrach, J. E., Chau, A., Emmerson, M., King, R. B., … Stevens, S. J. (2014). Going beyond "Whoa! That's Cool!" Achieving science interest and learning with the ICAN Intervention. In S. Karabenick & T. Urdan (Eds.), *Motivation-based learning interventions, Vol. 18, Advances in motivation and achievement* (pp. 107–140). London, UK: Emerald Group Publishing.

Renninger, K. A., Bachrach, J. E., & Hidi, S. E. (2019). Triggering and maintaining in early phases of interest development. *Learning, Culture and Social Interaction.* doi.org/10.1016/j.lcsi.2018.11.007

Renninger, K. A., & Hidi, S. E. (2016). *The power of interest for motivation and engagement.* New York, NY: Routledge.

Renninger, K. A. & Hidi, S. E. (2019). Interest development and learning. In K. A. Renninger & S. E. Hidi (Eds.), *The Cambridge handbook of motivation and learning* (pp. 265–290). Cambridge, UK: Cambridge University Press.

Renninger, K. A., & Hidi, S. E. (in press). Interest development as a dynamic process in the workplace. In C. Nye & J. Rounds (Eds.), *Vocational interests in the workplace.* New York, NY: Routledge.

Renninger, K. A., Nieswandt, M., & Hidi, S. (Eds.) (2015). *Interest and learning mathematics and science.* Washington, DC: American Educational Research Association.

Rounds, J., & Su, R. (2014). The nature and power of interests. *Current Directions in Psychological Science, 23*, 98–103. doi:10.1177/0963721414522812

Ryan, R., & Deci, E. L. (2017). *Self-determination theory: Basic psychological needs in motivation, development, and wellness.* New York, NY: Guilford.

Strong, E. K. (1943). *Vocational interests of men and women.* Stanford, CA: Stanford University Press.

Su, R. (2019). The three faces of interests: An integrative review of interest research in vocational, organizational, and educational psychology. *Journal of Vocational Behavior.* doi:10.1016/j.jvb.2018.10.016

Swarat, S., Ortony, A., & Revelle, W. (2012) Activity matters: Understanding student interest in school science. *Journal of Research in Science and Teaching, 49*(4), 515–537. doi:10.1002/tea.21010

van der Meer, L., Costafreda, S., Aleman, A., & David, A. S. (2010) Self-reflection and the brain: A theoretical review and meta-analysis of neuroimaging studies with implications for schizophrenia. *Neuroscience & Behavioral Reviews, 34*(6), 935–946. doi:10.1016/j.neubiorev.2009.12.004.

Wang, Z., & Adesope, O. (2016). Exploring the effects of seductive details with the 4-phase model of interest. *Learning in Motivation, 55*, 65–77. doi:10.1016/j.lmot.2016.06.003

3

PREPARING STUDENTS FOR THE FUTURE OF WORK

A Formative Assessment Approach

Alex Casillas, Patrick C. Kyllonen, and Jason D. Way

The role of schools in developing students' character and in preparing students for the workforce has been recognized at least since Horace Mann (1868). This theme was renewed in the Secretary's Commission on Achieving Necessary Skills (SCANS; Department of Labor, 1991), which identified interpersonal skills and personal qualities (responsibility, self-esteem, sociability, self-management, and integrity) as ones that "all American high school students must develop... if they are to enjoy a productive, full, and satisfying life" (p. i) and that are "needed for solid job performance" (p. iii). The importance of school is not limited to job preparation. As noted in the SCANS report, the school has a variety of functions, including to "prepare people to live full lives, to participate in their communities, to raise families, to enjoy the leisure that is the fruit of their labor. A solid education is its own reward and has value beyond specific skills" (p. i). Several relatively recent reports (National Research Council, 2012; Office of Economic Cooperation and Development, 2015) document evidence for the wide range of outcomes affected by school and the skills developed in school, including educational, social, civic, health, and workplace outcomes.

It is helpful to divide the skills that are acquired in school into three categories—cognitive ability, social (interpersonal) skills, and emotional and self-management (intrapersonal) skills. In this chapter, we focus on the latter two, which go by many names—noncognitive skills, soft skills, character skills, and 21st-century skills. For our purposes, in the chapter, we use the term *social-emotional learning (SEL) skills*, which has developed currency in the K–12 literature over the past decade or so, primarily due to the work of the Collaborative for Academic, Social, and Emotional Learning (CASEL, 2018).

There are several sources of evidence attesting to the importance of SEL skills in school and in the workplace. A number of employer surveys have identified SEL skills as among the most important skills employers seek when recruiting new graduates. In the annual employer survey conducted by National Association of Colleges and Employers (NACE, 2017), of the 20 skills identified as the "attributes employers seek on a candidate's resume," over half fall into the SEL category, including the ability to work on a team (78% of employers), strong work ethic (72%), leadership (69%), initiative (66%), flexibility (64%), detail-oriented (62%), organizational abilities (48%), friendly outgoing personality (26%), tactfulness (26%), and risk-taker (20%). Other employer surveys have produced similar lists, such as one by Casner-Lotto and Benner (2006), which identified critical thinking/problem-solving, oral and written communications, teamwork/collaboration, diversity, information technology, leadership, creativity/innovation, lifelong learning/self-direction, professionalism/work ethic, and ethics/social responsibility as the applied skills employers believed were "very important" for the new workforce entrant's success at work. In higher education, Lumina's Degree Qualifications profile and the AAC&U's value rubrics also point to the importance of such factors (Markle, Brenneman, Jackson, Burrus, & Robbins, 2013).

In addition to employer surveys, a number of prediction studies have shown high correlations between SEL skills measured during school and education and labor market outcomes measured many years later. The measures include Likert-scale personality self-assessments (Poropat, 2009), forced-choice measures (Salgado & Tauriz, 2014), ratings by others (Connelly & Ones, 2010; Oh, Wang, & Mount, 2011), 30-minute clinical interviews (Lindqvist & Vestman, 2011), and teacher ratings (Poropat, 2014; Segal, 2013). Outcomes range from educational attainment to supervisor ratings, training school success, earnings, unemployment, and chronic unemployment.

Given the empirical data supporting the positive association between SEL skills and education and labor market success, one question is whether any or all of these skills are teachable. There is evidence that education naturally teaches SEL skills. Students are rewarded for showing up, turning in their homework on time, not fighting with their teacher or other students, and learning from each other, and so it might be assumed that students are learning SEL skills in addition to mathematics, science, and language skills. In fact, there is evidence for a so-called "noncognitive" effect of education, in that the economic returns to education are substantially higher than the returns to the cognitive skills that students acquire in school (Bowles, Gintis, & Osborne, 2001; Garcia, 2014; Heckman, Stixrud, & Urzua, 2006; Levin, 2012). The benefits of early learning programs, which putatively target IQ, seem to be primarily noncognitive in nature (Heckman, 2006) in that the IQ gains fade after a few years, but the noncognitive effects persist (Borghans, Duckworth, Heckman, & ter Weel, 2008). Students who drop out of school but later obtain a general educational development (GED) have labor market performance that matches dropouts rather than degree holders, suggesting that although their cognitive skills are sufficient (they obtained a GED) their lack of noncognitive skills (what led to their leaving school) hampers them (Heckman, Kautz, & Humphries, 2014; Heckman & Rubinstein, 2001).

There is also some evidence for direct training effects. Despite the widespread assumption that personality is fixed from birth, meta-analysis have shown that personality naturally changes significantly over the life span (Roberts, Walton, & Viechtbauer, 2006) and that it can be changed substantially (approximately 0.5 standard deviation) by direct interventions, such as psychotherapy (Roberts et al., 2017) or major life transitions (Bleidorn, 2012). Perhaps more pertinent to the present concerns, two meta-analyses of SEL programs in schools (Durlak, Weissberg, Dymnicki, Taylor, & Schellinger, 2011; Taylor, Oberle, Durlak, & Weissberg, 2017) and after school (Durlak, Weissberg, & Molly, 2010) show substantial and sustainable effects of SEL training on a variety of outcomes, including social and emotional skills themselves, but also attitudes, positive social behaviors, conduct problems, emotional distress, well-being, decision-making, graduation, and achievement test scores. In addition, there is preliminary evidence that social-emotional skills can be developed through interventions in higher education (National Academy of Sciences, Engineering, and Medicine, 2017).

In summary, there seems to be some consensus on the important role of schools for developing social-emotional skills, and in the workforce's desire to identify new workers with such skills. There is also evidence that SEL skills can be taught and that doing so leads to a variety of positive outcomes. A question is how do we best go about teaching SEL skills? There are some suggestions from Durlak et al.'s (2011) study that successful SEL programs are ones that are "SAFE": (1) sequenced (connected and coordinated set of activities), (2) active (active learning orientation), (3) focused (at least one component dedicated to developing SEL), and (4) explicit (targets SEL skills, not positive development in general). We propose that SEL training can be accomplished with a formative assessment[1] system that targets SEL skills. We now turn to how we might go about doing that by leveraging design science guiding principles or criteria for the development of such a system.

Designing a Better Bridge for Future Workers by Leveraging Design Science

Design science is the scientific study and creation of artifacts, which are human-made (as opposed to natural) objects or processes developed to solve problems and improve practices (Simon, 1996). Design science has its roots in engineering (the "sciences of the artificial"; Simon, 1996), and although it has been influential in a number of applied fields including architecture and computer science, it is less known in educational and psychological assessment. We propose that tests, score reports, and interventions can be treated as artifacts and thus could be approached from a design science perspective.

In design science, three guiding principles or criteria are used to evaluate successful designs: desirability (Does a design solve a problem? Do people want it?), feasibility (How probable, from a technical perspective, is a solution? How defensible is it?), and viability (Is the design capable of producing a profit or attaining the intended goal?) (Brown, 2009). Using these design criteria to test our assumptions, we believe that an SEL formative assessment system would "build a better bridge" that helps students develop the knowledge and skills needed for making a successful transition or "crossing" into the workforce. This system would include not just an assessment delivered at a single time point, but an ongoing cycle of student assessment, instruction, and professional development (PD) for instructors, as informed by both assessment and instruction—all of which would lead to better immediate, short-term, and long-term outcomes for students. We consider the three design criteria and how the proposed assessment system fulfills them.

Desirability—Do people want a bridge? This criterion developed out of human-centered design practices, which focuses on developing solutions to problems by involving the human perspective in all steps of the problem-solving process (IDEO, 2015). The point of this criterion is to reinforce that a solution will be used by humans and thus must be user-friendly in order for a solution to be effective. Based on a variety of reports on workforce readiness skills dating more than 10 years, practitioners have rated SEL skills (e.g., persistence and work ethic, collaboration and teamwork, curiosity and flexibility) as highly desired by employers. For example, Casner-Lotto and Benner (2006) found that, when employers were asked to rank the most important skills for new entrants into the workforce, "applied" skills (e.g., professionalism/work ethic, teamwork/collaboration, oral communication, ethics/social responsibility) were consistently rated as the top five skills. In fact, compared to "basic" knowledge (e.g., English language, mathematics, science, reading comprehension), only one was consistently rated in the top five: reading comprehension (for detailed rankings, see Casner-Lotto & Benner, 2006, Tables 3–5). More recent research reports continue to reinforce this notion. For example, in a national survey of 8,969 respondents that included K-12 educators, postsecondary instructors, as well as workforce supervisors and human resource professionals, Elchert, Latino, Bobek, Way, and Casillas (2017) found that an overwhelming number of K-12 educators (90.4%), postsecondary instructors (86.3%), and workforce professionals (83.0%) consider SEL skills to be important for success in college[2] and work. Further, a recent report from LinkedIn (2018) shows that training for SEL skills in areas like leadership, collaboration, and communication is the number one training priority for workforce professionals, which included 1,800 talent developers, people managers, and executives (from a sample of 4,000 global professionals contacted via their LinkedIn profile). Thus, altogether, the evidence for the desirability of SEL skills in the workforce is strong, particularly given that organizations around the world are emphasizing a need to train for these skills and seem prepared to make a substantial monetary investment in this area.

Feasibility—Can we build a bridge? This criterion focuses on a solution having the empirical and technological support necessary to be delivered and implemented successfully. For the purpose of the proposed system, we focus on a low-stakes application; that is, we focus on a solution that is meant to help individuals develop their skills based on assessment, feedback, and intervention (as opposed to a high-stakes application such as selection or promotion). From an empirical perspective, there are hundreds—if not thousands—of primary studies and several influential reviews and meta-analyses (e.g., Barrick & Mount, 1991; Poropat, 2009; Roberts, Kuncel, Shiner, Caspi, & Goldberg, 2007; Sackett & Walmsley, 2014) that show personality, behavior, and SEL skills are important predictors of academic, work, and life outcomes above and beyond cognitive ability. In addition, there is a growing literature (e.g., Corcoran, Cheung, Kim, & Xie, in press; Durlak et al., 2011; Kautz, Heckman, Diris, Ter Weel, & Borghans, 2014; National Academies of Sciences, Engineering, and Medicine, 2017; National Research Council, 2012) that demonstrates that SEL skills are amenable to instruction and development. Together, this literature can be leveraged to build validity arguments and support claims that (1) SEL skills are associated with important outcomes, (2) we can measure these skills with reasonable levels of reliability and validity, and (3) these skills can be improved. Besides empirical support, another aspect of feasibility is whether technology can support a solution like an SEL formative assessment system. The technology needed is likely to involve an online platform accessible via a variety of Internet-connected devices (e.g., desktops, laptops, mobile) with a user-friendly interface that can administer an assessment, score said assessment, deliver reports, and provide personalized recommendations on resources that can be used to improve a user's SEL skills. Although this list of features may not have been feasible 15 years ago, we are happy to report that current assessment delivery technology fully supports such features. Indeed, there are some offerings that incorporate many of these features (e.g., ETS's [n.d.] WorkFORCE® Assessment for Job Fit).

Viability—Should we build a bridge? This criterion often focuses on financial aspects, including costs, to build and sustain a solution (Brown, 2009). Although profit is an important consideration when designing and developing a solution—particularly if it is a product or service that is offered for sale—in this thought exercise, we focus on other important considerations that are relevant to achieving the goal of helping individuals to be better prepared for the workforce. Specifically, we focus on two key issues: (1) using a common framework to which educators and workforce professionals can align, and (2) incorporating checks for fidelity of implementation. First, there are a number of SEL frameworks that have been advanced in the past few years (e.g., Camara, O'Connor, Mattern, & Hanson, 2015; Nagaoka, Farrington, Ehrlich, & Heath, 2015; National Research Council, 2012). Although each of them have relative strengths and weaknesses, what is important to this discussion is that they all use theory and empirical evidence to articulate a comprehensive framework by which knowledge and skills that are relevant to education and the workforce should be organized. Most importantly, they all serve as a way to create a common language among stakeholders (e.g., students, parents, educators, administrators, employers, and policymakers) that can be used to better align the skills needed by employers to those taught in the educational pipeline. Thus, these frameworks appear viable for serving as a foundation for a formative assessment system that can help to bridge the SEL skills needed in workforce settings. Second, fidelity of implementation is as important as the content of a solution. It is not unusual for implementation problems to be linked to lowered—or even null—efficacy (e.g., Marzano, 2013; Penuel, Fishman, Cheng, & Sabelli, 2011; for a comprehensive review of factors affecting implementation, see Durlak & DuPre, 2008). Thus, from our perspective, viable solutions need to include system-wide supports for implementation that include awareness campaigns (e.g., information about SEL skills), user training (e.g., PD and/or professional learning communities), documentation on how a program should be implemented as well as how it actually was implemented, and regular evaluation and discussion of lessons learned during implementation. All of these would be designed to realize the maximum potential for the efficacy of the solution. All in all, the evidence suggests that an SEL formative assessment system could be viable.

Knowing that an SEL formative assessment system is desirable, feasible, and viable is a critical first step in the design process. However, it is also critical to determine how the design will be developed. To this end, we recommend a principled approach to designing an SEL formative assessment system. This approach is described below, followed by an example of what elements an SEL formative assessment system might contain.

Principled Approach

To design and develop desirable, feasible, and viable assessments, it is important to follow design-based approaches, better known as principled approaches or evidence-centered design (see Ferrara, Lai, Reilly, & Nichols, 2016). These approaches provide guidance for considering factors external to the assessment along with the actual content of the assessment (Ferrara et al., 2016; Mislevy & Haertel, 2007; Nichols, 2013). In addition to measuring the construct of interest, under principled approaches, developers are reminded that having more data is not the same as having useful data (Mislevy, 2011). When creating assessments, developers may become preoccupied with measuring the intended construct without considering what information the assessment will provide, who the appropriate population is, how the assessment will be delivered, and how the information can inform the purpose for designing and developing a measure (e.g., diagnosis, intervention, training). Principled approaches address these important considerations and allow for assessment development across a variety of content areas with a broad range of assessment types.

When developing assessments under a principled approach, it is valuable to have a theory of action (a.k.a. theory of change) that keeps the intended purpose, users, uses, and consequences of the assessment in mind throughout design and development decisions. A theory of action is a way to describe the types of actions (in the form of an intervention, program, coordinated initiative, or solution) that bring about the intended outcomes and consequences of an initiative, such as the one articulated in this chapter. Each activity is tied to an outcome in a causal framework, revealing the web of activities required to bring about an intended outcome. A theory of action provides a working model against which to test hypotheses and assumptions about what design decisions will best bring about a solution that will accomplish the intended purpose (Taplin & Clark, 2012).

Description of the Formative Assessment & Instruction System Theory of Action

For the purpose of this chapter, we articulate a theory of action of a formative assessment and instruction system for assessing and developing SEL skills. The primary purpose of the system is to provide accurate information and feedback (to educators, administrators, students, and parents) on high school students' SEL skills that can inform instruction and interventions for helping students to improve their skills, succeed in educational contexts, and be better prepared to enter the workforce. Figure 3.1 provides a flowchart capturing a high-level theory of action, which is briefly described below in narrative form. The theory of action is divided into three overall portions: awareness and system design, a formative assessment and instruction cycle, and outcomes.

Awareness and System Design

User education and awareness of SEL. The theory of action begins with user education and awareness of SEL, what it is, and how these concepts can facilitate students' academic, workplace, and life success. This awareness may, in turn, lead to institutions (schools/districts) designing a solution (or purchasing an existing one, if it is sensitive to the local context) and making it available to their students. Unlike core academic skills solutions, which are well known in the marketplace, SEL is relatively new and may require a much more intentional and persistent awareness campaign to educate users on the appropriate (and less appropriate) ways to utilize this type of information.

Design. This part of the process captures the design of an SEL formative assessment system. Note that a school/institution could also choose to purchase and use an existing system. If designing a new system, the content should be informed by the existing research on SEL skills that predict outcomes of interest (e.g., the literature that shows conscientiousness predicts grade point average, higher year-over-year retention, and graduation rates) and resources

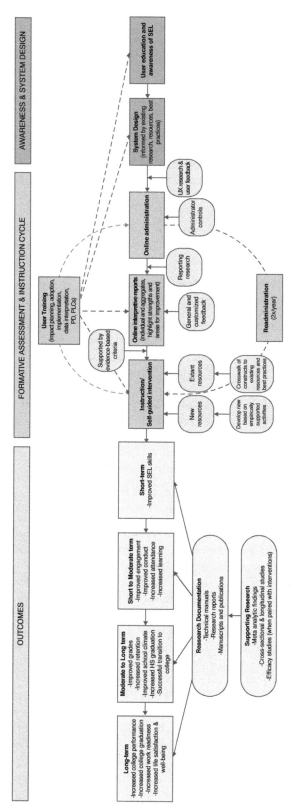

FIGURE 3.1 Proposed theory of action for an SEL formative assessment & instruction system.

that clearly identify these skills and break them down into measurable/observable pieces, such as ACT's Behavioral Performance Level Descriptors (PLDs; Casillas, Way, McKinniss, Colbow, & Hileman, 2016), which are empirically supported descriptions of the effectiveness levels of task-related, interpersonal, and self-regulatory behaviors needed to be successful in education and career contexts (for an example of PLDs for Persistence: Maintaining Effort, see Figure 3.2; for a review of the development of the PLDs, see Latino et al., 2017).

Listing Domain	Sustaining Effort
Component	Persistence
Sub-component	Maintaining Effort

Behavioral Knowledge and Skill Statements for Maintaining Effort	
Highly effective	• Almost always completes tasks even when he/she finds them boring, irrelevant, or unstimulating • Almost always maintains an appropriate level of effort even during challenging tasks and even without help • Works consistently at an appropriate level and knows when to take breaks
Effective	• Maintains an appropriate level of effort with help • Modifies his/her effort when he/she is working too quickly or slowly in order to get back on track
Somewhat effective	• Needs frequent intervention and help to complete a task he/she finds unstimulating • Sometimes works too quickly or slowly but can get back on track and complete tasks with supervision
Not effective	• Does not maintain an appropriate level of effort even with help • Abandons tasks that he/she finds unstimulating • Works too quickly and gets burned out or works too slowly and doesn't complete tasks

FIGURE 3.2 Example of PLDs for Maintaining Effort (subcomponent within Persistence) from the ACT Holistic Framework.

Reproduced by permission from Casillas, Way, McKinniss, Colbow, & Hileman, 2016.

Formative Assessment and Instruction Cycle

Administration. Administration of the SEL assessment system would ideally take place online. This would streamline the time and resources needed to administer and score the assessment, provide reports, and track progress on SEL skill development over time. Administration should be facilitated by simple and intuitive administrator controls, which could be refined on the basis of user experience (UX) research and iteration of the user interface.

Reports. After a student has completed an assessment, an interpretive report should be available highlighting areas where a student exhibits strength and also areas where a student can improve. These interpretive reports will be informed, in part, on the empirically established levels of behavioral effectiveness available in the SEL research literature and existing descriptions of effective SEL behavior (e.g., ACT's Behavior PLDs). Ideally, these reports could be refined on the basis of UX research and customer feedback. Reports should also be available at the aggregate level (classroom, school, and district) to allow educators and administrators to evaluate aggregate patterns of SEL skills and allow them to make instruction and resourcing decisions (Manning, Way, & Casillas, 2017). It is the unfortunate case that schools and districts often have limited resources available to assist their students with SEL skills. Therefore, if a teacher (or district) notices that a particular student (or school) is struggling with certain SEL skills, then the resources that are available can be directed to where there will be the most benefit, that is, to the students (or school) that needs them the most.

Instruction/self-guided interventions. A distinguishing feature of formative assessment systems is their direct connection to instruction (for groups and classrooms) and self-guided interventions (for individuals). In the case of an SEL formative assessment system, these should be based on the literature of effective SEL instruction and interventions, such as Durlak et al.'s (2011) meta-analysis showing that SEL interventions improve students' SEL skills (effect size = 0.57) and academic achievement (effect size = 0.27). A more recent meta-analysis of school-based SEL intervention research that met high methodological standards (Corcoran et al., in press) also found support for SEL interventions in school, such as predicting achievement in reading (effect size = 0.25), mathematics (effect size = 0.26), and science (effect size = 0.19). In addition, there are organizations such as OpenEd that contain online resources and offer more activities and opportunities for personalized instruction to individual students, as well as organizations like the National Council for Community and Education Partnerships (NCCEP) that have developed in- and after-school curriculum that emphasizes SEL skills (NCCEP, 2017). Finally, frameworks of SEL skills such as the Behavioral PLDs within ACT's Holistic Framework (Camara et al., 2015; Casillas et al., 2016) can guide the organization and scaffolding of curriculum, tools, and/or activities according to empirically established levels of behavioral effectiveness.

Re-administration. As is the case with any formative solution, part of its value lies in the re-administration of the assessment in order to track growth and examine change. Based on existing usage patterns and the research literature, we believe that the assessment component of a formative system could be administered approximately twice per academic year. Given this recommendation, a number of issues would need to be addressed in detailing a solution that goes beyond this high-level sketch. These would include how reports can accommodate tracking of changes (both in terms of UX and criterion-referenced reporting metrics that allow users to track meaningful changes in SEL skills), research on test–retest patterns and growth/change models for students in high school, as well as the need to develop multiple equated forms that demonstrate the psychometrically properties (e.g., reliability, accuracy) needed to support the intended interpretations across user groups (e.g., students, parents, educators, administrators).

User training. Given the relative novelty of SEL solutions in the market, it is important for an SEL formative assessment system to receive the support of a range of services that can assist users with a variety of adoption, implementation, and training needs. These include system adoption and implementation, embedding the system into district- and school-level plans, interpretation and dissemination of assessment results, PD options for educators and administrators, district and school SEL improvement planning, as well as professional learning communities that come together to discuss successes and address concerns. These services would go a long way to support intended uses of an SEL formative assessment system and to ensure it is implemented properly. Monitoring of the implementation of the system is an important point that should not be overlooked. As with any intervention, it is critical to ensure the SEL formative assessment system is implemented with fidelity in order for the maximum benefit to be attained. Schools and districts should periodically monitor the delivery of the assessment and curriculum to ensure that efficacious delivery of the system according to best practices. Further, it is important that school staff be the ones to deliver the interventions; for example, the Durlak et al.'s (2011) meta-analysis found that improvements in academic achievement as a result of SEL interventions were not found when those interventions were delivered by nonschool staff.

Outcomes

The outcomes section of the SEL theory of action is divided into four parts, depending on when the outcome is expected to occur after taking part in the SEL formative assessment system. The primary short-term outcome is an improvement in SEL skills. Short- to moderate-term outcomes include increased engagement in academic activities, improved conduct, increased attendance, and increased learning. Moderate- to long-term outcomes include improved grades (grade point average), increased retention, improved school climate, increased high school graduation rates, and a successful transition to college. Finally, long-term outcomes include increased college performance, increased college graduation rates, increased work readiness (i.e., increased likelihood of task performance, organizational citizenship, and decreased likelihood of counterproductive behavior), and increased life satisfaction and well-being.

As can be seen in the above discussion, having a theory of action allows designers, developers, and researchers to have a common understanding of the intended purposes, users, uses, and consequences of a solution. However, since the theory of action is written at a high level, we wanted to provide a more specific example to illustrate the use of an SEL formative assessment system.

Improving Persistence: A Use Case

As an example of how such a formative assessment system might work, let's consider a cycle of the assessment/intervention loop as shown in Figure 3.1 that focuses on the SEL skill of persistence, which has been documented in research studies as one of the most predictive SEL skills (Poropat, 2009). In this case, an assessment of persistence would be administered to establish a baseline measure of the skill for each student. After taking the assessment, each student would be provided an interpretive report that gives their assessment score and feedback that helps to contextualize the score and provide a basis for improving their persistence. However, even the best interpretive report is not sufficient for skill building. Therefore, the next step would be some kind of instruction or intervention, either self-guided, led by an instructor, or a combination, which shows students how to improve their persistence across a range of relevant scenarios. A few months later, the assessment would be re-administered in order to track students' skill growth and provide further feedback and guidance in an iterative or "formative" manner.

After giving feedback and interventions to help the students improve their persistence skills, the re-administration of the assessments would reflect the most immediate outcome of those improved skills. Increased persistence will be more likely to lead to better learning and engagement, as students learn not to get discouraged by difficult academic assignments, social pressures, or other challenges typically faced by high schoolers, where instead they persevere on their academic tasks and complete their work. Ultimately, their grades are more likely to improve, and students will be more likely to stay in school. Staying in school and getting better grades makes it more likely that students will graduate high school on time and have the knowledge and skills needed to successfully transition to college. In turn, this will make it more likely that students will persist in college-level coursework, successfully graduate from college, and be prepared to transition into the workforce. Throughout this process, students would be more likely to feel efficacious as a function of increased persistence and its positive outcomes, and thus would be more likely to feel confident in school, enjoy school, and maximize their learning.

There are several additional elements to be considered to ensure that the formative assessment system works as intended. First, PD, as mentioned previously, is critical to enable educators to be able to provide quality instruction on improving SEL skills (for a review of key components for PD, see DeSimone, 2009). This can include best practices for teaching SEL skills, detailed descriptions of various levels of effectiveness of SEL skills (see example of Persistence PLDs in Figure 3.2; Casillas et al., 2016), and sets of prebuilt activities that educators can either use or adapt to their classrooms (e.g., ACT Tessera Teacher Playbook; ACT, 2017). Additionally, it is important that interventions are implemented with fidelity, otherwise their positive benefits may not be fully realized (Durlak & DuPre, 2008). This could be addressed through PD activities, professional learning communities, and through teachers being observed by SEL subject-matter experts to provide constructive feedback and suggestions. Finally, there are various kinds of assessments and technology that could be leveraged to provide indicators of SEL skills and implementation fidelity. Assessments could range from simple self-report assessments, experience sampling, choosing among potential responses to hypothetical situations (i.e., situational judgment tests), gamified assessments where the assessment aspect is less salient and tasks are more engaging, and teacher behavioral observations of student SEL skills. Technology allows even more options to present engaging assessment and instruction, as well as ensure that interventions are implemented with high degree of uniformity and fidelity. Students could take online assessments that include animations or video clips, play an online game or activity designed to assess certain skills, receive interactive reporting that allows them to take a deeper dive into their assessment scores, and view live or recorded online lessons focused on improving SEL skills. Online delivery of assessments and instruction provides a higher degree of implementation fidelity, as it is easier to ensure each student is receiving the same content and quality UX as they move through the formative assessment system.

Conclusions and Future Directions

This chapter has communicated the value of developing students' SEL skills in preparation for entering the workforce and proposed features of a formative assessment system that would achieve this goal, while following design science principles of desirability, feasibility, and viability. As described at the beginning of the chapter, SEL skills are critical to workforce readiness in terms of both predicting important work outcomes and in terms of employer desirability. However, the oft-discussed "skills gap" shows that we are still a long way from meeting the workforce demand for work-ready employees (for a thoughtful and wide-ranging discussion of this topic, see Burrus, Mattern, Naemi, & Roberts, 2017).

Educational institutions, employers, and governments can leverage design science to bridge the skills gap between K–12 and workforce and design SEL formative assessment and training systems that will enable future workers to develop the skills they need throughout their educational journey and cross the bridge that allows them to be successful not just at work but also in life.

There are additional factors that should be considered during the design and development of a system such as the one described in this chapter. The first is beyond the scope of this chapter and involves identifying institutional constraints and hurdles to implementing such a system in K–12 and postsecondary institutions and possible ways to overcome such hurdles. An incomplete list would include aspects such as constraints on classroom time, teacher availability, financial resources, empowering educators through PD and professional learning communities to deliver SEL curriculum, and so on. One possible solution to some of the constraints (e.g., teacher time) is placing more emphasis on the importance of SEL skills and their associated outcomes to make the case to administrators and policymakers that classroom time spent on this topic has beneficial short-, moderate-, and long-term effects[3] and return on investment (see, for examples, Taylor et al., 2017). Further, supports for educators such as PD, professional learning communities, and help with evaluating implementation fidelity of instruction will help SEL formative assessment systems to be successful.

Stakeholders also need to emphasize the importance of holistic approaches that include empirically supported frameworks that can be leveraged for communication purposes, as well as serve as a common foundation from which to develop formative systems. Further, engaging in design thinking (i.e., approaches based on design science) by designing assessments and interventions with the end in mind (i.e., an important outcome of education should be a workforce with a broad range of SEL competencies) will help to avoid creating solutions that are looking for a problem to solve (e.g., a one-shot SEL summative test that will "magically" address workforce readiness needs) but that only contributes noise to an already noisy discussion. Especially important in the design process is the need for iteration, which is common in research—as it is part of the scientific process—but is less commonly seen in education and workforce practices, which are replete with examples of applying the "latest trend" without taking the necessary time for iterating through variations of a solution. Equally important as iteration is evaluation. Without proper evaluation of a solution, including UX, examination of individual components, and fidelity of implementation, it is difficult to determine the solution's efficacy and to pinpoint where iteration is needed and where it is "good enough." Finally, evaluation can help us to answer the ultimate question of any scaled approach aimed to help individuals develop skills: What works for whom when (or under what circumstances)?

Of course, no one solution can ever address all of the needs surrounding workforce readiness, but we believe that a system such as the one articulated in this chapter has a great deal of potential for helping prepare the students of today to be the hardworking, cooperative, resilient, and creative employees of tomorrow.

Notes

1 The purpose of formative assessment is to monitor student learning to provide ongoing feedback to instructors for improving their teaching and to students for improving their learning; formative assessments tend to be low stakes. In contrast, the purpose of summative assessment is to evaluate student learning at the end of an instructional unit, course, or term of study by comparing the results against some standard or benchmark; summative assessments tend to be high stakes (Black & Wiliam, 1998).

2 We use the term "college" to refer to a broad range of possible postsecondary opportunities rather than just a traditional four-year university. This includes, but is not limited to, two-year degree-granting institutions, certificate programs, vocational training, and so on.

3 For example, time spent on helping students to develop their self-management and self-control skills will lead to better behaved students, thus lowering the amount of time that teachers need to spend dealing with classroom misconduct. In turn, this will lead to additional instruction time and more learning opportunities for students. Therefore, time spent developing students' SEL skills can not only lead to better students (and improved classroom learning environments) but, over time, to better workers.

References

ACT. (2017). *ACT Tessera teacher playbook*. Iowa City, IA: ACT.

Barrick, M. R., & Mount, M. K. (1991). The big five personality dimensions and job performance: A meta-analysis. *Personnel Psychology, 44*(1), 1–26.

Black, P., & Wiliam, D. (1998). Assessment and classroom learning. *Assessment in Education: Principles, Policy, & Practice, 5*(1), 7–74. doi:10.1080/0969595980050102

Bleidorn, W. (2012). Hitting the road to adulthood: Short-term personality development during a major life transition. *Personality and Social Psychology Bulletin, 38*(12), 1594–1608.

Borghans, L., Duckworth, A. L., Heckman, J. J., & ter Weel, B. (2008). The economics and psychology of personality traits. *Journal of Human Resources, 43*(4), 972–1059.

Bowles, S., Gintis, H., & Osborne, M. (2001). The determinants of earnings: A behavioral approach. *Journal of Economic Literature, 39*(4), 1137–1176.

Brown, T. (2009). *Change by design: How design thinking transforms organizations and inspires innovation*. New York, NY: Harper Business.

Burrus, J., Mattern, K., Naemi, B., & Roberts, R. (2017). *Building better students: Preparation for the workforce*. New York, NY: Oxford University Press.

Camara, W., O'Connor, R., Mattern, K., & Hanson, M. A. (2015). *Beyond academics: A holistic framework for enhancing education and workplace success*. Iowa City, IA: ACT.

Casillas, A., Way, J., McKinniss, T., Colbow, A., & Hileman, R. (2016). *ACT behavioral performance level descriptors*. Iowa City, IA: ACT. Retrieved from https://www.act.org/content/dam/act/unsecured/documents/ACT-Behavioral-Performance-Level-Descriptors-rev2.pdf

Casner-Lotto, J., & Benner, M. W. (2006). *Are they really ready to work? Employers' perspectives on the basic knowledge and applied skills of new entrants to the 21st century US workforce.* Washington, DC: Partnership for 21st Century Skills.

Collaborative for Academic, Social, and Emotional Learning (CASEL). (2018). *CASEL.* Retrieved from https://casel.org/

Connelly, B. S., & Ones, D. S. (2010). An other perspective on personality: Meta-analytic integration of observers' accuracy and predictive validity. *Psychological Bulletin, 136*(6), 1092–1122. doi:10.1037/a0021212

Corcoran, R. P., Cheung, A., Kim, E., & Xie, C. (in press). Effective universal school-based social and emotional learning programs for improving academic achievement: A systematic review and meta-analysis of 50 years of research. *Educational Research Review.* doi:10.1016/j.edurev.2017.12.001

Desimone, L. M. (2009). Improving impact studies of teachers' professional development: Toward better conceptualizations and measures. *Educational Researcher, 38*(3), 181–199.

Durlak, J. A., & DuPre, E. P. (2008). Implementation matters: A review of research on the influence of implementation on program outcomes and the factors affecting implementation. *American Journal of Community Psychology, 41*(3–4), 327–350.

Durlak, J. A., Weissberg, R. P., & Molly, P. (2010). A meta-analysis of after-school programs that seek to promote personal and social skills in children and adolescents. *American Journal of Community Psychology, 45*(3–4), 294–309.

Durlak, J. A., Weissberg, R. P., Dymnicki, A. B., Taylor, R. D., & Schellinger, K. B. (2011). The impact of enhancing students' social and emotional learning: A meta-analysis of school-based universal interventions. *Child Development, 82*(1), 405–432.

Elchert, D., Latino, C., Bobek, B., Way, J., & Casillas, A. (2017). *The importance of behavioral skills and navigation factors for education and work success.* Iowa City, IA: ACT.

ETS. (n.d.) *WorkFORCE Assessment for Job Fit.* Retrieved from https://www.ets.org/workforce/about

Ferrara, S., Lai, E., Reilly, A., & Nichols, P. D. (2016). Principled approaches to assessment design, development, and implementation. In A. A. Rupp & J. P. Leighton (Eds.), *The Wiley handbook of cognition and assessment: Frameworks, methodologies, and applications* (pp. 41–74). West Sussex, UK: John Wiley & Sons.

Garcia, E. (2014). *The need to address noncognitive skills in the education policy agenda* (Briefing Paper #386). Washington, DC: Economic Policy Institute. Retrieved from: https://www.epi.org/files/2014/the-need-to-address-noncognitive-skills-12-02-2014.pdf

Heckman, J. J. (2006). Skill formation and the economics of investing in disadvantaged children. *Science, 312*(5782), 1900–1902.

Heckman, J. J., & Rubinstein, Y. (2001). The importance of noncognitive skills: Lessons from the GED testing program. *The American Economic Review, 91*(2), 145–149.

Heckman, J. J., Stixrud, J., & Urzua, S. (2006). The effects of cognitive and noncognitive abilities on labor market outcomes and social behavior. *Journal of Labor Economics, 24*(3), 411–482.

IDEO. (2015). *The field guide to human-centered design.* San Francisco, CA: IDEO.

Kautz, T., Heckman, J. J., Diris, R., ter Weel, B., & Borghans, L. (2014). *Fostering and measuring skills: Improving cognitive and noncognitive skills to promote lifetime success* (No. w20749). Cambridge, MA: National Bureau of Economic Research.

Latino, C. A., Way, J., Colbow, A., Bouwers, S., Casillas, A., & McKinniss, T. (2017). *The development of behavioral performance level descriptors.* Iowa City, IA: ACT. Retrieved from https://www.act.org/content/dam/act/unsecured/documents/R1620-developing-behavioral-plds-2017-04.pdf

Levin, H. M. (2012). More than just test scores. *Prospects, 42*(3), 269–284.

Lindqvist, E., & Vestman, R. (2011). The labor market returns to cognitive and non-cognitive ability: Evidence from the Swedish enlistment. *American Economic Journal: Applied Economics, 3*(1), 101–128.

LinkedIn. (2018). *2018 workplace learning report: The rise and responsibility of talent development.* Sunnyvale, CA: LinkedIn Learning. Retrieved from https://learning.linkedin.com/content/dam/me/learning/en-us/pdfs/linkedin-learning-workplace-learning-report-2018.pdf

Manning, S., Way, J., & Casillas, A. (2017). *Measuring social and emotional learning development with behavioral performance level descriptors.* Iowa City, IA: ACT. Retrieved from https://www.act.org/content/dam/act/unsecured/documents/R1671-measuring-sel-with-plds-2017-10.pdf

Markle, R., Brenneman, M., Jackson, T., Burrus, J., & Robbins, S. (2013). *Synthesizing frameworks of higher education student learning outcomes.* ETS Research Report Series, ETS RR-13-2. Princeton, NJ: Educational Testing Service.

Marzano, R. J. (2003). *What works in schools: Translating research into action.* Alexandria, VA: Association for Supervision and Curriculum Development.

Mislevy, R. J. (2011). *Evidence-centered design for simulation-based assessment* (CRESST Report 800). Los Angeles, CA: National Center for Research on Evaluation, Standards, and Student Testing (CRESST).

Mislevy, R. J., & Haertel, G. D. (2007). Implications of evidence-centered design for educational testing. *Educational Measurement: Issues and Practice, 25*(4), 6–20. doi:10.1111/j.1745–3992.2006.00075.x

Nagaoka, J., Farrington, C. A., Ehrlich, S. B., & Heath, R. D. (2015). *Foundations for young adult success: A developmental framework* (Concept Paper for Research and Practice). Chicago, IL: University of Chicago Consortium on Chicago School Research.

National Academies of Sciences, Engineering, and Medicine. (2017). *Supporting students' college success: The role of assessment of intrapersonal and interpersonal competencies.* Washington, DC: The National Academies Press. https://doi.org/10.17226/24697

National Association of Colleges and Employers. (2016). *Job outlook 2017.* Bethlehem, PA: Author.

National Council for Community and Education Partnerships. (2017). *Career & College clubs* (7th ed.). Washington, DC: National Council for Community and Education Partnerships.

National Research Council. (2012). *Education for life and work: Developing transferable knowledge and skills in the 21st century.* Washington, DC: The National Academies Press.

Nichols, P. (2013). *What is PDE?* London, UK: Pearson. Retrieved from https://www.pearson.com/content/dam/one-dot-com/one-dot-com/global/Files/efficacy-and-research/schools/004___NGLA_Nichols_WhatisPDE_Formatted_1213.pdf

Oh, I.-S., Wang, G., & Mount, M. K. (2011). Validity of observer ratings of the five-factor model of personality traits: A meta-analysis. *Journal of Applied Psychology, 96*(4), 762–773. doi:10.1037/a0021832

Organization for Economic Co-Operation and Development. (2015). *Skills for social progress: The power of social and emotional skills.* OECD Publishing. doi:10.1787/9789264226159-en

Penuel, W. R., Fishman, B. J., Cheng, B. H., & Sabelli, N. (2011). Organizing research and development at the intersection of learning, implementation, and design. *Educational Researcher, 40*(7), 331–337.

Poropat, A. E. (2009). A meta-analysis of the five-factor model of personality and academic performance. *Psychological Bulletin, 135*(2), 322–338.

Poropat, A. E. (2014). A meta-analysis of adult-rated child personality and academic performance in primary education. *British Journal of Educational Psychology, 84*(2), 239–252. doi:10.1111/bjep.12019

Roberts, B. W., Kuncel, N. R., Shiner, R., Caspi, A., & Goldberg, L. R. (2007). The power of personality: The comparative validity of personality traits, socioeconomic status, and cognitive ability for predicting important life outcomes. *Perspectives on Psychological Science, 2*(4), 313–345.

Roberts, B. W., Luo, J., Briley, D. A., Chow, P., Su, R., & Hill, P. L. (2017). A systematic review of personality trait change through intervention. *Psychological Bulletin, 143*(2), 117–141.

Roberts, B. W., Walton, K., & Viechtbauer, W. (2006). Patterns of mean-level change in personality traits across the life course: A meta-analysis of longitudinal studies. *Psychological Bulletin, 132*(1), 1–25.

Sackett, P. R., & Walmsley, P. T. (2014). Which personality attributes are most important in the workplace? *Perspectives on Psychological Science, 9*(5), 538–551.

Salgado, J. F., & Tauriz, G. (2014). The five-factor model, forced-choice personality inventories and performance: A comprehensive meta-analysis of academic and occupational validity studies. *European Journal of Work and Organizational Psychology, 23*(1), 3–30.

Secretary's Commission on Achieving Necessary Skills. (1991). *What work requires of schools: A SCANS report for America 2000.* Washington, DC: US Department of Labor.

Segal, C. (2013). Misbehavior, education, and labor market outcomes. *Journal of the European Economic Association, 11*(4), 743–779. doi:10.1111/jeea.12025.

Simon, H. A. (1996). *The sciences of the artificial.* Cambridge, MA: MIT press.

Taplin, D. H., & Clark, H. (2012). *Theory of change basics: A primer on theory of change.* New York, NY: Actknowledge. Retrieved from http://www.theoryofchange.org/wp-content/uploads/toco_library/pdf/ToCBasics.pdf

Taylor, R. D., Oberle, E., Durlak, J. A., & Weissberg, R. P. (2017). Promoting positive youth development through school-based social and emotional learning interventions: A meta-analysis of follow-up effects. *Child Development, 88*(4), 1156–1171.

4

ADVANCING WORKFORCE READINESS AMONG LOW-INCOME AND MINORITY HIGH SCHOOL STUDENTS

Barbara Schneider and Lindsey Young

Solving a Workforce Readiness Problem

Most young people, whether they are in industrialized or developing countries, expect to continue their formal education after secondary school (OECD, 2017). For many adolescents, however, these ambitions are unlikely to be fulfilled (Schneider, Kim, & Klager, 2017). There are fewer job opportunities for young people today, especially those without some postsecondary education or training (Manyika et al., 2017). Community life has been replaced by the virtual spaces of social media, reshaping relationships, access to knowledge, and communication throughout a host of societal institutions (Putnam, 2015). Access, persistence, and completion of one's education continue to be the major interventions that countries recognize as critical for supporting young people's economic stability and political growth. However, this is particularly challenging in countries where there are not enough educational institutions or financial resources for all those who desire to attend secondary school, making enrolling in postsecondary school a remote possibility. Even in developed countries, educational opportunities remain inaccessible for certain economic and social groups. This is perhaps best understood in the United States, where there are wide differences by socioeconomic status, race and ethnicity, and family resources, all of which impact postsecondary school enrollment.

In 2016, the U.S. Department of Labor reported that the percentage of high school completers who entered college immediately after graduation was 83% for those from high-income families. There was no measurable gap between the enrollment rates of students in low- and middle-income families, with 64% from middle-income and 67% in low-income families enrolling in college immediately after high school graduation. The percentage difference between these groups is considerably smaller than the 12% gap 20 years ago. Today the gap between high- and low-income families has been almost cut in half, from 30% in 2000 to 16% in 2016. Understanding these changing estimates is critical for contextualizing college access and persistence in the United States. First, the financial security that once clearly distinguished those categorized as middle-income or lower-middle-income from those who are low-income has become questionable (Morduch & Schneider, 2017).[1] Occupations that once were the stalwart of middle-income households have become less reliable; for instance, teachers earn less in some states than those in jobs considered low-income (https://www.cnn.com/health).[2] Rising college costs have made higher education less affordable for a greater proportion of the population. These changes in affordability raise serious questions about the type of postsecondary education young people should pursue, especially given the uneven college persistence numbers between those from different income levels and racial and ethnic groups.

Second, while the proportion of low-income students who now enroll in college immediately after graduation has risen to nearly 70% in the United States (Bureau of Labor Statistics, 2018), the type of institutions such students attend becomes an important consideration with respect to students' future education options and labor market opportunities. Among young people in high-income families (defined as those earning over $100,000 a year), 61% attend four-year colleges, compared to enrollment rates of 45% for those in the $60,000–$99,999 range, 33% for those in the $30,000–$59,999 range, and 39% for those below $30,000. Twenty-one percent of those in the highest income bracket attend two-year colleges, 11% are working, and only 6% are neither enrolled in college nor working the year after high school graduation. For young people in families with incomes under $100,000, the number working nearly doubles (18% for those in the $60,000–$99,999 range, 24% for those in the $30,000–$50,9999 range, and 19% for those below $30,000). Among those not employed and not in college, the proportion of young people in the lowest income category is over three times greater than those in high-income families, at 19% (17% for those in the $30,000–$59,999 range and 10% in the next highest income bracket [Cooper, 2018]).

While enrollment rates have climbed, especially among students in lower income families (Snyder, de Brey, & Dillow, 2016), college completion rates continue to vary significantly by race and ethnicity. Within a 6-year period, 62% of Whites and 63% of Asians received their degree, whereas 46% of Hispanics and 38% of Blacks did so (Tate, 2017). Students who enroll in a four-year institution are more likely to receive their degree than students seeking a two-year degree. Few students transfer from a four-year to a two-year institution to finish their degrees, though Whites and Asians are more likely to do so compared to Hispanics and Blacks. Degree completion matters with respect to lifetime earnings, and students with a bachelor's degree can expect to earn about 65%

more over their lifetime than someone with only a high school diploma (Baum, Ma, & Payea, 2013; Chetty, Friedman, Saez, Turner, & Yagan, 2017).

These uneven completion rates by race and ethnicity are producing enormous financial and social costs for students as well as society (Bailey & Dynarski, 2011; Michelmore & Dynarski, 2016). Bachelor's degree completion not only means a higher income, but better health outcomes and increased social and political participation (Cohen & Syme, 2013; Hillygus, 2005; Oreopoulos & Petronijevic, 2013). Though, in most industrialized countries, a bachelor's degree accrues multiple benefits, degrees from two-year colleges and technical schools also increase the odds for higher labor market participation and wages compared to those who fail to complete high school or only attain a secondary school diploma (OECD, 2017).

The dramatic changes in labor market demands and the rise of technological innovations have created a priority for increased post-high school education— not only in industrialized countries but throughout the globe (OECD Horizon, 2020, 2017). While the pathways to receiving a postsecondary degree (especially for marginalized groups such as recent immigrants and low-income and minority students) vary by country, they are often fraught with multiple challenges regardless of their country's economic context (OECD, 2017). Many students receive the message that they should pursue more education and training after high school, but they often lack information regarding the different types of education and training options available to them, along with their associated costs. Oftentimes, they also lack social support from their families, and the type of preparation they received in high school excludes them from being a competitive applicant regardless of their future work and educational goals (Burkander, 2014).

This chapter begins by examining some of the economic and social constraints facing low-income and minority students in the United States as they consider their lives after high school. Some of these obstacles include the wide variation in parent behaviors and expectations that are devoted to educational preparation, including maintaining high educational aspirations (Schneider, 2015), monitoring and engaging in school work, and relying on and building social networks that can advance their children's education and career choices (Kim & Schneider, 2005). This chapter identifies a number of programs and interventions that have been created and implemented to address the difficulties many low-income and minority students experience. This is followed by a discussion of a new intervention directed at providing disadvantaged and vulnerable student populations access to support systems that can improve their postsecondary education and training choices, workforce readiness, and persistence to degree or certificate completion. We conclude by providing recommendations for the advancement of workforce readiness opportunities for low-income and minority students.

The Uncertain World of Work

Seventy-five years ago, graduation from high school was considered a major accomplishment. Today, most high school graduates worldwide expect to attend some form of postsecondary education. Although many of these young people will not reach their aspirations, their expectations for a higher degree match labor market predictions. For example, it has been estimated that the need for college graduates in the United States will be nearly twice (36 million) that of those with only a high school diploma (20 million) by 2024 (Bureau of Labor Statistics, 2015). However, it is not only a degree that will help young people succeed in their future lives; many economists and others predict the future will require deep knowledge within a specific field, the ability to communicate with diverse populations, effective critical thinking and problem-solving skills, and the ability to work collaboratively with others.

There are also strong predictions among labor economists that most work and jobs are unlikely to last a lifetime (World Economic Forum, 2016). Brighter, more stable jobs and professions in the future economy will be in fields such as science, technology, engineering, and mathematics (STEM), which are expected to grow. Yet, few students who attend college (both two- and four-year institutions) choose STEM majors in fields in which there is a labor shortage, particularly among underrepresented minorities and women (National Science Board, 2018). Other occupations that are also expected to grow are those in healthcare support occupations and in the service industry, but these tend to be low-paying and unstable, with little opportunity for advancement (Manyika et al., 2017). Experts agree that rapid changes in technology are taking place, but the impact of these changes on the future workforce is under debate. For example, while 48% of technology builders and analysts who responded to a survey conducted by the Pew Research Center stated that many jobs currently performed by humans will be replaced by artificial intelligence by 2025, 52% believe this will not displace more jobs than it creates in that time period (Smith & Anderson, 2014).

One major change that has affected the adolescent population is technology and increased access to information via the Internet. Rapid changes in technology have greatly impacted how adolescents, in particular, interact with one another and gather information. Today, more than 50% of teenagers text their friends daily using instant messaging (79%), video chat (59%), and other types of communication platforms (Pew Research Center, 2018). Smartphone ownership is increasing: 77% of all Americans own smartphones, up from 35% in 2011 (Pew Research Center, 2018). Ninety-five percent of high-income adults (>$100K) own a smartphone, compared to 64% of low-income adults (<$30K) (Anderson, 2017). Almost 75% of adolescents have access to a smartphone, with Black teens being the most likely to have access, at 85% (Lenhart, 2015). Ninety-five percent of teens report going online daily, with over half (56%) going online several times a day, and 24% online "almost constantly" (Lenhart, 2015).

While Whites, Blacks, and Hispanics are equally likely to own a smartphone, minorities rely on their phones for Internet access more frequently. For example, 13% of Hispanics and 12% of Blacks are smartphone-dependent, compared to only 4% of Whites (Anderson, 2015). Whereas 97% of high-income adults have access to multiple devices—such as a desktop or laptop computer—to get online, only 56% of low-income adults have such access (these differences in percentages are similar for broadband access: 94% for high-income adults compared to 53% for those who are low income [Anderson, 2017]). Those living in rural areas are two times as likely not to use the Internet as those who reside in urban or suburban areas (Anderson, Perrin, & Jiang, 2018).

These discrepancies in how individuals access information are very problematic, especially considering their potential to limit education and career opportunities. Minorities are more likely to use their phones to research information about jobs and to submit a job application (Anderson, 2015). Recent estimates by the Pew Foundation indicate that some 5 million school-age children do not have a broadband Internet connection at home, with low-income families (those earning less than $30,000) accounting for a disproportionate share (Anderson, 2017). Lower income Americans are more than twice as likely as those in other income groups to be classified as "digitally unprepared." For low-income and minority adolescents, smartphone dependency and lack of access to laptops and other computer devices at home and in schools (where access can be limited) can restrict their future plans, especially considering how education and career information is distributed today. Young people need opportunities that allow them informed choices about future education possibilities as they cope with an uncertain labor market where technology plays an increasingly fundamental role.

One of the widely accepted developmental tasks of adolescence used to be the formation of a consolidated sense of identity—a commitment to a set of values, beliefs, and goals to pursue (Erikson, 1950, 1968). However, recent researchers argue that identity formation today does not necessarily coalesce in adolescence or even later (Settersten, Ottusch, & Schneider, 2015). Instead, among many young adults, there is continual ruminative exploration of self and career, where the identity of "who I am" remains uncertain (Beyers & Luyckx, 2016). As uncertainty about what future jobs will be available (and for how long) is coupled with rapid changes in technology, the growing pressure for advanced degrees places today's adolescents in an ambiguous life-course position requiring flexibility, strategic information gathering, and strong support networks. Regardless of their economic and social resources, most adolescents face these pressures. However, these decisions are likely to be problematic for adolescents in families and schools lacking access to the often-obscure information and extensive support networks required for successful construction of educational and occupational plans. For adolescents with limited social and economic resources, decisions are overwhelmingly complicated. There is considerable anxiety and indecisiveness regarding which postsecondary pathway to pursue when considering its associated costs and the lack of assurance that a reasonable job awaits them upon attaining their degree.

College Knowledge and College Eligibility

The educational preparation that many low-income and minority students receive can be considered as one source of the disconnect between educational attainment and labor market opportunities that poses uncertainty for many young people. While this process starts in the early grades, it becomes patently obvious when examining the transition from high school to college. One way to understand the mismatch between educational preparation and postsecondary choices is to distinguish what constitutes college eligibility and college knowledge (Roderick, Nagaoka, & Coca, 2009). College eligibility refers to having taken college-preferred academic courses, received high grades and above-average class rank, and achieved college entrance exam scores that allow entry into typical four-year postsecondary institutions. College knowledge refers to behaviors such as preparing for and taking college entrance exams, applying to colleges, and seeking financial aid (including scholarships and other forms of support). Importantly, college eligibility consists of externally validated metrics linked with college acceptance, while college knowledge is comprised of external proxies and is subject to bias and misinterpretation of actual college entrance criteria and financial support (Fitzpatrick & Schneider, 2016). Initiatives to improve postsecondary enrollment have largely focused on one of these two forms of college readiness (for college knowledge, completing the Free Application for Federal Student Aid; for college eligibility, requiring more rigorous courses in math and science for high school graduation). Rarely have these initiatives been coupled in any meaningful way, often leading highly qualified students into (1) less-competitive colleges or (2) institutions that cost more than initially expected.

The school plays a critical role in the transition to college, though it is not the only one; family units, peer groups, and communities also form spaces where young people interact and develop their ambitions, social interactions, and normative belief systems. These other contexts, much like schools, are beset with their own challenges as young people try to make social connections, often finding themselves with weak social network supports to help them navigate work, education, community resources, and interpersonal relationships. In low-income urban and rural communities, where high school postsecondary enrollment rates tend to fall below statewide averages, these in- and out-of-school social supports are particularly challenging (Burkander, 2014; Schneider, 2015). The College Ambition Program (CAP) was created to address these concerns, aiming to aid students through their transition from high school to college. CAP (funded by the National Science Foundation) began six years ago with a small number of treatment schools serving low-income and minority students.

Increasing College Eligibility and Knowledge

Today, CAP is in 15 treatment schools located in urban areas (i.e., Detroit, Lansing, and Grand Rapids) and rural townships in the central part of Michigan. The population of students in CAP schools that are participating in this project is 46.9% Black, 12% Hispanic/Latino, 6.4% Asian, 3.2% two or more races, and slightly less than 1% Native American or Hawaiian. In the rural CAP schools, which are overwhelmingly White, the average household income is lower than the national and state average (Keaton, 2012). More importantly, these rural schools do not have a college-going culture; some parents are reluctant to send their adolescents to four-year colleges, especially ones that are residential (Burkander, 2014). CAP's focus is to help young people access higher education institutions given their personal preferences (e.g., reputation, school size, and location), academic record, and social and economic resources.

CAP is staffed by a site coordinator—a half-time teacher employed by the school (most often certified in either science or mathematics)—who manages the day-to-day operations of the center. Available before, during, and after school, site coordinators (a) reinforce the importance of attendance and perseverance for classroom work; (b) provide tutorial assistance; (c) strengthen bridges with teachers and staff in the school; and (d) arrange college visits and offer advice about college choices and financial aid. Additionally, tutoring is offered by college undergraduates whom we recruit and match with the race and ethnicity of the students. Tutors provide students with near-age role models to help them visualize themselves as college students (Schneider, Broda, Judy, & Burkander, 2013).

CAP also works with community organizations to take advantage of existing resources that support a college-going environment for the students. Through these community organizations, CAP has leveraged resources for college visits, obtained scholarship support, and provided tax advice to parents who find that their present tax status hinders their children from access to federal financial aid. While the results for CAP treatment schools are positive (Schneider, 2015), we recognized the limits of CAP to raise college enrollment rates in its initial form, especially for serving the most disadvantaged high school students in Detroit. For example, CAP surveys show that while tutoring activities are helpful to the students, it is simply unrealistic to raise ACT scores from 14 to 21, the mean of most four-year colleges. To augment CAP services and increase college enrollment rates further, the CAP team has been developing a digitized mobile-friendly platform to help students acquire the out-of-school experiences that colleges value for admission.

A Digitized Augmentation for Learning Postsecondary Access and Workforce Readiness

Recognizing society's need for technologically adaptive youth, CAP has evolved to include a playlist system that digitizes students' college-preparedness training while also streamlining the matching of students with an internship of their choosing. The aim here is to prioritize real-world experiences over traditional methods of learning, along with the transfer and formation of knowledge. The central idea is that learning is more likely to occur when knowledge is personalized and culminates in the creation of an artifact that can be monitored and disseminated through digital technology. This model allows the learner to take personal ownership by creating and experiencing out-of-school opportunities that are markers of performance, perseverance, and achievement valued by oneself and others—including postsecondary institutions and the labor market. Recent research shows the positive effects of personalized, customized learning experiences using badges and gamified learning in a number of settings. Implementing theories of connected learning, this type of venue gives students personal ownership over two crucial areas of their school career: (1) the college admission process and (2) subject-specific knowledge and experience in fields such as STEM. By adding such support into the existing high school curriculum and providing digitized scaffolds for increased learner involvement, students are presented with tasks that are motivating and innovative.

Working with businesses and college administrators, we designed several new supplements to the CAP resource base that we are implementing and testing this year. Students in current CAP schools are offered opportunities to participate in a free, widely accessible playlist program delivered on a digitized platform that monitors and, as described, rewards personalized learning on collections of remixable modules that comprise a common theme. These playlists are tailored to students' interests and strengths and are designed to induce motivation and teach college readiness material and particular skill sets that enhance students' success in the classroom.

When students complete such a playlist, they earn a badge—a publicly shareable, digital credential that shows evidence of a substantive learning outcome. The experiences on the playlists are developed by CAP personnel in collaboration with business and university partners to ensure that the badges and final "capstone" projects provide clear paths to higher education and careers. The progression from playlists to badges, capstone experiences, and college admission is shown in Figure 4.1.

Playlists are organized and grouped into pathways containing related content: College-Preparedness, Workplace Readiness, and Workplace Experience. Currently, the College-Preparedness pathway is being implemented in the high schools. The last two pathways, which are still under construction with the assistance of university and business partners, are specifically designed to prepare students for future internships in local businesses and educational communities. These pathways are more complex, as they need to be tailored to students' individual needs and interests.

FIGURE 4.1 Playlist roadmap for advancing to college.

Within the College-Preparedness pathway, there are several playlists that are designed to support students through the college application process, including: "Organizing and Preparing for the College Process," "Standardized Testing," "Crafting Your College Essay," "Paying for College," and "Building Your Extracurricular Resume." The playlist begins with an introductory page, acquainting students with the content of the module. Following the introductory page, students are taken through a series of modules that contain informational and actionable activities. Students engage in these activities and upload their material into a digital portfolio, which is shared, monitored, and discussed with their CAP site coordinator. Within a specific playlist, such as "Crafting Your College Essay," there are motivating and experiential modules that introduce content (which the students may or may not know) and a set of activities. Modules within "Crafting Your College Essay" include (a) "Why do I need to write an essay?"; (b) "Writing an excellent college application essay"; (c) "Selecting a topic and planning your writing"; (d) "Creating your first draft"; and (e) "Crafting your final draft." When the students successfully complete the activity, they receive a reward: for the essay playlist, the reward is a book on writing a successful college essay. Each completed playlist includes a review slide which serves to (1) remind students of what they have learned and (2) preview the content of the next playlist.

Over the past several months, we have piloted the financial playlist module in a randomized experiment with 100 students in Detroit-area high schools. It was encouraging that in the schools we targeted, over half of the graduating students began the program and worked through the activities, with students who attended CAP centers showing a significant increase over non-CAP visitors by over 10%. Conducting an analysis of planned college enrollment, we found a significant increase in the number of students who were applying to college that used the playlist modules, in contrast to the control condition. However, this was a limited test—not causal, but a "nudge" worthy of a more fully developed experiment.[3] We argue that these types of activities may be especially useful as support tools for high school students who are involved in other types of programs designed to help them acquire skills and knowledge for postsecondary school and training programs.

Developing Deeper Learning and Social and Emotional Skills

CAP is an informational and preparatory program designed to facilitate college-going, especially in those STEM disciplines where there are unequal representations of females and minorities (such as in the physical sciences or computer science).[4] Most recently, critics have been concerned with the lack of skills that many postsecondary graduates do not possess but that are needed by the labor market. Such skills are not just content-based but are those that also include intra- and interpersonal competencies such as problem-solving, communication, and collaborating. A number of commissions and studies were launched a decade after 2000 to examine this broad disconnect between cognitive, social, and emotional competencies and labor market demands. One of the most well known of these initiatives was the *Partnership for 21st Century Skills*, which argues that for students to be successful in college and careers, they are required to be proficient in critical thinking, problem-solving, communication, collaboration, creativity, and innovation (*Partnership for 21st Century Skills*, 2010, p. 2).[5] The release of this report was greeted with support from both the education and business community; within a very short period of time, a number of new reforms were introduced that were designed to improve both academic skills and cognitive strategies that create support for fostering social and emotional development. The range of the *21st Century Skills* report was global, and a large number of OECD countries also incorporated it in their new education policies and regulations (Ananiadou & Claro, 2009).

One of the most significant outcomes of the *21st Century Skills* report was a second effort by the National Research Council to review (1) what is meant by deeper learning, 21st-century skills, college and career readiness, and other such labels; (2) how these terms relate to each other; (3) the research that instantiates the relationships between these skills and success in education, work, and other adult civic and ethical responsibilities; and (4) what interventions could be used to identify the enactment of such skills both in and out of school. The ensuing report, *Education for Life and Work: Developing Transferable Knowledge and Skills for the 21st Century*, helped to reify and extend the reforms initiated by the *21st Century Skills* report. Other important reports were issued worldwide, also calling for a broader and deeper skill set that would help young people pursue a realistically prepared life pathway. The report suggested that while cognitive competencies had been studied quite extensively, inter- and intrapersonal skills (such as being organized, responsible, and hardworking) had not received the same attention but should be taken into account in light of emerging labor market demands for these social and emotional skill sets.[6] The report suggested that taking this broader perspective on what types of skills young people needed for the future was likely to support deep learning and transferrable social and emotional competencies.

Following the release of these reports and others, both in the United States and abroad, many studies and commissions were established to revive educational programs to make them more carefully matched to learning and working in complex environments—not necessarily just in content learning but also in developing cognitive skills such as problem-solving, imagination, perseverance ("grit"), flexibility, and cooperation. This emphasis on new skills was quickly adopted by the entire educational system, with multiple programs designed to strengthen academic, social, and emotional learning implemented into existing and new career and technical education (CTE) programs. While a number of these programs focused on elementary schools, others were developed to reenergize existing and new initiatives to strengthen high school students' career and technical skills, especially in STEM fields.

One place where U.S. federal reform efforts were directed was secondary schools—interestingly, comparable types of initiatives were also started in European and OECD countries, precipitated by OECD's (2015) report, *Skills for Social Progress: The Power of Social and Emotional Skills*. Making a similar case to the United States, this report describes why these types of programs are needed and why new policies and practices should be undertaken in OECD countries and partner economies. The central, global issue is how all children can be provided better educational pathways that meet their educational needs and the demands of the labor market. For students in secondary schools, where many of these programs have been initiated, the emphasis tends to be on hands-on workplace learning. This gap is being filled by a number of different types of programs; some of these are part of the secondary school system, such as in-school vocational or technical programs found in many northern European countries. Others are offered as associate degree or certificate processes. In many of these programs, students can engage in apprenticeships or intern experiences where they learn on-the-job training by working with professionals. Sometimes these programs are designed whereby students earn a salary with the assurance of a job when completing a specific training program. Many of these types of programs blend face-to-face learning and technology-based teaching, giving students opportunities in workplace settings where they can experience first-hand how to work in groups, problem solve, communicate, and present a confident, assured sense of self.

Transitions Programs from School to Work Reflecting the 21st-Century Framework

Vocational education is one of the most common programs designed to prepare students for the world of work. Within some countries, such as Germany and Finland, students decide (before entering 11th grade) whether they desire to pursue a technical program or a university education. Upon entering the vocational program, students receive some type of work-education hybrid program, which can include actual involvement in a place of work. In the United States, traditional types of vocational programs have shown a marked decline over the past several decades (Bills, 2009). However, there has been a more recent revival of work-related programs in high schools, which encourage students to enter programs where there are new initiatives such as career academies, youth apprenticeships, tech preprograms, co-op programs, and work-based learning centers.

In the past, students placed into vocational programs were typically viewed as less academically oriented and unlikely to attend postsecondary school following high school graduation (Carroll & Muller, 2018; Oakes & Saunders, 2008).

This stratification of the high school curriculum was often seen as inequitable, in which the students placed in vocational programs were often the least academically able and/or disproportionately minority students. Not surprisingly, these types of tracking practices have been criticized, and high schools have attempted to alter programs so that students are not channeled into specific programs viewed as unfit for academic work. In some countries, this tracking system has been viewed quite differently and students have seen the technical track as an opportunity to learn an employable skill set that would allow them into the marketplace. However, many countries are finding that students in these tracks may want to change their minds about entering certain occupations or are deciding to enter postsecondary school after completing secondary school. Options are now being put into place so a student can apply to attend postsecondary school regardless of their choice of track in secondary school. In some countries, educational systems use a course-by-course tracking system instead of these track programs, in which more academically able students are guided or selected into more advanced-level courses, typically in mathematics, science, and humanities.

Even though there have been changes in these once intractable placements and attempts to make them more porous, students still tend to identify with one track rather than another. Chmielewski (2014), examining responses from 15-year-olds on the 2003 Programme for International Student Assessment, found that about 45% of students identify themselves as belonging to an academic or vocational track. Comparing track placement programs with those that use course tracking, she found that not only are students more segregated when high schools divide their programs into vocational and academic tracks, but academic achievement also varies significantly between them. In the middle of their high school experience, students in the vocational track tend to have lower mathematics scores than those in the academic track. She argues that both types of programs have profound effects for how secondary students experience their high school program and are likely to influence future plans.

The real question is whether having these dual types of programs and experiences in high school increases the likelihood of students developing skill sets that allow them to successfully enter the labor market. A recent international literature review of various types of elementary and secondary technical and academic programs (Conn, Park, Nagakura, Khalil, & Corcoran, 2017) found that students who complete vocational education and training programs that most closely match with specific industries are more likely to find employment.[7] However, the effects of CTE programs, which are designed to prepare students for the labor market and postsecondary degrees (including internships, apprenticeships, and in-school programs), are often indistinguishable and not reproducible (Jacobs, 2017).

CTE programs have been suggested as the place to teach soft skills necessary in the labor market. Available in the United States for over 100 years, these programs have seen periods of increasing and decreasing interest. With the increased interest in academic programs beginning in the 1980s and through No Child Left Behind, CTE was in sharp decline; however, with the recent reports discussed above and increased interest in the States, Jacobs (2017) reports that, in 2015, 39 states instituted 125 new laws, policies, or regulations relating to CTE programs, allocating funding to a sizable number of them. Despite the allocation of revenue and programs, however, few of these types of programs have been evaluated. Jacobs cites only two empirical studies that he considers rigorous. The first, on career academies in the early 1990s, found that the academies had no impact on high school graduation, postsecondary enrollment, or educational attainment; however, high-risk males enjoyed a 17% increase in earnings compared to the control group (there was no significant difference between females in the treatment and control condition).[8] The second study, using a set of regional vocational and technical high schools, found an increase in high school graduation rates but no increase in mathematics and reading exam scores.[9] These initial results from CTE programs are worrisome, especially since the results were achieved using strong statistical techniques (treatment and control condition in the first and regression discontinuity in the second). However, what is clearly missing are longitudinal studies of these programs. The difficulty arises not so much with what is likely to occur for these treated cohorts in the near future but their longer term earning power in our increasingly unstable labor market. Clearly, this is an underdeveloped area and one where empirical work is needed.

Training Tomorrow's Workers, Today

Personalized education and internships abound, but we need to be certain that the internships students participate in truly help them develop the skills they need for the future. For students with limited social networks that do not allow them entry into many professions, quality internships are difficult to find. Students having trouble with their classes may not get the opportunity to pursue traditional internship opportunities that provide the kinds of work experiences needed by the future generation to succeed in an ever-changing, technologically advancing workplace. CAP aims to provide students with skills that are immediately transferrable to the workplace, while connecting businesses with their next generation of employees. CAP, however, represents only one type of option in the suite of programs currently being developed to assist young people in making career decisions that incorporate both a strong educational path and one that is combined with postsecondary and work-related options.

The major difficulty most of these programs have is in trying to develop a balance between a specific level of education that makes one employable in multiple occupations and where there is a strong linkage between education and a restricted set of occupations.[10] The origins of this argument can be traced to Shavit and Muller (1998), who examine important cross-national differences in educational systems, including whether the country provides general or specific vocational education, whether the education system is nationally standardized, the extent to which the system is stratified by instituting early tracking into nonmobile programs (compared to mobile choice), and the extent of credential inflation.

These ideas are especially useful for understanding the challenges that most countries are encountering in trying to incorporate educational programs that prepare students for work, especially today, where there is an emphasis on preparing students for a postsecondary education program even for specialized technical fields. The problem that occurs is that to aid students entering work programs after high school, many vocational or career tech programs are still places overrepresented by low-income, minority, and often the least academically prepared students. While students in these CTE programs may initially receive higher wages, one could expect that advances in technology will likely result in obsolescence and human displacement, much like what has occurred with similar programs in the past.

There are a number of problems we face globally, with credential inflation—where jobs require more education, regardless of skill sets (Collins, 2002)—leaving those with technical skills and degrees out of the labor market. For example, examining a variety of occupations, the percentage of job postings now requiring a bachelor's degree is considerably higher than the percentage of workers holding less than a bachelor's degree and currently employed in fields such as management, administrative services, sales, business, and health care. One reason behind degree inflation is the belief that bachelor's degree holders are better workers, not only with respect to knowledge but also with respect to flexible thinking, time management, and other social skills (Burning Glass Technologies, 2014).

However, in some countries, young people with recent bachelor's degrees find there is no market for their talents or knowledge. It has been argued that even though they are not in jobs requiring a bachelor's degree, they are likely to benefit from their education by making better life choices regarding their health, social relationships, and civic engagement; furthermore, when new labor market opportunities are introduced, they are likely to have some advantages over others who have job experiences but lack credentials. Yet, in the short run, for those individuals who are over-credentialed for the current job market, there are small assurances that employment opportunities may change. These individuals often report deep regrets for their investment in an advanced degree that did not result in a job that affords a reasonable financial gain over the deferred time, tuition costs, and losses in income they expended.

These are unquestionably difficult education and work readiness quandaries— too much education for the present marketplace and rising credentials for work that in the past did not require advanced education or training. Nonetheless, it seems that right now—although there are certainly variations in the immediate labor demands of countries making rapid technological changes—a system that provides everyone with strong general skills and leaves specific skill training up to work environments might be a better alternative. This might be a more equitable system than one that minimizes the value of a deep, general education for some and not others. Encouraging strong general skills for everyone, especially in the K-12 environment, fits best with the uncertain, unstable labor market that many have predicted is likely for the foreseeable future in numerous countries. Without a strong general education at the elementary and secondary level for everyone, the winners are likely to remain those individuals with high family incomes and strong social networks that can help to identify and advance their career prospects.

Notes

1 Researchers have shown that most families go through periods of economic turbulence (Brown, Haltiwanger, & Lane, 2006), that being poor is sometimes not forever, and that those not identified as "poor" can experience periods of poverty. What has changed is that those not identified as "poor" are finding that their resources are less than anticipated and their periods of poverty longer and more catastrophic, making it difficult to financially re-coup their losses. Even the luxury of intergenerational assets—like inherited homes from earlier good union jobs—have disappeared or become more difficult to keep secure. These conditions for families of all races and ethnicities are forcing new limitations on children's educational mobility within income categories once considered middle class (including some families with postsecondary education—see Morduch and Schneider [2017]).
2 See numbers from the Bureau of Labor Statistics (2018).
3 See Castleman and Page (2015) on college nudge experiments.
4 See National Science Board (2018); and Perez-Felkner, McDonald, Schneider, and Grogan (2012).
5 Expert consensus reports are produced by a committee of experts convened by the National Academies—often in the name of the National Research Council—and other divisions within the academies to study a specific scientific or technical issue of national importance. These reports are often viewed as authoritative because of their independence, ability to recruit top scientists to produce them, and the studies' rigorous peer review process.
6 This argument has been made by economists: see Almlund, Duckworth, Heckman, and Kautz (2011); and Deming (2017).
7 The Conn et al.'s (2017) review is quite extensive, and vocational education is not the only topic that they investigate—they also examine apprenticeships, cooperative education, career academies, and other mechanisms of delivery, including e-learning in postsecondary education and information interventions. The problem is the heterogeneity of impact from the various types of programs and that the programs themselves are quite diverse, ranging from elementary through postsecondary school. The more focused review—though considerably shorter—by Jacobs (2017), which examines only the U.S. context, highlights the lack of serious methodological studies of CTE programs, especially in light of their current popularity and funding.
8 See Kemple and Willner (2008) for the original report.
9 See Doughtery (2018) for the original report.
10 See DiPrete, Eller, Bol, and van de Werfhorst (2017) on these differences and their impact across countries.

References

Almlund, M., Duckworth, A., Heckman, J., & Kautz, T. (2011). *Personality psychology and economics*. NBER Working Paper No. 16822. Retrieved from http://www.nber. org/papers/w16822

Ananiadou, K., & Claro, M. (2009). *21st century skills and competences for new millennium learners in OECD countries*. OECD Education Working Papers, No. 41. Paris: OECD Publishing.

Anderson, M. (2015). *Racial and ethnic differences in how people use mobile technology*. Washington, DC: Pew Research Center.

Anderson, M. (2017). *Digital divide persists even as lower-income Americans make gains in tech adoption*. Washington, DC: Pew Research Center.

Anderson, M., Perrin, A., & Jiang, J. (2018). *11% of Americans don't use the internet. Who are they?* Washington, DC: Pew Research Center.

Bailey, M., & Dynarski, S. (2011). *Gains and gaps: Changing inequality in U.S. college entry and completion*. NBER Working Paper No. 17633. Retrieved from http://www.nber. org/papers/w17633

Baum, S., Ma, J., & Payea, K. (2013). *Education pays 2013: The benefits of higher education for individuals and society*. College Board. Retrieved from https://trends.collegeboard. org/sites/default/files/education-pays-2013-full-report.pdf

Beyers, W., & Luyckx, K. (2016). Ruminative exploration and reconsideration of commitment as risk factors for suboptimal identity development in adolescence and emerging adulthood. *Journal of Adolescence, 47*, 169–178. doi:10.1016/j.adolescence.2015.10.018

Bills, D. B. (2009). Vocationalism. In A. Furlong (Ed.), *Handbook of youth and young adulthood: New perspectives and agendas* (pp. 127–134). New York, NY: Routledge.

Brown, C., Haltiwanger, J.,& Lane, J. (2006). *Economic turbulence: Is a volatile economy good for America?* Chicago, IL: University of Chicago Press.

Bureau of Labor Statistics. (2015). *Occupational employment projections to 2024*. U.S. Department of Labor Statistics. Retrieved from https://www.bls.gov/opub/mlr/2015/article/occupational-employment-projections-to-2024.htm

Bureau of Labor Statistics. (2018). *College enrollment and work activity of recent high school and college graduates summary*. U.S. Department of Labor Statistics.

Burkander, K. N. (2014). *Culture, class, and college: A mixed-method contextual understanding of undermatch* (3635423) (Doctoral dissertation). Retrieved from ProQuest Dissertations Publishing.

Burning Glass Technologies. (2014). *Moving the goalposts: How demand for a bachelor's degree is reshaping the workforce*. Retrieved from https://www.burning-glass.com/wp-content/uploads/Moving_the_Goalposts.pdf

Carroll, J., & Muller, C. (2018). Curricular differentiation and its impact on different status groups including immigrants and students with disabilities. In B. Schneider & G. Saw (Eds.), *Handbook of sociology of education in the 21st century* (pp. 251–274). New York, NY: Springer.

Castleman, B., & Page, L. (2015). Summer nudging: Can personalized text messages and peer mentor outreach increase college going among low-income high school graduates? *Journal of Economic Behavior and Organization, 115*, 140–160.

Chetty, R., Friedman, J., Saez, E., Turner, N., & Yagan, D. (2017). *Mobility report cards: The role of colleges in intergenerational mobility*. NBER Working Paper No. 23618. Retrieved from http://www.nber.org/papers/w23618

Chmielewski, A. (2014). An international comparison of achievement inequality in within- and between-school tracking systems. *American Journal of Education, 120*, 293–324.

Cohen, A., & Syme, S. (2013). Education: A missed opportunity for public health intervention. *American Journal of Public Health, 103*(6), 997–1001. doi:10.2105/AJPH. 2012.300993

Collins, R. (2002). The dirty little secret of credential inflation. *The Chronicle Review, 5*, B20. Retrieved from https://www.chronicle.com/article/The-Dirty-Little-Secret-of/20548

Conn, K., Park, E. H., Nagakura, W., Khalil, S., & Corcoran, T. (2017). *Strategies for strengthening the technical workforce: A review of international evidence.* CPRE Research Reports. Retrieved from https://repository.upenn.edu/cpre_researchreports/96

Cooper, P. (2018). College enrollment surges among low-income students. *Forbes.* Retrieved from https://www.forbes.com/sites/prestoncooper2/2018/02/26/college-enrollment-surges-among-low-income-students/#6fae38e4293b

Deming, D. (2017) The growing importance of social skills in the labor market. *Quarterly Journal of Economics, 132*(4), 1593–1640.

DiPrete, T. A., Eller, C. C., Bol, T., & van de Werfhorst, H. G. (2017). School-to-work linkages in the United States, Germany, and France. *American Journal of Sociology, 122*(6), 1869–1938. doi:10.1086/691327

Doughtery, S. (2018). The effect of career and technical education on human capital accumulation: Causal evidence from Massachusetts. *Education Finance and Policy, 13*, 119–148.

Erikson, E. H. (1950). *Childhood and society.* New York, NY: W.W. Norton & Company.

Erikson, E. H. (1968). *Identity: Youth and crisis.* New York, NY: W.W. Norton & Company.

Fitzpatrick, D., & Schneider, B. (2016, March). *Linking counselor activities and students' college readiness: How they matter for disadvantaged students.* Paper presented at the annual conference of the Society for Research on Educational Effectiveness, Washington, DC.

Hillygus, D. S. (2005). The missing link: Exploring the relationship between higher education and political engagement. *Political Behavior, 27*(1), 25–47. doi:10.1007/s11109-005-3075-8

Jacobs, B. (2017). *What we know about career and technical education in high school.* The Brookings Institute. Retrieved from https://www.brookings.edu/research/what-we-know-about-career-and-technical-education-in-high-school/

Keaton, P. (2012). *Numbers and types of public elementary and secondary schools from the common core of data: School year 2010–2011.* U.S. Department of Education. Washington, DC: National Center for Education Statistics.

Kemple, J., & Willner, C. J. (2008). *Career academies: Long-term impacts on labor market outcomes, educational attainment, and transitions to adulthood.* New York, NY: MDRC.

Kim, D., & Schneider, B. (2005). Social capital in action: Alignment of parental support in adolescents' transition to postsecondary education. *Social Forces, 84*, 1181–1206.

Lenhart, A. (2015). *Teens, social media, and technology.* Washington, D.C: Pew Research Center.

Manyika, J., Lund, S., Chui, M., Bughin, J., Woetzel, J., Patra, P., ... Sanghvi, S. (2017). *Jobs lost, jobs gained: Workforce transitions in a time of automation.* McKinsey Global Institute.

Michelmore, K., & Dynarski, S. (2016). *The gap within the gap: Using longitudinal data to understand income differences in student achievement.* NBER Working Paper No. 22474. Retrieved from http://www.nber.org/papers/w22474

Morduch, J., & Schneider, R. (2017). *The financial diaries: How American families cope in a world of uncertainty.* Princeton, NJ: Princeton University Press.

National Science Board. (2018). *Science and engineering indicators 2018.* Alexandria, VA: National Science Foundation.

Oakes, J., & Saunders, M. (2008). *Beyond tracking: Multiple pathways to college, career, and civic participation.* Cambridge, MA: Harvard Education Press.

OECD. (2015). *Skills for social progress: The power of social and emotional skills.* Paris, France: OECD Publishing.

OECD. (2017). *Education at a Glance 2017: OECD Indicators.* Paris, France: OECD Publishing. doi:10.1787/eag-2017-en

OECD Horizon 2020. (2017). *Work programme 2018–2020.* London, UK: European Commission.

Oreopoulos, P., & Petronijevic, U. (2013). *Making college worth it: A review of research on the returns to higher education.* NBER Working Paper No. 19053. Retrieved from http://www.nber.org/papers/w19053

Perez-Felkner, L., McDonald, S. K., Schneider, B., & Grogan, E. (2012). Female and male adolescents' subjective orientations to mathematics and the influence of those orientations on postsecondary majors. *Developmental Psychology, 48*(6), 1658–1673. Advance online publication. doi:10.1037/a0027020

Pew Research Center. (2018). *Mobile fact sheet.* Washington, DC: Pew Research Center.

Putnam, R. D. (2015). *Our kids: The American dream in crisis.* New York, NY: Simon & Schuster.

Roderick, M., Nagaoka, J., & Coca, V. (2009). College readiness for all: The challenge for urban high schools. *The Future of Children, 19*(1), 185–210. doi:10.1353/foc.0.0024

Schneider, B. (2015). AERA presidential address, the college ambition program: A realistic transition strategy for traditionally disadvantaged students. *Educational Researcher, 44*(7), 394–403.

Schneider, B., Broda, M., Judy, J., & Burkander, K. (2013). Pathways to college and STEM careers: Enhancing the high school experience. *New Directions for Student Leadership, 2013*(140), 9–29. doi:10.1002/yd.20076

Schneider, B., Kim, S., & Klager, C. (2017). Co-development of education aspirations and postsecondary enrollment especially among students who are low income and minority. *Research in Human Development, 14*(2), 143–160. doi:10.1080/15427609.2017.1305811

Settersten, R., Ottusch, T., & Schneider, B. (2015). Becoming adult: Meanings of markers to adulthood. *Emerging Trends in the Social and Behavioral Sciences,* 1–16. doi:10.1002/9781118900772.etrds0021

Shavit, Y., & Muller, W. (1998). *From school to work: A comparative study of educational qualifications and occupational destinations.* New York, NY: Clarendon Press.

Smith, A., & Anderson, J. (2014). *AI, Robotics, and the Future of Jobs.* Retrieved from http://www.pewinternet.org/2014/08/06/future-of-jobs/

Snyder, T. D., de Brey, C., & Dillow, S. A. (2016). *Digest of Education Statistics 2015.* NCES 2016-014. Washington, DC: National Center for Education Statistics, Institute of Education Sciences, U.S. Department of Education.

Tate, E. (2017). Graduation rates and race. *Inside Higher Ed.* Retrieved from https://www.insidehighered.com/news/2017/04/26/college-completion-rates-vary-race-and-ethnicity-report-finds

World Economic Forum. (2016). *The future of jobs: Employment, skills, and workforce strategy for the fourth industrial revolution.* Retrieved from http://www3.weforum.org/docs/WEF_Future_of_Jobs.pdf

PART II
Employment

5

WORKFORCE READINESS IN TIMES OF CHANGE

Employer Perspectives

Richard A. Guzzo

Employers constantly face challenges of preparing for success in the future. Sometimes those challenges are self-induced as when a business elects to enter an unfamiliar market. Sometimes they arise because an organization, like others in its same niche, is caught up in a wave of change affecting all in that niche, as when a new competitor emerges advantaged by its unique innovation (think early Amazon competing with bookstores). At other times, employers find themselves needing to respond to the same large waves of change that almost all are responding to such as technology advances, globalization, and ups and downs in population demographics. Whatever the origins, employers frequently are compelled to consider how best to acquire, prepare, re-equip, replace, reconfigure, adapt, or otherwise alter the nature of their workforces for future success.

This chapter adopts an employer-centric perspective on workforce readiness. Three case studies illustrate. The things that ignite the concern about workforce readiness are unique to each: the evolving nature of one sector of a nation's economy, transformative technology-driven change in an industry, and one company's pursuit of a new business strategy. Each case describes what workforce capabilities (e.g., skills, abilities, knowledge, and experiences) define readiness in that situation, the processes by which those capabilities were identified, and initial actions to enhance readiness.

Of universal relevance to all employers' workforce readiness efforts are two concepts, external and internal labor markets. External labor markets are the sources of an employer's new hires or contracted workers. Rather than some undifferentiated quantity, external labor markets are best thought of as being bounded in ways meaningful to an employer's needs, such as by geography (e.g., a nation's workforce), a specific skill set (e.g., coding), and combinations

---

INTERNAL LABOR MARKET DYNAMICS

Employers have unique configurations of processes for hiring, placing, retaining, managing, motivating, and developing employees. Together, these influence outcomes such as who stays with the employer, who performs well, who gets promoted, and who learns and changes. Ideally, today's internal labor market dynamics are creating tomorrow's needed workforce, but managing these dynamics is complex. For example, multiple practices can simultaneously affect the same outcome, as when pay, job rotations, coaching, and other practices all influence employee retention. Also, any one practice (e.g., training) can affect multiple outcomes (e.g., knowledge, performance, retention, promotability). Further, interdependencies exist such that one employer's investments in, say, employee learning may have different outcomes than another employer's because of differences in context, such as when in one enterprise learning is tightly integrated with changes of job assignments and compensation while not so in another. As a consequence, it is unrealistic to think that there will be one best path forward to readiness—for example, "reskilling through MOOCs for all." Further details about internal labor market dynamics can be found in Nalbantian et al. (2004) and Guzzo and Nalbantian (2014).

---

of relevant attributes (e.g., coding in Python in eastern European countries). The supply of capabilities in an external labor market is shaped by educational institutions, government policies, population demographics, and the nature of the economy. The internal labor market is comprised of those people already working for an employer. Internal labor market dynamics refer to practices such as hiring, rewarding, training, transferring, promoting, coaching, and so on that are constantly shaping the capabilities inherent in an employer's workforce as well as events and experiences in the workplace that those practices influence. External and internal labor markets offer alternative points of leverage for workforce readiness. Depending on circumstances, an employer may emphasize one or the other as the primary source of its future workforce.

Case #1: Workforce Readiness in a Changing Economy

Employers are part of an ecosystem. As such, they can act in concert with other entities to address workforce readiness. This case presents one such example, centered on anticipated changes in Canada's economy with regard to foreign trade. While countries that transition from "closed" to global economies can experience dramatic workforce readiness challenges such as China did in the late 1970s and early 1980s as it adopted some forms of Western-style capitalism (e.g., accepting foreign investment, encouraging entrepreneurism), the challenges described in this case are less dramatic and are limited to one economic sector, international trade. Employers in this sector have accepted the premise that the nature of Canada's international trade is changing in response to the rise of new and more diverse trading partners, increased complexity of global supply chains, and an expected shift toward more trade in the form of services relative to manufactured goods and extracted resources. Given the criticality of trade to Canada's economy (Cross, 2016), employers banded together with representatives of government, educational institutions, and other interested stakeholders to make a systematic assessment of the readiness of Canada's workforce to meet the expected demands of future international trade and to identify strategies for increasing readiness.

The case described here draws heavily on the report issued by the Forum for International Trade Training (FITT, 2013). The work was carried out under the auspices of FITT supported by a core team of researchers advised by members of business, education, and government. Employers contributed to the process in many ways, such as by lending representatives to task forces and steering committees, reviewing findings, and being participants in the research process. The research process first focused on identifying the skills required for international trade and then gauging where gaps are most likely to arise between the expected demand for those skills and their likely future supply. Research findings thus provided a foundation for specifying actions to prevent gaps from arising. At the highest level of abstraction, the process is straightforward:

- Identify the skills, knowledge, and other attributes ("capabilities" here for convenience) required of those segments of the national workforce engaged in international trade;
- Quantify the current and future supply of those segments and their capabilities, estimate the future demand for those capabilities, and specify where the largest supply-demand gaps will be for the relevant capabilities; and
- Formulate strategies for closing those gaps.

In many ways, this process enacted at the national level is very much like processes that any individual employer could engage in "in miniature" when assessing its own workforce's readiness. At both the employer and national levels, however, a seemingly straightforward process is actually a complicated journey full of nuanced issues, judgment calls, imperfect or missing data, and diverse viewpoints swirling in a milieu of futurism. Nonetheless, several scientific disciplines can make important contributions to this process.

Identifying Occupations Critical to International Trade

What workforce capabilities are required for international trade? The search for answers in this case began with Canada's National Occupational Classification (NOC) system which at the time identified 519 distinct occupations in the Canadian economy. The NOC, however, did not identify which occupations are most relevant to international trade. So, a two-pronged "bottom–up" and "top–down" approach was adopted to identify occupations—and thus the capabilities essential to those occupations—required for international trade.

In the bottom–up analysis, all 519 occupations in the NOC were independently classified by five subject-matter experts (SMEs) into core and non-core occupations for trade. Core occupations were defined as those directly involved in international trade processes (e.g., shipping and receiving), those essential to areas of the Canadian economy that generate substantial revenues from abroad (e.g., mining), and occupations (e.g., managing) deemed to have high relevance to trade. The five SMEs then met to compare their respective lists and resolve differences by discussion to consensus. This resulting list of occupations was then reviewed independently by a project steering committee and by outside advisors, resulting in a list of 109 occupations identified as candidates to be considered core to international trade.

The top–down approach was more quantitative. Using data from Statistics Canada, it began by identifying the 15 sectors of the Canadian economy which generate a large share of their revenues from international trade. These included sectors in manufacturing, energy, business services, computers and electronics, banking, insurance, and wholesale trade. Next, the 20 occupations that occur most frequently in each of these 15 sectors were identified, again using data from Statistics Canada. Redundancies that occurred when the same occupation appeared in more than one industry sector were eliminated, as were entry-level jobs such as laborers. The top–down approach resulted in 112 occupations identified as candidates to be considered core to international trade.

The products of the two approaches were integrated in the following way:

- The 350 occupations not identified as core by either of the approaches were eliminated from further consideration.
- The 52 occupations identified as core by both approaches were accepted without further review.
- The remaining 117 occupations—57 from the bottom–up and 60 from the top–down approaches—were further assessed by the SMEs in a discuss-to-consensus procedure, followed by a review by the project steering committee, to determine the final list.
- In the end, 95 occupations were identified as core to Canada's international trade.

The full list of occupations can be found in the Appendix B of the FITT's (2013) report. No assertion was made that all workers in these occupations are engaged in international trade activities. Consider a purchasing manager. Some who work in this job regularly engage in international transactions while others may never. Rather, it is the capabilities of workers in these occupations that are important.

Further, the changing nature of international trade can bring about new jobs—new configurations of tasks and activities—that have not yet had the opportunity to be recognized and cataloged in the NOC's taxonomy. Consequently, employers participated in a series of facilitated expert panel discussions to identify such new and emerging occupations relevant to trade. The panels were composed of volunteers representing a mix of industries, company sizes, and locations across the country. Table 5.1 reports the ten emerging occupations identified through this process. Employers saw these occupations as distinct from existing occupations because (1) new capabilities are required in some of these jobs or (2) these new roles require atypical or unusual combinations of known capabilities. While recognizing these occupations as important, no workforce data existed with regard to these emerging occupations; thus, they were excluded from the next step of the analysis.

TABLE 5.1 Emerging Occupations in International Trade

Ecommerce—conducting business through the Internet including social media use and customer intelligence

Environmental risk—assessing risk of business practices on local environments

Global account management—cross-border oversight and management of customer relationships

Global IT systems—design, development, implementation of systems that manage the flow of information across borders

International risk management—assessing and managing enterprise-wide risks of doing business across borders

International business development—international sales based on knowledge of customer segments, local business practices, and trade agreements and regulations

Trade facilitation—coordinating the flow of information and contracting among multiple parties involved in international trade

Regulatory compliance—oversight and advice to ensure compliance with country and local laws and regulations

Trade finance—analysis and guidance regarding foreign investments and cross-border payments

Value-chain management—creating and directing multiparty partnerships at all points in a supply chain (e.g., sourcing, production, assembly, distribution, logistics, marketing, and sales)

Quantifying Supply, Estimating Demand, and Specifying Gaps

The goal of addressing gaps between future workforce supply and demand was not to make precise numerical estimates but rather to provide an evidence-based categorization of supply-demand gaps as high, medium, or low in the types of occupations most relevant to international trade. Such a simple categorization scheme would help prioritize efforts to achieve workforce readiness.

Quantifying future workforce supply was made easy by relying on estimates of workforce growth, publicly available from Statistics Canada, in each of the 95 key occupations. Demand is more difficult to estimate. One source of insight, again using data available from Statistics Canada, was the proportion of each industry's revenues that come from foreign sources. Another was the proportion of an occupation's total workforce working in the industries of interest. So, for example, occupations that have low (or negative) workforce growth rates and that are concentrated in industries with above-average proportions of revenues coming from foreign sources would be occupations where expected supply-demand gaps would be categorized as high.

The analysis yielded a number of specific-to-Canada insights. For example, jobs in three occupational groups—management, business/finance/administration, and natural/applied sciences—were found to be relatively highly concentrated in industries with large revenues from foreign trade. However, in only the first two of those occupational groups were supply-demand workforce risks deemed to be high, mostly due to comparatively lower rates of entry into and higher rates of exits from the two groups. The Management workforce in Canada is appreciably older than that in Natural/Applied Sciences, for example, and thus managers are expected to exit the workforce at comparatively higher rates over the next several years. Sometimes shortfalls of worker supply in an occupation can be overcome quickly through intensive schooling. However, because of the value of experience to managerial work, extensive more time may be required to overcome its shortfall. One final observation of interest is that workers in occupations core to international trade are more highly educated—that is, a greater proportion of people working in those occupations hold bachelor's degrees and higher—relative to those working in other occupations, pointing to the broad importance of higher education to workforce readiness for international trade.

Setting Strategies for Closing Gaps

Three broad sets of stakeholders were identified as initiators of action to reduce gaps: government, educational providers, and employers engaged in foreign trade (FITT, 2013). Many of the suggested actions are the province of only one stakeholder. For example, it is uniquely within the domain of the Canadian government to change immigration policies in ways that favor the admission of immigrants with skills well matched to employment in international trade. Educational institutions have great autonomy to design degree and certificate programs that enhance graduates' readiness for employment in international trade-related jobs. Employers, too, can act individually or in concert through industry associations to build relevant capabilities, such as knowledge of regulations governing international commerce. Numerous recommended actions call for collaboration among two or three of the major stakeholders. For example, one action called for two stakeholders, employers and the government, to act in concert to facilitate the placement in the private sector of individuals leaving the Canadian Armed Forces because many leave with valuable cross-cultural exposure and with experience in activities relevant to international trade, such as managing logistics across national borders. A three-stakeholder action is illustrated by educational institutions which, with government support where appropriate, offer relevant degree-granting and credentialing programs of study with employers advising on curricula and offering internships in the private sector integrated into a curriculum.

Uniquely from the employer's perspective, the existing external labor market can immediately be leveraged in ways that do not require time spent waiting for future workers to complete their programs of study or military service. One such way is by recruiting workers who are not currently employed in international trade-related occupations but who already possess capabilities needed for international trade. Customs brokers are occupations core to international trade and require such things as customer service abilities, attention to detail, familiarity with long-form contracting, compliance skills, and the ability to work with deadlines. Real estate agents require many of the exact same capabilities. Real estate agents mostly are engaged in local, not international, commerce but illustrate an occupation whose members would have, by virtue of the nature of the work they perform, capabilities readily transportable to employers in international trade. Many occupations have capabilities transportable into one or more of the 95 core occupations, thus mobility across occupations is a potentially important external labor market tactic that employers can leverage for greater workforce readiness.

Case #2: Leadership Readiness in Digital Manufacturing

Manufacturing organizations face profound workforce readiness challenges due to changes in technology-driven production processes. Robots continue to be the face of technological change in manufacturing. It is estimated that over 2.5 million robots will be operating in industrial processes in 2019, reflecting a 12% average annual growth rate of implementation (International Federation of Robotics, 2017). The workforce implications of robots, like the implications of other technologies, can include job loss, job change, and job creation (National Academies of Sciences, Engineering, and Medicine, 2017). Robots are perhaps popularly thought of as machines that eliminate employment opportunities altogether, pushing individuals out of the workforce or displacing them into other jobs. But robots may not eliminate jobs so much as change them, such as by taking over highly complex or exacting tasks that humans may not be able to perform as quickly or to the standards that a machine can repeatedly meet. When activities pass from worker to robot, the worker is freed to take on new activities in a now-redefined job. Another example of job change comes from collaborative robots ("cobots") that operate alongside and in interaction with humans. Further, introducing robots into workplaces can also create new-new jobs for developing, programming, and maintaining them.

Another of the technology-related changes contributing to manufacturing's workforce readiness challenges is the rapidly expanding use of sensors to monitor production processes, people, and equipment. Sensors can collect enormous numbers of observations—often high-velocity, high-volume data—during a production process, for example, and that data can be acted on in real time through algorithms that can intelligently direct a change to be made in a production process to deter errors and to bring measured values back to within accepted tolerances. Networked sensors—the Internet of things (IoT)—can communicate, share data, and amplify the usefulness of sensor-based data. Sensors and the IoT have implications not only for the skill requirements of workers on a manufacturing line but also for engineers who design production processes as well as for analysts who are in position to make use of the outsized sensor-based data sets to pinpoint sources of unwanted errors, discover opportunities for heightened efficiency, and craft models that predict such things as when maintenance will be required.

Additive manufacturing, a new and rapidly evolving process, is also affecting the nature of work. The term additive manufacturing refers to the process of building things by adding layer upon layer—extremely thin layers—of material such as a plastic or a metal that binds into finished outputs. Those outputs typically are parts that become integrated into larger products although, at the forefront of additive manufacturing, complex systems of parts are being fashioned as whole entities. Sometimes referred to as 3-D printing and direct digital manufacturing, the process involves computer-aided design and control of what are usually very precise requirements of process and product. The benefits of additive processes are potentially enormous, including lower cost of production through the use of less expensive materials, achieving in one step what might otherwise require multiple steps to produce, and the capacity to create customized objects with shapes and features that could not be created through traditional processes. Additive manufacturing also changes what is required of employees, such as programming skill, the ability to visualize, and knowledge of materials.

Technology-driven changes in manufacturing have implications for leadership, and the readiness of future leaders in digital manufacturing is the focus of this case. One employer's early steps to meet this challenge are described here.

General Electric (GE) is a digital industrial company. At the time of the work described in this case, GE operated hundreds of production facilities globally, served customers in over 180 countries, and provided products and services such as aircraft engines, power generation and oil and gas production equipment, medical imaging, and financing. Currently, the company is in a state of transformation to focus on aviation, power generation, and renewable energy as core and will sell or spin off other lines of business. Thus, GE's concern for leadership readiness is focused on its digital manufacturing environments.

GE has a long history of developing leaders from within. That is, through years of service, select employees gain the requisite skills and expertise essential to performing well in positions of leadership. These capabilities are acquired through a mix of training and development programs as well as ample experience-based learning acquired by rotating through different positions, facilities, functions, and lines of business. It is not uncommon for a manager of a production facility to have spent 20 years with the company prior to taking on that leadership position, for example. GE utilizes its internal labor market to "build" its leadership talent over "buying" it from the external labor market. The degree of technological change being experienced by the manufacturer prompted its concerns about whether today's model for developing leaders from within will be effective for leadership in the digitized workplace.

Capabilities and Leadership Readiness

A starting point for GE is its existing leadership competency model. That model specifies a set of domains (e.g., quality, operations, and finance) relevant to leadership responsibilities in manufacturing. Within each domain, the model further identifies specific competencies and knowledge areas (e.g., problem-solving, coaching, and financial risk management) that have been tagged as especially relevant to the domain. Further, the model provides guidance for recognizing differing levels of mastery of a competency or knowledge area, from "aware of" through "can do it" through "can lead others to do it." Ideally, training and development programs plus directed career experiences develop high levels of mastery of many competencies. But might there be leadership capabilities not yet accounted for in the model that will become critical in the increasingly digital manufacturing environment? The interest of this employer is to successfully adapt the existing competency model and the talent management practices aligned to it to ensure the availability of leaders ready for its future workplaces.

The Investigative Process

Although the company would say that none of its production facilities is at a fully realized state of digital manufacturing, several of its facilities around the world are demonstrably deeper into the digital era than others. The company took advantage of this by making higher digitization facilities targets of study. Specifically, it was in these facilities that the current experiences of leaders and leadership teams were investigated to learn about the unique demands being placed on them by digital environments.

Qualitative research methods were used. The work began with a series of structured one-on-one interviews with manufacturing plant leaders and their leaders. These interviews queried the general experience of implementing advanced digital manufacturing, how the day-to-day activities of plant leaders changed as result of digitization, and specific changes in the knowledge, skills, abilities, and competencies required of leaders in these new environments. The interviews also explored views on how best to develop or acquire the new capabilities, including issues such as the value of experience in the firm versus the value of experience in digital environments outside the company. Interviews were followed by immersive visits to higher-digitization plants. The visits served several purposes. They gave researchers the opportunity to see first-hand digitization in action and to more fully appreciate the contexts in which it is occurring. The visits also enabled multiple discussions to occur with site leaders and leadership teams regarding the issues of interest, discussions that were grounded in each specific work context. Visits also provided the opportunity to interact informally with employees in jobs at various points along production lines or in supporting roles. Notes from interviews and observations were synthesized and key findings identified. The final step in the investigative process involved "testing" selected key findings through telephone interviews with individuals from operations, innovation, and human resource functions at four other manufacturing organizations, themselves at different stages of digitization. The objectives of these final interviews were to see if the findings "ring true" in other settings and to see if anything was missed in the internal research.

Meeting the New Leadership Requirements in Digital Manufacturing

The research found that certain staples of knowledge and experience important to effective leadership in manufacturing are expected to remain so, such as having shop floor experience and understanding cost containment methods. It was also found that the digital environment expands what is required of leaders. Expanded leadership capabilities in this company's digital manufacturing environments include:

- Conceptual thinking, including the ability to visualize. Digital environments not only change the way work is done but change how leaders can "see" linked processes and their outputs.
- Social skills, such as networking. Digitization raises the bar for leaders' social skills by creating numerous opportunities for increased connectivity

among people, not just among things. Additionally, digitization enables individuals with nontraditional backgrounds to contribute in a manufacturing facility, such as individuals with knowledge of computers, data visualization skills, or data analytic capability. Employees with such backgrounds are atypical for manufacturing facilities and those employees are likely to come with workplace expectations and preferences that differ from those of in-place manufacturing workers. Effective leaders will require social skills to integrate and position such newcomers for success.

- Innovation and change management capabilities. The information-rich digital environment creates occasions for insight and innovation at multiple stages in a production process. Digital environments put a premium on leaders' capacity to facilitate data-driven innovation within and among teams responsible for different production stages and to oversee the implementation of new ways of doing things.
- Strategic thinking capabilities. With digitization, the plant leader's role is expected to become more strategic than it is now. The digital age brings with it fluidity, adaptation, and replanning sparked by volumes of data and insights into the performance of the plant at any point in time. Data-driven, on-the-spot strategic thinking, often done collaboratively with the local team, is a heightened demand on plant leaders.

Given its culture and long track record of developing leadership from within, the company is predisposed to continue to rely on its internal labor market to meet future leadership needs. While some greater concession may be made to hiring leadership-level talent into the firm, internal development is likely to dominate, and all means of development are open to revision. For example, changes in the company's leadership training programs have been made or will be made to orient those programs to create capabilities suited to digital environments. Also, advancement into leadership positions historically often has occurred within a single line of business. However, many of the required digital-era leadership capabilities (e.g., conceptual thinking, networking) are transportable across business lines within the company. Consequently, a greater emphasis on cross-line-of-business mobility to fill leadership roles is a viable tactic, where one line of business identifies candidates strong in digital-era capabilities currently working elsewhere in the company and "imports" those individuals to meet its leadership needs. Greater comingling of nontraditional and traditional employees in production facilities is also a way of developing experience-based proficiency in leading people with diverse backgrounds in digital environments. Different tactics will suit different employers, and not all manufacturers can be expected to follow GE's practices. Indeed, one of the employers interviewed in the final step of the research rejected the GE approach, declaring that it will rely on the external labor market for its future digital leaders.

Case #3: Workforce Readiness for a New Business Strategy

With some regularity, employers revisit their business strategies. Typically that process starts by looking outward, scanning competitors and the marketplace for new ways to grow revenues and profits. When new strategic directions are adopted employers sometimes, but not always, then look inward and ask "Is our workforce ready to make the new strategy successful?" This case describes how one company that did exactly that.

The company is a mid-sized firm ("MidCo"). It provides products and services that help its clients work more efficiently and better manage customer relationships. Changes in the ways in which software-based services are provided and data stored—such as cloud-based solutions—shape the strategic possibilities for this company, as do the growth of opportunities to expand into underserved markets. Following an extensive review and analysis of business opportunities, the company adopted a new strategy with the objective of doubling revenues in a five-year period. The new strategy had several components to it, including introducing the company's existing offerings into new overseas markets, acquiring or partnering with smaller companies that have complementary software products so to expand its overall portfolio, and investing heavily in new product development to increase the number of products and the speed at which they are brought to market. Having laid out the strategy and committed to it, the company leadership then turned its attention to the readiness of its current workforce for success with it.

Skill Requirements for the New Strategy

If a company adopts a strategy that says "we're going to do X" and X is something that other businesses already do, it is often easy to know what skills, knowledge, and abilities are required. A healthcare organization opening up its first walk-in urgent care clinic is such an example. MidCo did not feel that it had comparator organizations that would serve as easy referents for specifying the workforce capabilities critical to achieving its strategic objectives. So, the company elected to rely on the pooled expertise and opinions of its leaders to identify requirements of its workforce under the new strategy.

The process began with a review of documents that codified the new business strategy followed by individual interviews with executive team members to generate an initial specification of employee skills, knowledge areas, and experiences thought to be critical to the success of the new strategy. The "working list" of these attributes were further refined, clarified, and reduced to a set of 13. While each of the 13 attributes could indeed be important to future business success, the company felt a need to establish which among them were the most important as this would aid in prioritizing actions to ensure the availability of needed capabilities.

To establish rank-order importance, the company carried out a survey to capture the views of 83 of its leaders who occupied positions in and one and two levels below the executive level. The 13 attributes were investigated using a "MaxDiff" approach that is designed to yield a clear ordering of importance among attributes (Marley & Louviere, 2015). In this approach, respondents were presented with a series of subsets of 4 of the 13 attributes and asked to indicate which among the attributes in a subset was most the important and which was the least important to the success of the new strategy. Subsets were constructed such that the 13 attributes were balanced in terms of being presented an equal number of times with each other. Analyses yield a ratio–scale ordering of the importance of the 13 workforce attributes to the new strategy. The survey also captured perceptions of the current workforce vis-à-vis the needed workforce. Using a five-point scale anchored by "no gap" (1), "moderate gap" (3), and "extensive gap" (5), respondents reported their perceptions of gaps between the current level and the needed level of a capability for the strategy to succeed. Figure 5.1 shows the 13 attributes (skills, experiences, and knowledge areas), the relative importance of the attributes to the business strategy, and the relative magnitude of the perceived gaps between current and needed capabilities.

Company leadership found the pattern of findings in Figure 5.1 startling: The capabilities it deemed most important to future business success were the very capabilities most lacking in the current workforce. For example, the top right quadrant—higher importance, larger gaps—lists capabilities germane to features of the new strategy such as those related to new product development and entering into business partnerships. Also in this quadrant are general

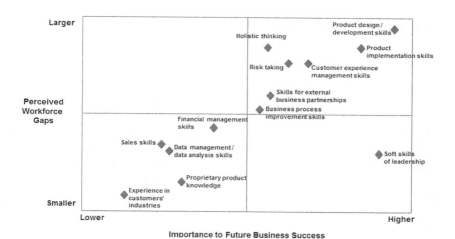

FIGURE 5.1 Workforce skills for business success in MidCo: importance and gaps.

capabilities supportive of the strategy (e.g., risk-taking, regarded as important to identifying new products and services and bringing them to new buyers, and holistic thinking, regarded as important to successfully bringing customers bundles of revenue-generating services).

Planning for the New Workforce

So how might MidCo come to have the workforce it needs for future success? One option—the internal labor market approach—would be to reskill the existing workforce through education and coursework, for example, or through structured experiences. Survey responses indicated that 80% of the leaders described the current workforce as a product of building versus buying, consistent with workforce data indicating modest turnover rates and appreciable employee tenure. However, when asked about the future, only 15% of the respondents endorsed a build-workforce-capability-from-within approach as the way preferred way forward. Clearly, company leadership believed that it needed to emphasize hiring, not development, as the better way to secure required workforce capabilities. MidCo's new business strategy was causing it to pivot from a "build" to a "buy" strategy to achieve workforce readiness.

Further, new hires and new places were seen as going hand-in-hand. Linked to the choice to draw new talent into the enterprise, leadership believed that the company needed to explore additional, alternative locations—in effect, to go where the talent is rather than try to attract it to its headquarters. Being a US corporation, MidCo actively explored alternative US-based locations as well as overseas locations, some where the company intended to expand its business and some where it did not expect to make sales but where it believed that the right workforce capabilities would be abundant.

Concluding Observations

Readiness is Not Just About Entry-Level Employment

The concept of workforce readiness most often is applied to initial employability, especially with regard to youth or generally any new entrants or re-entrants into the workforce. As such, readiness typically concerns fundamental skills relevant to almost all employers everywhere. Lists of such skills provide guidance for educators and others seeking to equip new workforce participants with what it takes to be employable (e.g., National Network of Business and Industry Associations Employers, 2015). Figure 5.2 illustrates one such list, ordered by importance to general employability as rated by 521 members of the Society of Human Resource Management (Lezotte & Marder, 2017). Employers and prospective employees benefit greatly from the well-specified definition of readiness at the entry level.

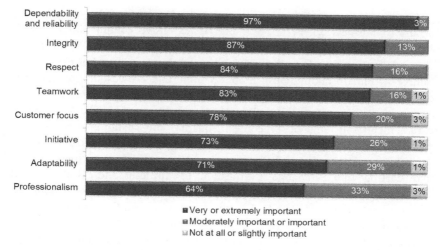

FIGURE 5.2 Entry-level skills and their importance.
Source: Lezotte, D. & Marder, B. (2017).

The concept of workforce readiness, however, also applies to the already-employed, the highly skilled, and the experienced. All three case studies presented here illustrate this. Importantly, the cases show that the meaning of readiness for the experienced worker shares little with its meaning for the entry-level workers. Experienced workers have mastered the basic requisites of employability (see Figure 5.2), one reason for the difference. But the major reason that readiness means something very different for experienced workers is that, for them, readiness is highly context specific. The case presented here about workforce requirements and a new business strategy illustrates such specificity of context, as does the case of leadership readiness in digitized manufacturing. An experienced worker can indeed be unready for a new environment, thus it would be a shame to restrict the concept of readiness to only entry-level employability.

Readiness is Loaded with Uncertainty

Readiness requires the specification of "for what." Compared to the familiar demands of entry-level employment, the "for what" is far less knowable when looking into uncertain futures, as the cases presented here illustrate. The perils of defining readiness in circumstances of uncertainty are easily imagined, yet the need to establish a useful description of what readiness will look like is real and persistent. Are there lessons to be taken from the three case studies about how best to navigate the uncertainty inherent in specifying the meaning of workforce in an uncertain context?

One lesson is to avoid exercises in armchair futurism. All too often this occurs in business when, for example, an extensive compilation of trends and prognostications is created and then the question is posed, "What does it all mean for our workforce?" Here is one such list shown to business leaders (source to remain anonymous): mobile computing, crowdsourcing, the IoT, big data, robots, autonomous vehicles, artificial intelligence, advanced manufacturing, multigenerational workforces, global demographic changes, gender parity, increasing longevity, income inequality, and changing social norms. Any one of those issues is legitimate; taken all at once, they are enormously unhelpful to enterprises seriously seeking to address workforce readiness. Rather than starting with a "change is all around us" mindset, the cases described here are instructive for their focus on an agreed-to, reasonably well-bounded (if complex) anticipated change. Establishing a narrowed focus grounded in a particular context thus appears to be an important element in reducing uncertainty and turning the abstract concept of readiness into something workable, in part by providing a common frame of reference and minimizing the risks of failure due to overreach.

Another lesson concerns the value of multiple approaches to data. Quantitative projections made from good here-and-now measurements are very valuable, such as forecasts of the occupational supply that begin with solid numbers about the number of people in an occupation now, the rate of occupational entry, and age-related demographics. On balance, though, most of the data relevant to defining workforce readiness will be qualitative in nature. Consequently, the value of classic methods of "doing research with words" (Gephart, 2013) in management contexts is very high, as is evident from the cases. Interviews with executive leaders, for example, initiated data collection in the cases on business strategy change and digital leadership. In the latter case, fieldwork and observational methods were also essential sources of data. Several other methods of data analysis were also evident in the cases, including the use of reasonably sophisticated survey techniques, content analysis of documents, and facilitated expert panel discussions. Skills in qualitative methods are critical to gaining data-based insights into the details of what workforce readiness means in a business context. Overall, flexible, adaptive applications of both qualitative and quantitative methods are keys to success.

Readiness Brings a Labor Market Dilemma

As the cases here illustrate, employers make different choices about the extent to which they will rely on external and internal labor markets. These choices are usually more about proportionate rather than absolute reliance on one over the other. Future workforce needs can lead employers to recalibrate, even radically alter, the extent to which they rely on one labor market over the other.

The emergence of alternative work arrangements represents different ways for employers to transact with their external labor markets. Such arrangements—gig workers, on-call workers, contract workers, agency-sourced temporary workers, freelancers, independent contractors, and the otherwise self-employed—are on the rise. Katz and Krueger (2016) report that the percentage of US workers engaged in alternative work arrangements grew from about 10% in 2005 to nearly 16% as of late 2015. The most populous among these is self-employment, which is about 10% of the US workforce (Bureau of Labor Statistics, 2018), and the category with the greatest rate of growth is contract workers (Katz & Krueger, 2016). Short-term affiliations with any one organization and limited scope of responsibilities are typical features experienced by individuals in these forms of employment.

The rise of alternative work arrangements is attributable to many factors. Technologies that support remote working and flexible work times, for example, may enable certain individuals to participate in the workforce who might not otherwise be able to do so at all (e.g., retirees, people with at-home responsibilities, the disabled, and those living in rural areas). Personal preferences also fuel their rise. For example, individuals who do not need to work for the income may find in alternative work arrangements a wished-for freedom to engage in only those work activities that most appeal to them. Employers, too, have a strong hand driving the growth of these arrangements. One reason is cost reduction. Lower wages, fewer benefits costs, lower overhead costs related to maintaining physical workplaces and employee record-keeping are all sources of cost savings for employers.

Employers face a classic investment quandary when choosing between internal and external labor markets. Those employers electing to achieve workforce readiness through their internal labor markets—that is, by engaging in training, coaching, managed career experiences, and rewarding to create and retain desired workforce capabilities—are making what are often long-term investments. Such investments are real costs to the employer. However, the employer controls those investments and will be first in line to reap their payoffs. In contrast, organizations electing to rely on external labor markets for workforce readiness can also make investments designed to help ensure that workers with desired future capabilities will be available. These investments, which can take the shape of expenditures on education and community services to influence the general workforce readiness, are almost certain to be smaller than those made in internal labor markets. However, the disposition of those investments is far less under the control of any one employer and any payoffs will be shared with many others.

A core strategic dilemma for employers concerned with future workforce readiness, then, is the resolution of the better bet: minimize short-term costs (the external labor market bet) or incur costs today in exchange for advantageous future returns (the internal labor market bet). For employers whose business success heavily relies on entry-level or short-term workers—for example, those in industries such as hospitality, food service, and mass retail—the better bet seems clear. But for other employers the better bet may be the internal labor market. These other employers may be those whose business success relies on the continued mastery and development of proprietary knowledge and work processes, for example, or employers relying on the preservation of distinctive organizational cultures for business advantage. Employers, however, surely will encounter challenges when making a bet on the internal labor market. One such challenge is the growth of alternative work arrangements: These keep individuals out the very type of employment relationship on which internal labor markets are predicated. Another, and perhaps greater, challenge is the prevailing emphasis on cost reduction. Meeting short-term financial goals can undercut commitments to long-term investments, as does the press to return value to outside shareholders now rather than later. How well employers manage this labor market dilemma—and how well they overcome challenges when the better bet is on the internal labor market—will be critical to success in achieving workforce readiness.

References

Bureau of Labor Statistics. (2018). The employment situation—January, 2018. Retrieved from https://www.bls.gov/news.release/pdf/empsit.pdf

Cross, P. (2016). *The importance of international trade to the Canadian economy: An overview.* Fraser Institute Research Bulletin. Retrieved from Fraserinstitute.org

Forum for International Trade Training. (2013). *International Trade Workforce Strategy.* Ottawa. Retrieved from https://fittfortrade.com

Gephart, R. P. Jr. (2013). Doing research with words. In J. M. Cortina & R. S. Landis (Eds.), *Modern research methods for the study of behavior in organizations* (pp. 265–317). New York, NY: Routledge.

Guzzo, R. A., & Nalbantian, H. (2014). Assessing learning's impact on careers. In C. D. McCauley, D. S. De Rue, P. R. Yost, & S. Taylor (Eds.), *Experience-driven leadership development* (pp. 523–528). New York, NY: Wiley.

International Federation of Robotics. (2017). *The impact of robots on productivity, employment and jobs.* A positioning paper by the International Federation of Robotics, April, 2017.

Katz, L. F., & Krueger, A. B. (2016). *The rise and nature of alternative work arrangements in the United States, 1995–2015.* NBER Working Paper No. 22667. The National Bureau of Economic Research. Retrieved from http://www.nber.org/papers/w22667. doi:10.3386/w22667

Lezotte, D., & Marder, B. (2017). *Evaluating the skills and assessment methods used by employers in the entry-level hiring process: Summary of research conducted for The Joyce Foundation.* Mercer Technical Report, 1 September 2017. Mercer commissioned and collaborated with SHRM on a survey funded by the Joyce Foundation about KSAs organizations are focusing on currently and in the future.

Marley, A. A. J., & Louviere, J. J. (2005). Some probabilistic models of best, worst, and best–worst choices. *Journal of Mathematical Psychology, 49*(6), 464–480.

Nalbantian, H., Guzzo, R. A., Kieffer, D., & Doherty, J. (2004). *Play to your strengths*. New York, NY: McGraw-Hill.

National Academies of Sciences, Engineering, and Medicine. (2017). *Information technology and the U.S. workforce: Where are we and where do we go from here?* Washington, DC: The National Academies Press. doi:10.17226/24649

National Network of Business and Industry Associations. 2015. *Common employability skills: A foundation for success in the workplace*. Report retrieved from http://national network.org/our-products.

6

THE MILITARY AS A SOURCE FOR CIVILIAN WORKFORCE DEVELOPMENT

Nathan D. Ainspan, Karin A. Orvis, and Lynne M. Kelley

When asked to list the organizations that have the greatest impact on the development of the United States (U.S.) workforce, the Department of Defense (DoD) may not likely be listed toward the top the list. However, as this chapter illustrates, the U.S. military has a critical role as one of the largest and most prominent forces in the nation's workforce development. Since its inception, the U.S. Armed Forces has been an integral part of the nation's workforce development. The DoD is the world's largest employer, with employees in a broad variety of occupations that also exist in the civilian employment sector. It not only provides an extensive amount of training to these employees but also is a unique employer in that it anticipates and trains its employees to be prepared for future employment and to eventually leave the organization. Approximately 200,000 service members currently transition from the military and enter the civilian sector every year, making this talent pipeline from the DoD larger in scope and impact than many other national training and educational programs.

In 2011, U.S. political leaders began focusing greater attention on how to best prepare service members for a successful transition from military service to civilian life, including the civilian workforce. DoD programs and policies, such as the Transition Assistance Program (TAP), were significantly enhanced and continue to evolve. DoD is also engaging with human resource (HR) leaders, hiring managers, and other critical stakeholders involved in the nation's civilian workforce development to ensure that society works to maximize the value transitioning service members and veterans can bring to the civilian workforce. DoD's ability to provide an effective pathway into the nation's civilian workforce relies on service members experiencing successful transitions into civilian employment; this occurs when civilian employers fully leverage the range of technical and nontechnical skills that service members gain from the military. For civilian employers, a military background on a resume can serve as a signaling device that an applicant conquered significant challenges, gained skills, and attained accomplishments and key experiences, similar to how diplomas from higher education institutions signal training and accomplishments. Employers who understand the military's culture and occupational training and can translate service members' transferable skills and experiences will have a competitive advantage over other employers that do not understand how to harness this talent.

This chapter describes the national importance of successful military-to-civilian transitions and explains the integral role of the DoD in America's workforce development. It provides a description of occupations in the military workforce for civilian employers to better understand the breadth of this workforce for their civilian workforce recruitment efforts. Also, DoD training and education for service members is explained, highlighting the benefits to civilian employers. Finally, the TAP, the DoD program that provides training to ensure service members successfully transition into civilian life is explained, concluding with specific recommendations for employers seeking to find and hire from this pipeline of talent.

The National Imperative of Successful Transitions

The successful transition of service members from military service into civilian employment is a national imperative for the United States; however, the nation is not currently fully leveraging this workforce development pathway. Skilled technical jobs is one example. These jobs, which make up 12 percent of the American workforce (Rothwell, 2015), require a high level of knowledge in a technical domain, but do not require a bachelor's degree for entry (National Academies of Science, Engineering, and Medicine, 2017). The National Academies identified a critical national workforce shortage in this area, which will exacerbate over time if efforts are not taken to address this shortage. The DoD, alongside other federal, state, and local entities, holds a critical role in improving this situation and ensuring the United States maintains a trained workforce with these skills. The National Academies recommended that DoD continue to enhance its efforts regarding military-to-civilian transition, increase coordination with civilian policymakers and educators, and enhance its outreach to civilian employers. The National Academies also recommended civilian employers increase their understanding of the skills, training, and experiences service members acquire in the military, and develop appreciation for the benefits veterans bring to the civilian workplace. This enhanced understanding and appreciation should help increase the talent flow of service members from the military into these skilled technical jobs. This is but one example of how civilian employers should look to DoD when recruiting new employees into their organizations. The advantage of capitalizing on this talent pipeline can be sizable—every year, a new talented pool of service members will transition from the military (roughly 200,000, with experience across a diverse range of occupations). If America's civilian workforce is not fully leveraging these individuals' broad skill sets and experience (acquired as a result of years of training, education, and on-the-job experience provided during military service, as described later in this chapter), the nation's competitiveness in the global economy will feel the impact.

The nation also has a financial interest in ensuring successful transitions for service members. Under American law, each unemployed veteran is eligible to collect unemployment compensation through a program geared for military veterans, called the Unemployment Compensation for Ex-servicemembers (UCX) program, which is funded by DoD. If a greater effort is taken to ensure successful transitions to meaningful civilian employment, UCX funds could potentially be spent on other DoD focus areas (such as training and military equipment). In 2011, UCX funding peaked to one billion dollars in payments to nearly 100,000 veterans. Since then, UCX payments have gone down with 310 million dollars paid out to roughly 20,000 individuals in 2016 (U.S. Congressional Budget Office, 2017). Further, similar to civilians, veterans may apply for unemployment insurance (UI) after their UCX ends if they are still unemployed. In addition to the money spent on UCX and UI, unemployed veterans also impact the nation's economy by not contributing to the nation's tax base through income taxes they would otherwise contribute.

Reducing unemployment or underemployment (i.e., employed in a position greatly below qualifications) for America's veterans is critical, not only for the nation's global competitiveness and financial future but also for the psychological and financial futures of individual veterans and their families. Unemployment or underemployment can hit veterans particularly hard. Those who self-select into the military tend to have attributes that favor action and activity, as well as a sense of duty, discipline, mission, and purpose (Hall, 2013). Veterans may be more likely to be missing these key elements if unemployed or underemployed, which could create negative psychological consequences, such as depression and anxiety.

Finally, one of DoD's missions is to look out for the best interest of service members, even as they transition to civilian life, by preparing them to be "career ready." DoD has also become aware that successful military-to-civilian transitions can be viewed from a national security perspective. Successful transitions of current service members will impact the effectiveness of its future recruiting efforts and DoD's ability to maintain an effective force that can defend the nation. Since 1973, the All-Volunteer Force replaced the military draft in America and required that America build its military by encouraging young adults to join. In order to do this, DoD continually needs to demonstrate the benefits of and value gained from military service. Research on the proclivity and interest of young adults to serve in the military demonstrated that one of the most commonly cited factors influencing a young adult's

decision to join the military is the expectation that military service will provide experience and career-related skills (U.S. Department of Defense Joint
Advertising, Market Research and Studies, 2016, 2017). Successful veterans
serve as ambassadors for military service by demonstrating that the military
is a high-quality career option, which also serves as an effective pathway for
gaining higher education, credentialing, and a future career in the civilian
workforce after leaving military service.

In sum, successful military-to-civilian transitions, with veterans attaining
productive civilian careers, have numerous substantial benefits to the nation.
Society needs to better understand the military's Profession of Arms, as well
as recognize this population as a talent pipeline into the civilian workforce in
order to maximize the value veterans can bring to our civilian communities.

The Military Workforce and Occupations

The sheer size of the DoD workforce alone makes it a critical component of our
nation's workforce development. The DoD is the largest employer in the world
with over 3.5 million employees (both civilian and military). DoD has approximately 2.4 million personnel serving in uniform. This number includes personnel from the Active Component (full-time service members, approximately
1.3 million), as well as the Reserve Component (members of the Reserves and
National Guard, approximately 1.1 million) who work full-time jobs in their
communities, but can be activated for training activities, national emergencies, or
during times of war (U.S. Department of Defense, Office of the Deputy Assistant
Secretary of Defense for Military Community and Family Policy, 2018).

DoD is one of the most diverse employers in our nation, as its members
represent the diverse country they serve. Although the military's demographics
do not completely mirror the diversity of the civilian population (e.g., because
of the military's stringent admission policies and criteria for entry, as well as
members must volunteer to serve, see Appendix for more details), the DoD's
workforce reflects more of the nation's diversity than other workforces. As an
example, the military was one of the first employers in America to integrate
racially and it has offered leadership positions to women and members of minorities earlier and at a greater pace than other organizations.

In the U.S. military, service members progress through formal ranks. Each
increase in rank corresponds to a larger realm of responsibility and leadership
(e.g., managing more people, more missions, or missions of greater importance)
and is associated with a greater time in military service. There are two rank
structures: (1) Enlisted, whose service members make up the majority of the
military and train (and may supervise others) in specific technical areas; and
(2) Officer, whose members are the managers and leaders of the organization.
Across both rank structures, and at all ranks, the military represents a diverse
range of occupations. Roughly 86 percent of the more than 8,000 occupations

in the military have a strong linkage or moderate overlap with civilian occupations (based on the knowledge, skills, and abilities listed in the Department of Labor's Occupation Information Network) and less than 10 percent are combat-related (U.S. Department of Defense, Office of the Under Secretary of Defense for Personnel and Readiness, 2018). In short, virtually every civilian employer can find one or more military job fields that directly correspond to the occupations for which it hires. Table 6.1 outlines the major occupational groups for the four branches of military service within the DoD, with the number of service members for each occupation type.

TABLE 6.1 Examples of Major Occupational Categories by Military Service and Total

Occupation	Ranks	Army	Air Force	Marine Corps	Navy	DoD Total
Administrative	Enlisted	5,575	14,095	11,691	18,244	49,605
Combat specialty	Enlisted and officers	123,326	4,381	44,483	14,417	186,607
Construction	Enlisted	15,050	5,203	6,377	3,692	30,322
Electronic and electrical equipment repair	Enlisted	29,276	29,988	16,673	48,921	124,858
Engineering, science, and technical	Enlisted and officers	64,630	66,183	31,272	51,351	213,436
Executive, administrative, and managerial—officer	Officer	13,142	6,730	2,450	6,908	29,230
Health care	Enlisted and officers	39,643	24,272	—	30,688	94,603
Human resource development	Enlisted and officers	18,114	9,356	3,037	7,515	38,022
Machine operator and production	Enlisted	4,374	6,283	2,488	8,404	21,549
Media and public affairs	Enlisted and officers	6,320	7,323	2,629	4,012	20,284
Protective service (e.g., military police and emergency management officers)	Enlisted and officers	24,032	34,938	6,451	14,147	79,568
Support service (e.g., logistics, transportation, and supply professionals)	Enlisted and officers	11,538	5,928	2,248	9,346	29,060
Transportation and material handling	Enlisted and officers	57,934	46,545	28,755	43,879	177,113
Vehicle and machinery mechanic	Enlisted	43,725	43,290	21,168	46,984	155,167

Source: Data from the Defense Manpower Data Center and summarized by the U.S. Department of Labor, Bureau of Labor Statistics (2017), *Occupational Outlook Handbook*, Military Careers, on the Internet at https://www.bls.gov/ooh/military/military-careers.htm (retrieved February 02, 2018).

Military Training, Education, and Credentialing Efforts Benefiting the Civilian Workforce

Because DoD recruits military employees primarily out of high school (proportionately few join after college) and demands proficiency in numerous areas and technical occupations, it is one of the largest providers of training and education in the nation. This training and education can be leveraged by the civilian workforce when service members transition from the military to civilian life, employing their prior skills and training to their civilian employment. DoD provides both training and education to its members.

Members may first encounter this training at one of the prestigious service academies (i.e., U.S. Army's Military Academy, West Point, NY; U.S. Naval Academy, Annapolis, MD; U.S. Air Force Academy, Colorado Springs, CO; U.S. Coast Guard Academy, New London, CT; and U.S. Merchant Marine Academy, Kings Point, NY). The military services also have a direct presence on many university campuses through the Reserve Officers' Training Corps, which like the service academies, prepares students to become commissioned officers. DoD runs accredited graduate-level institutions at various locations (e.g., National Defense University, Washington, DC; Army War College, Carlisle, PA; Army Command and General Staff College, Fort Leavenworth, KS; Naval War College, Newport, RI; Naval Postgraduate School, Monterey, CA; Air Force Institute of Technology, Wright Patterson Base, OH; Air University, Maxwell Base, AL). The Air Force also runs the Community College of the Air Force, a worldwide, multicampus accredited community college which confers 23,000 Associate of Applied Science degrees annually (U.S. Department of Defense, Office of the Under Secretary of Defense for Personnel and Readiness, 2018).

In addition to these institutions, each military service has extensive training commands that oversee training requirements across their service. These training commands ensure that the training and professional development courses are providing the right skills at the right time to service members. As part of this structure, every occupation and virtually every major military installation have some training activity along with its own training centers.

With regard to education, the magnitude of the DoD's educational assistance programs rivals many of America's largest university systems. Even when excluding the aforementioned training activities and the formal, on-duty training and education provided to service members and examining *only* the voluntary education programs (i.e., elective educational opportunities pursued during a service member's off-duty/nonwork hours), the DoD provided voluntary education opportunities to 255,729 service members who took 726,305 classes through over 2,700 accredited academic institutions in Fiscal Year 2017 (U.S. Department of Defense, Office of the Under Secretary of Defense for Personnel and Readiness, 2018). By comparison, the entire University of California system has 238,000 students on 10 campuses, and the University of Texas enrolls 221,000 students at 14 locations (The University of California, 2018; The University of Texas, 2016).

In addition to providing formal education and training, DoD provides on-the-job training with technical instruction though its formal apprenticeship program, called the U.S. Military Apprenticeship Program. Most apprenticeships require over 4,000 work hours to complete (U.S. Department of Defense, Office of the Under Secretary of Defense for Personnel and Readiness, 2018). Apprenticeship completion provides service members with documented, recognizable work experience that can provide greater opportunities for immediate civilian employment following transition. Civilian employers also have the opportunity to gain early access to service members as prospective employees before they become veterans through the DoD SkillBridge Authority. Under this unique program, transitioning service members (up to six months before separation or retirement) can obtain valuable civilian job skills training, apprenticeships, and internships from private sector employers, while continuing to receive their military pay and benefits. Companies in dozens of growing industries—from welding and advanced manufacturing to information technology—are already participating. In Fiscal Year 2017, over 2,000 transitioning service members participated in this program; and, historically over 90 percent of participants obtain post-service employment as a result (U.S. Department of Defense, Office of the Under Secretary of Defense for Personnel and Readiness, 2018).

Another area where DoD contributes to the nation's workforce is via the development of employee non-technical skills (e.g., leadership, teamwork) that compliment employee technical skills (e.g., information technology, accounting). In fact, civilian employers from organizations of all sizes and industries continually report a desire to hire individuals with these non-technical skills (Feffer, 2016). Recently, the RAND Corporation completed research codifying the non-technical skills service members develop throughout their military service, both via professional military education/training and on-the-job experiences (Hardison et al., 2017). Specifically, RAND identified 19 skills that service members acquire through military service, such as leadership, decision-making, teamwork, oral and written communication, handling work stress, dependability, attention to detail, and managing and supervising the work of others. RAND discovered that service members are likely to have well-developed non-technical skills because—unlike many civilians—they have received formal, extensive, professional training targeting these skills. In addition, they refine these skills via on-the-job experiences, such that they become ingrained as elements of the individual's character and personality. These skills are closely linked to the skills identified by the Department of Labor as the "essential skills" needed in the 21st-century workforce (ACT Inc., 2000; Stuart & Dahm, 1999). For civilian employers, this recent research substantiates that military service on a resume can be used as signal for not only high technical skills but also the sought-after non-technical skills they desire but have difficulty finding in the civilian realm. As an example, the Center for Creative Leadership conducted research on leaders in the Army and civilian leaders and found that Army leaders showed significantly higher proficiency ratings on many of the non-technical skills compared to civilian leaders (Young, 2017). Hence, this illustrates another talent area for civilian employers that they can find from service members who are transiting from military to civilian employment.

The DoD Transition Assistance Program

As mentioned previously, DoD has a strong interest in the successful transition of its service members. DoD ensures service members successfully transition into civilian life, including civilian employment, through its robust program, TAP. TAP was first introduced in 1991 (as the American military was drawing down its forces after the end of the Cold War), as the mechanism that would provide departing service members (in the last months of their military careers) with the tools, training, and resources they could use to help them transition out of the military, find employment, and begin their civilian lives. This legacy TAP offered good resources, but it became clear that the education, tools, and resources could be further expanded to better serve our transitioning service members. This became particularly prominent when the U.S. economy was facing an overall economic downturn and high unemployment rates, particularly for our military veterans. For example, the unemployment rate in 2011 for veterans was 12 percent compared to an overall rate of 9 percent. Further, young male veterans between 18 and 24 years of age experienced significantly higher levels of unemployment in 2011 at 29.1 percent, compared to their peers at 17.6 percent (U.S. Department of Labor, Bureau of Labor Statistics, 2018).

Acknowledging the difficulties that veterans were having with their transition into the civilian workforce, the White House and Congress responded. In August 2011, President Obama called for significant improvements in the transition assistance provided to service members to ensure they are "career ready" as they transition to civilian life. As a result, the Interagency Veterans Employment Initiative Task Force was formed to rethink transition and ensure transitioning service members are optimally prepared for transition to civilian life. This Task Force included the DoD (and each military service); the Departments of Veterans Affairs (VA), Labor (DOL), Homeland Security, and Education; the Office of Personnel Management; and the Small Business Administration and formed the foundation of the current formal interagency governance structure responsible for the design, implementation, evaluation, and continuous improvement of the TAP. The Task Force provided an implementation plan to the White House in December 2012 that described a phased roll-out of a fundamentally redesigned TAP centered on the career readiness of our transitioning service members, broadly defined.

Likewise, due to the passage of the Veterans Opportunity to Work (VOW) to Hire Heroes Act in November 2011, several elements of transition assistance became mandatory for all service members (from the Active and Reserve Components) who were retiring, separating, or being released after 180 days or more on continuous Title 10 Active Duty status (except in certain limited circumstances). Per this law, transitioning service members must now attend (a) preseparation/transition counseling (which details the full range of programs and services available to assist them during their transition, including the TAP curriculum, and introduces the service member to the transition requirement of developing their own Individual Transition Plan), (b) the DOL Employment Workshop, and (c) VA Benefits briefings. In accordance with the VOW Act and the White House–approved Task Force implementation plan, the redesigned TAP was fully implemented across all DoD military services, at over 185 locations worldwide, by the end of 2014. Notable key features of the current TAP include the following:

- **Career Readiness Standards:** Career Readiness Standards are a set of career preparation activities and associated deliverables that service members must complete to demonstrate that they are "career ready" prior to transitioning from the military. Examples of the Career Readiness Standards include development of a viable Individual Transition Plan which documents the service member's personal circumstances, needs, and transition goals (e.g., employment, education, financial goals); completion of a job application package, to include a resume; completion of a post-transition budget; evaluation of the transferability of one's military skills/experiences to the civilian workforce and completion of a gap analysis of what additional education, credentials, or skills one may need for their desired career path.
- **A revamped curriculum:** The TAP employs a standardized adult learning-based curriculum, with standardized learning objectives, across all military services called Transition GPS (Goals, Plans, Success). This curriculum was designed to support each member's personal transition goals and attainment of the Career Readiness Standards. The Transition GPS curriculum currently includes a core curriculum and three additional two-day specialized training tracks that are tailored to meet the needs and personal goals of the service member (e.g., whether seeking to pursue additional higher education, career technical training and credentialing, or entrepreneurship interests). Currently, the following curriculum modules are taught during the TAP:
  - *Resilient Transitions*—Discusses transition-related stressors for the individual and their family, key military and civilian cultural differences that service members may experience, and resources and support available both pre- and post-transition.
  - *Financial Planning*—Provides information and tools that service members need to identify financial responsibilities, obligations, and goals after transition, including key differences with regard to topics such as

taxes, health care, and benefits and compensation. This module prepares service members to create viable post-transition budgets.

- *Military Occupational Code Crosswalk*—Explains how service members can document and translate their military skills (both technical and non-technical skills) and experience to the civilian workforce using language that civilian employers will understand. The module also helps service members document any gaps that may exist between their current skills/experience and what they need to meet their future career goals.
- *DOL Employment Workshop*—Provides industry best-practice information needed for successful employment transition, such as job search techniques, labor market information, resume development, as well as interviewing, networking, and salary negotiation skills.
- *VA Benefits Briefings*—Provides information on benefits and services that are available from the (VA), including eligibility criteria and how to apply for veteran's health and education benefits, home loan guaranty, insurance, and disability benefits.
- *Accessing Higher Education Track*—Provides information to assist service members in identifying education requirements that support their personal career goals, including a focus on researching and comparing institutions, educational funding, and the admissions and application process.
- *Career Exploration and Preparation Track*—Provides information and tools for service members to self-assess their skills, knowledge, values, and interests to shape their future career goals and career planning, and includes information on how to identify reputable apprenticeship, credentialing, and training programs.
- *Entrepreneurship Track*—Provides information on the benefits and challenges of self-employment and describes the steps required for pursuing business ownership.
- **Capstone:** At least 90 days before service members transition from military service, they will participate in a Capstone event intended to validate and verify that they have met the Career Readiness Standards, ensure they have developed a viable Individual Transition Plan, and provide an opportunity for a "warm handover" to agency partners. A warm handover is for service members who require (or desire) additional assistance who are referred to additional or remedial training opportunities. Service members will be offered a warm handover to agencies and organizations that provide them continued benefits, services, and support as veterans. As an example, a transitioning service member unable to create an effective resume would be connected with a local representative from an American Job Center run by the DOL. This individual would then work directly with the service member to help them develop a viable resume, as well as provide a host of other employment-related services. Service member, TAP installation staff, and commander participation in the Capstone

process is a key aspect of the TAP that builds a culture of shared accountability for career readiness.

• **Career Planning and Transition Preparation Across the Military
  Life Cycle:** Perhaps the most significant change in the TAP is that career planning and transition preparation now occurs over the entire span
  of a service member's military career—from accession into the military
  through transition out of military service (at various key touchpoints such
  as one's first permanent duty station/home station, promotion, and deploy-
  ment). Service members are encouraged to begin thinking early in their
  military service about their post-military careers and to obtain training,
  certifications, and higher education to help them prepare for future civilian
  career opportunities. The ongoing process aligns military career development with the service member's personal post-military goals. This represents a significant culture change for the DoD—a change from a culture
  that avoided conversations about transition and civilian career planning to
  one that acknowledges that every member will transition from military to
  civilian life (whether that time is four, 10, or 20 years down the line) and
  thoughtful preparation is key. In short, the earlier service members start
  preparing for their transition and future civilian career, the more successful
  they will be in achieving their post-transition goals.

To ensure the TAP continues to provide relevant and current information to
service members, an Interagency TAP Evaluation Plan, which was approved by
the U.S. Office of Management and Budget, was created to continually assess,
evaluate, and update the program. As part of this plan, DoD and its interagency
partners assess program processes, output, and outcomes in order to provide
accountability, improve customer satisfaction, and ensure program effectiveness.
Annual updates to the TAP are also based on findings from behavioral science
(e.g., industrial psychology's approach to competency modeling and the pedagogy literature on how to effectively teach adult learners), research conducted
and commissioned by interagency TAP partners (e.g., the RAND non-technical
skills research referenced previously), surveys and focus groups of transitioning
service members and veterans about their experiences with the TAP and about
their post-military careers and lives, and the passage of any new legislation.
Further, program outputs and employment/educational outcomes that reflect
the desired long-term end state of the TAP are also tracked and evaluated. Such
a rigorous program benefits employers and the nation as a whole, as service
members now spend significant time preparing for their future civilian career.

Recommendations for Civilian Employers

Many civilian employers understand the crucial role that transitioning service members and veterans can have in contributing to their workforce talent
and thus to their overall competitiveness in the national and global economy.

As such, they have developed progressive recruitment and selection programs to tap into this talent pool so that they can leverage the technical and non-technical skills of transitioning service members and veterans (e.g., Amazon, Walmart, Microsoft, and Hilton). However, the business case for hiring transitioning service members and veterans may still not be understood by all. Recent research from the Society for Human Resource Management (2016) found that only 36 percent of employers will seek talent from nontraditional sources, including sources targeting transitioning service members and veterans. It may be that many civilian hiring managers and business leaders lack familiarity with the military and the skill set and experiences that transitioning service members and veterans could bring to their workforce (Carter, Schafer, Kidder, & Fagan, 2017). This chapter seeks to help remedy this issue.

It may also be that other civilian hiring managers and business leaders desire to hire transitioning service members and veterans yet face challenges. According to this same 2016 SHRM survey, 68 percent of the surveyed HR professionals reported that they were facing challenging recruiting conditions in the current market, and 84 percent saw a skills shortage in the previous year. HR professionals also reported that although their companies are interested in hiring military veterans to fill their human capital needs, they have difficulties finding veterans and translating their military experiences into civilian terms. The following are recommendations and resources available to help civilian employers overcome such challenges in recruiting, hiring, and retaining transitioning service members and veterans.

Connecting and Recruiting

- The DOL offers employer resources for finding and hiring transitioning service members and veterans. Through https://veterans.gov/ you can contact a Veterans Employment Coordinator to get free one-on-one assistance in creating a veteran hiring plan. You can also link to your state job bank through this website. Once registered, your jobs will be automatically posted to veterans.gov through the U.S. jobs National Labor Exchange. You can also contact a Veterans Employment Representative at your local American Job Center (AJC). Let them know you want to hire a veteran. They will help you identify qualified veterans. This is a free service. Visit the AJC website to locate the center closest to you at http://www.careeronestop.org/Site/businesses.aspx.
- Hiring Our Heroes is a nationwide initiative run by the U.S. Chamber of Commerce Foundation to help transitioning service members, veterans, and military spouses find meaningful employment opportunities. Attend a Hiring Our Heroes Transition Summit, Job Fair, Community-Based Hiring Event, or Sports Expo Hiring Event. Consider creating a "Corporate Fellowship Program" through Hiring Our Heroes. These programs match transitioning service members and spouses with participating companies. Find out more at https://www.uschamberfoundation.org/hiring-our-heroes.

- Service members transition from approximately 185 distinct locations across the world. Identifying these geographic recruiting hubs to target populations of transitioning service members will enhance your veteran recruiting success. Reach out to these local military installations to share training and employment opportunities. You can go to the DoD's TAP website, https://www.dodtap.mil, which will link you to each military services' TAP website for specific locations.
- Create an apprenticeship or internship program to connect with transitioning service members before they leave the service. Capitalize on the DoD SkillBridge initiative, which allows service members to receive civilian job skills training up to six months prior to separation. Find out more at https://dodskillbridge.com. Employers may also apply for national and/or state funding to create or expand apprenticeship programs through the DOL's American Apprenticeship Grants program. Find out more at https://www.doleta.gov/oa/aag.cfm.
- Partner with organizations near military installations to leverage hiring opportunities and to share best practices, as well as with organizations and collectives that have expertise in this area (e.g., the Blackstone Group, the Bush Institute, the Veterans Job Mission, the Institute of Veterans and Military Families, and LinkedIn).
- Leverage the knowledge and network of Veteran Service Organizations that can help you connect with veterans. The VA has a directory of these organizations at https://www.va.gov/vso/VSO-Directory.pdf.
- Enhance your recruiting capabilities by creating and utilizing veteran-specific programs and recruiters to help bridge the cultural gap between your organization and the veterans interested in your company. Ensure your marketing materials are honest, accurate, and have the right tone. Veterans frequently share their experiences regarding employers with their peers, making word of mouth recruiting crucial to your efforts. Ask veterans in your company about their experiences and have them review your recruiting materials for their honest feedback.
- Let success breed success: Veterans tend to have strong veteran networks and listen to their fellow veterans when it comes to learning about job opportunities. Encourage your veteran employees to share their stories with other service members and veterans. Encourage them to go to hiring events and give them the time to attend meetings and activities held by Veteran Service Organizations.
- Many service members joined the military and got promoted because they tend to have mission-driven personalities. Emphasize the mission of your company in your recruiting efforts, focus on how they can contribute to this effort, and ensure that you give these employees a sense of purpose and mission in their careers.
- If you have customer-facing products and staff, realize that your veteran recruiting efforts begin in your interactions with service members and their

families. Some companies make extensive efforts to extend great customer service to service members and their families (e.g., extending payment deadlines to the families of deployed service members) as part of their veteran recruiting efforts. Service members and families will remember these positive experiences when it comes time to pursue civilian employment.

- Transitioning service members and veterans may have a difficult time describing the skills that they gained in the military (particularly nontechnical skills) in their resumes and during interviews. This may happen because many service members are routinely exposed to other service members with similar skills, so they may not realize how valuable or unusual their skills are in the civilian workforce. Your company's resume reviewers and interviewers may need to take some extra efforts to extract these skills and characteristics. Ask these applicants to provide examples of their experiences in different military assignments, and you are likely to hear desirable technical and nontechnical skills emerge. Leverage the knowledge of other veterans in your organization to help you further translate resumes based on your organization's needs. For further information and tips, see RAND's *What Veterans Bring to Civilian Workplaces* toolkit at https://www.rand.org.

Onboarding and Retention

- Research demonstrates that two of the most effective recruiting and retention tools for veteran employees are mentoring and peer groups (Allen et al., 2004; Allen et al., 2009; and Van Aken, Monetta, & Scott, 1994) These can include formal veteran-to-veteran mentoring programs, informal mentoring relationships, or corporate affinity groups. Ensure support from the top executives in your organization for these programs, that they are properly resourced, and that veterans (and non-veterans interested in the issue) are afforded the time to participate.
- Understand and appreciate that the military has a different culture. Work to integrate this new culture in your organizational diversity efforts. Do your research to understand the military system, its culture, and its language. The resources in this chapter can provide you with some of this information. The military is built on honesty and respect, so if you do not know something about veterans be honest in your interactions with them, show respect, and admit gaps in your knowledge.
- Form internal strategic communications highlighting commonalities between your corporate culture and veteran capabilities, values, and opportunities; share these commonalities across your organization to include hiring managers and recruiters.
- Provide veteran employees with clear goals and regular and frequent feedback. The military culture is known for communicating goals clearly, explaining how to measure and obtain these goals, and then providing open, honest, and

regular feedback about the goals. Service members are accustomed to knowing what is needed to accomplish the mission, and receiving regular, quick checks on their performance, including needed improvements. As veterans in your company, they will expect the same, so do not hesitate to provide this.

Conclusion

American service members receive extensive education and training in applicable career skills as soon as they enter the military, starting with boot camp/basic training and then through formal training for their specific occupations. As service members become more proficient in their occupation and are promoted to higher ranks, they receive additional occupation-specific training and credentialing, as well as other professional and leadership development opportunities. To complement this formal training and education, each service member gains diverse on-the-job experience. The military is known for placing its members in extraordinary, stressful experiences requiring fast decision-making with limited knowledge and resources, with a lot riding on their decisions. These are learning opportunities experienced by every service member. As such, service members commonly assume enormous responsibilities and leadership roles that exceed what their civilian counterparts are doing at comparable ages. For example, a 20-year-old enlisted service member will be directly responsible for millions of dollars of equipment, managing a dozen of their peers in a dangerous and risky situation, and making decisions and recommendations to their senior leaders, while their civilian counterparts are still in college or are just getting started in the workforce.

Society must better understand, recognize, and leverage the military's Profession of Arms as a talent pipeline into the civilian workforce to maximize the value veterans can bring to their civilian communities and the broader national economy. American civilian employers are implored to fully utilize this talent pool over approximately 200,000 transitioning service members a year. If America does not fully leverage veterans' skills and experiences (acquired during military service) in the civilian workforce, our overall competitiveness in the global economy will also feel the impact. Successful military-to-civilian transitions rest not only on (1) the individual service member, but also on (2) the federal government, such as through the DoD TAP, as well as (3) the civilian sector, such as through actions of civilian employers. Together, we can accomplish this national strategic challenge.

Disclaimer

The views, opinions, and/or findings contained in this chapter are solely those of the authors and should not be construed as an official position, policy, or decision of the DoD, unless so designated by other documentation.

Self-selection	The DoD's All-Volunteer Force means that those who volunteer are motivated to join and make many sacrifices for a greater purpose. The more types of individuals who have the interest, personality, and character to think of joining the military in the first place are a smaller subset of the larger U.S. population.	Research has found that the propensity to join the military tends to run in families, as the children and grandchildren of military veterans are more likely to sign up to serve than the children of non-veterans (Carter et al., 2017).
Criteria for entry	Even if someone was interested in joining, the military's strict criteria for who it will admit (e.g., in terms of intelligence, education, physical agility, and endurance), further reduces the number of people who can serve so that it represents a less representative, yet more elite, subset.	The DoD estimates that only 29 percent of the youth population of America (between the ages of 17 and 24 years) are eligible to serve in the military and that only 17 percent of this population would qualify and be available to serve (U.S. Department of Defense, 2013).
Culture and promotions	After self-selecting into the military, a service member exists in a culture and an organization with values that are different from the culture of civilian organization (Hall, 2013).	For example, the military has an "up or out" system (its leadership structure is a pyramid and members are expected to leave the military at certain points if they do not receive promotions); members who are high performers and thrive in this culture will succeed and receive promotions, while those who cannot perform or adjust will leave service.
Individual traits	While the military draws in a wide range of personalities and cultural backgrounds, its culture and requirements have the effect of attracting and intensifying certain personality traits and attributes that will make the individuals in military service different from the civilian population (DeVries & Wijnans, 2013).	These include higher levels of conscientiousness, a willingness to leave the safety and security of home, and a willingness to sacrifice everything in their lives to protect others.
Education	The DoD workforce is more educated than the rest of the United States, as service members enter with at least a high school degree for initial entry into the enlisted ranks and a college degree for entry into the officer ranks. DoD then requires various training and encourages service members to pursue formal education throughout their military careers via both military training and civilian colleges and universities. The GI Bill, which generally covers the full cost of college tuition and living expenses for military veterans and their dependents, is another self-selection factor that draws individuals to serve in the military.	According to the DoD's surveys of young adults, 49 percent of America's youth population cite education benefits as the main reason that they join the military (U.S. Department of Defense Joint Advertising, Market Research and Studies, 2016), while a survey of veterans found 53 percent provided this as their reason for joining the military (Zoli, Maury, & Fay, 2015). In total, this focus on education and credentials creates a workforce that is more educated than the rest of the U.S. population.
Age	Since most members join the military as young adults, the military population is younger on average than the civilian workforce.	Approximately 44 percent of uniformed active duty personnel are 25 years old or younger (U.S. Department of Defense, Office of the Deputy Assistant Secretary of Defense for Military Community and Family Policy, 2017).

References

ACT Inc. (2000). *Workplace essential skills: Resources related to the SCANS competencies and foundation skills.* Retrieved from https://wdr.doleta.gov/OPR/FULLTEXT/00-wes.pdf

Allen, T. D., Eby, L. T., Poteet, M. L., Lentz, E., & Lima, L. (2004). Career benefits associated with mentoring for protégés. A meta-analysis. *Journal of Applied Psychology, 89,* 127–136.

Allen, T. D., Finkelstein, L. M., & Poteet, M. L. (2009). *Designing workplace mentoring programs: An evidence-based approach.* Oxford, UK: Wiley-Blackwell Publishing.

Carter, P., Schafer, A., Kidder, K., & Fagan, M. (2017). *Lost in translation: The civil-military divide and veteran employment.* Washington, DC: The Center for New American Security. Retrieved from https://www.cnas.org/publications/reports/lost-in-translation.

DeVries, M. R., & Wijnans, E. (2013). Personality and military service. In B. A. Moore & J. E. Barnett (Eds.), *Military psychologists' desk reference.* New York, NY: Oxford University Press.

Feffer, M. (2016). HR's hard challenge: When employees lack soft skills. *HR Today.* Retrieved from https://www.shrm.org/hr-today/news/hr-magazine/0416/pages/hrs-hard-challenge-when-employees-lack-soft-skills.aspx

Hall, L. K. (2013). Military culture. In B. A. Moore & J. E. Barnett (Eds.), *Military psychologists' desk reference.* New York, NY: Oxford University Press.

Hardison, C. M., McCausland, T. C., Shanley, M. G., Saavedra, J. M., Wong, J. P., Clague, A., & Crowley, J. C. (2017). *Methodology for translating enlisted veterans' non-technical skills into civilian employers' terms.* Santa Monica, CA: The RAND Corporation. Retrieved from https://www.rand.org/pubs/research_reports/RR1919.html.

National Academies of Science, Engineering, and Medicine. (2017). *Building America's skilled technical workforce.* Washington, DC: The National Academies Press. Retrieved from https://www.nap.edu/download/23472.

Rothwell, J. (2015). *Defining skilled technical work.* Prepared for the National Academies Board on Science, Technology, and Economics Policy, Project on the "The Supply Chain for Middle-Skilled Jobs: Education, Training, and Certification Pathways." Washington, DC: The National Academies of Science, Engineering, and Medicine. Retrieved from https://sites.nationalacademies.org/cs/groups/pgasite/documents/webpage/pga_167744.pdf

Society for Human Resource Management. (2016). *New talent landscape. Recruiting difficulties and skills shortages.* Alexandria, VA: Society for Human Resource Management. Retrieved from https://www.shrm.org/hr-today/trends-and-forecasting/research-and-surveys/Documents/SHRM%20New%20Talent%20Landscape%20Recruiting%20Difficulty%20Skills.pdf.

Stuart, L., & Dahm, E. (1999, January). *21st century skills for 21st century jobs.* Washington, DC: U.S. Departments of Commerce, Education, and Labor and the National Institute of Literacy and the Small Business Administration. Retrieved from https://digitalcommons.ilr.cornell.edu/cgi/viewcontent.cgi?referer=https://www.google.com/&httpsredir=1&article=1153&context=key_workplace.

University of California. (2018). *The UC system.* Retrieved from https://www.universityofcalifornia.edu/uc-system.

University of Texas. (2016). *Fast facts 2016.* Retrieved from https://www.utsystem.edu/documents/docs/publication/2017/fast-facts-2016.

U.S. Congressional Budget Office. (2017). *Transitioning from the military to the civilian workforce: The role of unemployment compensation for ex-servicemembers.* Washington, DC: U.S. Congressional Budget Office. Retrieved from https://www.cbo.gov/system/files/115th-congress-2017-2018/reports/52503-transitionreport.pdf.

U.S. Department of Defense. (2013). *Qualified military available study.* Washington, DC: U.S. Department of Defense.

U.S. Department of Defense Joint Advertising, Market Research and Studies. (2016). *New recruit survey.* Washington, DC: Department of Defense Joint Advertising, Market Research and Studies.

U.S. Department of Defense Joint Advertising, Market Research and Studies. (2017). *Youth polls.* Washington, DC: Department of Defense Joint Advertising, Market Research and Studies.

U.S. Department of Defense, Office of the Deputy Assistant Secretary of Defense for Military Community and Family Policy. (2018). *Profile of the military community: 2017 demographics: Profile of the military community.* Washington, DC: U.S. Department of Defense, Office of the Deputy Assistant Secretary of Defense for Military Community and Family Policy. Retrieved from http://download.militaryone source.mil/12038/MOS/Reports/2017-demographics-report.pdf.

U.S. Department of Defense, Office of the Under Secretary of Defense for Personnel and Readiness. (2018). *Department of Defense report: Credentialing program utilization.* Washington, DC: U.S. Department of Defense, Office of the Under Secretary of Defense for Personnel and Readiness.

U.S. Department of Defense, Undersecretary of Defense for Personnel and Readiness. (2018). *Defense manpower data center occupational database.* Washington, DC: U.S. Department of Defense, Undersecretary of Defense for Personnel and Readiness.

U.S. Department of Labor, Bureau of Labor Statistics. (2017). *Occupational outlook handbook: Military careers.* Washington DC: U.S. Department of Labor, Bureau of Labor Statistics. Retrieved from https://www.bls.gov/ooh/military/military-careers.htm.

U.S. Department of Labor, Bureau of Labor Statistics. (2018). *Data tools: Data retrieval: Labor force statistics (Current Population Survey).* Washington, DC: U.S. Department of Labor. Bureau of Labor Statistic. Retrieved from https://www.bls.gov/webapps/legacy/veterans_by_age_and_sex.htm.

Van Aken, E. M., Monetta, D. J., & Scott, S. D. (Spring, 1994), Affinity groups: The missing link in employee involvement. *Organizational Dynamics, 22*(4), 38–54.

Young, S. (2017). *How veterans outscore their counterparts on leadership.* Center for Creative Leadership. Retrieved from https://www.ccl.org/blog/veterans-outscore-civilian-leaders.

Zoli, C., Maury, R., & Fay, D. (2015, November). *Missing perspectives: Servicemembers' transition from service to civilian life. Data-driven research to enact the promise of the Post-9/11 GI Bill.* Syracuse, NY: Institute for Veterans and Military Families. Retrieved from https://ivmf.syracuse.edu/wp-content/uploads/2016/05/MissingPerspectivesACC_03.02.18.pdf.

7

O*NET AND THE NATURE OF WORK

Erich Dierdorff and Kemp Ellington

The need for both scholarship and policy on issues of workforce readiness has long existed, where such readiness refers to the formal work-related processes and interventions to build knowledge, skills, abilities, and other factors (KSAOs) that lead to important workforce outcomes for individuals, organizations, and society. While this focus has a rich history, addressing issues of workforce readiness appears to be particularly urgent in the contemporary world of work that is now replete with reorganization, reformation, and reconstitution of employment arrangements, technology, and information (Okhuysen, Lepak, Labianca, Smith, & Steensma, 2013). Recent examinations of the U.S. economy make this urgency especially striking, where forecasts have suggested that nearly one-third of all workers will need to transition out of their existing occupational roles by 2030 (Manyika et al., 2017). Such transitions hold substantial and far-reaching effects for individuals, organizations, and the nation. Not only do these types of forecasts highlight the rapidity and scope of workplace changes; they also suggest the centrality of "occupations" in the discourse that attempts to understand, predict, and address concerns of workforce readiness.

In this chapter, we seek to extend the conversation about workforce readiness by making the case for why and how an occupation-centric approach can inform scholarship and practice. We begin by discussing what it means to approach workforce readiness from an occupational standpoint as well as the potential value it brings. Next, we demonstrate how many of these opportunities already exist and can be supported by currently available resources to researchers and practitioners. We illustrate this point by describing the U.S. Department of Labor's Occupational Information System (O*NET), arguably one of the most comprehensive systems of its kind, as well as its potential applications to bolster workforce readiness. Third, we present results that exemplify the utility of an occupational approach to workforce readiness. Here, we examine O*NET data to illustrate the kinds of deeper insight an occupational approach can provide. More specifically, we examine occupational clusters that delineate along several critical "21st-century" skills that have been put forth as especially valuable, yet underdeveloped, in the current labor force. We conclude with a discussion of several key challenges associated with efforts to promote and sustain workforce readiness, as well as offer recommendations for how we might proceed.

Workforce Readiness and Occupations

The concept of workforce readiness is inextricably linked to the concept of an occupation, and this relationship provides a number of benefits for researchers and practitioners. It is interesting to note that many who contribute to the domain of workforce readiness already recognize the importance of occupations, at least implicitly so, when they rely on occupation-based data for analysis and interventions. For example, occupationally linked data such as wages, credentialing, employment statistics, and so forth are frequently brought to bear when informing career choice decisions, professional development opportunities, as well as broader industry outlooks, overall workforce trends, and economic development opportunities. Yet, we believe the value that comes with leveraging an occupational approach remains underutilized in workforce readiness scholarship and practice.

Occupations have been defined as "collections of work roles with similar goals that require the performance of distinctive activities as well as the application of specialized skills or knowledge to accomplish these goals" (Dierdorff, Rubin, & Morgeson, 2009, p. 974). Closely looking at this definition makes it easy to see how issues of workforce readiness are directly connected to the concept of occupation. Workforce readiness entails the acquisition of relevant competencies that span knowledge, skill, and abilities, as well as the capacity or preparedness to apply these competencies to work-related behavior and performance. In this way, workforce readiness encompasses the readiness to fulfill the various demands required by a given occupation, adapt to evolving practices or technology within an occupation, and the readiness to effectively transition into new occupational roles when such needs arise.

There are three reasons that an occupational approach holds particular value for addressing workforce readiness. First, invoking an occupational lens provides a "common language" for examining the multitude of factors that come into play when studying workforce readiness. As is clearly illustrated throughout this book, stakeholders invested in issues of workforce readiness come from a variety of disciplines, each with its own vernacular and models. Such variety is indeed beneficial, yet it does present challenges when it comes to integrating these streams of scholarship. Occupations, by definition, create contextually bounded objects of study that demarcate the major domains of variables that affect workforce readiness, including the demands of work (e.g., activities), attributes required of workers (e.g., knowledge, skills, abilities), and a host of associated economic variables (e.g., labor demand and supply, wages). Thus, occupations centrally link these various data and create a shared language that "promotes the communication of ideas between researchers in different disciplines, as well as between practitioners, laypersons, governmental agencies, and academics" (Peterson et al., 2001, p. 481).

A second reason an occupational approach to workforce readiness is valuable is that it offers considerable flexibility for both practical applications and data-driven insights for research and policy. Occupations are inherently multilevel in nature. They taxonomically exist at a level above individual jobs and at a level lower than industries (Dierdorff & Morgeson, 2007). Occupations also span and are embedded in multiple industries, as well as cut across multiple organizations (Dierdorff & Morgeson, 2009; Nolan, Morrison, Kumar, Galloway, & Cordes, 2011; Trice, 1993). These features make occupations a highly flexible unit of analysis for examining the diverse set factors involved in workforce readiness. Furthermore, many disciplines, such as industrial/ organizational psychology and labor economics, tend to delineate workforce data by occupation or clusters of occupations. This makes additional integration and insight increasingly feasible for workforce readiness researchers because it permits analyses to go "up or down" in terms of descriptive specificity. For example, occupational data can be the linking mechanisms between industry- or regional-level economic data and job- or individual-level data. From a practical standpoint, an occupational approach views jobs not as unique entities, but rather as differences and similarities evident on generalizable, cross-job descriptors (Mumford & Peterson, 1999). This approach allows for multiple views of workforce readiness and its consequences, whereby different sets of factors can be emphasized for different individuals in different types of situations. In workforce development, for example, a focus for recent graduates might be on the ability requirements and vocational interests associated with occupations, whereas a focus for displaced workers might be on skill demands and previous work activities to determine the optimal occupations in which to transition.

Finally, a third reason an occupational perspective is useful for addressing workforce readiness is that it brings to bear a rich body of existing scholarship, which can better delineate the landscape of pertinent individual and situational factors to consider. For instance, a well-recognized concept supported by occupational theory and research is the notion of "person-occupation fit," which generally refers to the congruence or match between individuals' interests, needs, and abilities and the characteristics, requirements, and contexts of their occupations (Holland, 1985; Kristof, 1996; Vogel & Feldman, 2009). Extensive research has demonstrated that person-occupation fit is associated with a host of important outcomes, such as individuals' job and career satisfaction, performance, and underemployment (Dawis & Lofquist, 1994; Feldman, 2002; Spokane, 1985; Tranberg, Slane, & Ekeberg, 1993). Such evidence suggests that conceptualizing workforce readiness in terms of person-occupation fit can provide a useful framework from which to examine how macro-level influences, such as regional economic growth or industry concentrations, come to influence lower level factors, such as occupational employment opportunities, occupational performance requirements, and individual KSAO capabilities.

As we mentioned earlier, it is not that occupations are absent from current conversations about workforce readiness, but rather remain underutilized in our opinion. However, there are reasons to believe that this situation can be remedied especially when one considers the rich occupational data that are already being collected by government and private organizations. In the section that follows, we discuss one such source of occupational information: the Department of Labor's O*NET system. We briefly summarize the kinds of data that O*NET can bring to bear for addressing issues of workforce readiness. We also discuss several examples of how such data can be applied to efforts to study and foster workforce readiness for individuals, organizations, and the nation.

Addressing Workforce Readiness with O*NET

O*NET was originally designed as the replacement for the *Dictionary of Occupational Titles* (U.S. Department of Labor, 1991) to create a more flexible and updateable system for capturing and disseminating domestic occupational information. From the beginning, an essential purpose of O*NET was promoting national competitiveness and readiness by facilitating the development and maintenance of a skilled domestic workforce (Dye & Silver, 1999). The data collected and disseminated by O*NET are expansive and nationally representative, making them a highly relevant tool for studying and addressing issues of workforce readiness. O*NET currently covers 974 distinct occupations, which can be cross-referenced to other classification systems such as the *Standard Occupational Classification* system. The wide variety of occupational information covered by O*NET is conceptually structured into a hierarchal framework. This "Content Model" is organized into six domains that span work- and worker-oriented information that is both occupation-specific and cross-occupational in nature. Table 7.1 provides a summary of these descriptors.

Although occupational information can be obtained in a number of ways, O*NET provides a unique and efficient way to apply an occupational approach to workforce readiness. It is important to note that, by design, the majority of information in O*NET is descriptively broad because the system is intended to encompass the labor force as a whole. Thus, O*NET emphasizes data that generalize across organizations and occupations. One inherent trade-off with this wide scope is that the structure and content of O*NET may not provide direct or obvious applications (Converse, Oswald, Gillespie, Field, & Bizot, 2004).

TABLE 7.1 Summary of the O*NET Content Model

Domain	Descriptor Types	Descriptor Categories or Details	Select Examples
Occupation requirements	Generalized work activities	Information input, mental processes, work output, and interacting with others	Getting information; performing administrative activities; selling or influencing others
	Intermediate work activities	332 activities common across many occupations and industries	Administer basic health care or medical treatments; perform human resources activities; evaluate the quality or accuracy of data
	Detailed work activities	2,070 activities performed across a small to moderate number of occupations within a job family	Give medications or immunizations; Conduct eligibility or selection interviews; Verify accuracy of financial information
	Work context	Interpersonal relationships, physical work conditions, and structural job characteristics	Structured/unstructured work; Freedom to make decisions; Hazardous work conditions
Worker requirements	Basic skills	Content and process skills	Speaking; Science; Critical thinking; Active learning
	Cross-functional skills	Social skills, complex problem-solving skills, technical skills, systems skills, and resource management skills	Negotiation; Social perceptiveness; Judgment and decision-making; Time management
	Knowledge	Business and management; manufacturing and production; engineering and technology; mathematics and science; health services; arts and humanities; law and public safety; communications; and, transportation	Economics and Accounting; Building and construction; Biology; Medicine and dentistry; Telecommunications
	Education	Required level of education; job-related certification; and, instructional program required	Required level of education; Professional certification

Worker characteristics	Abilities	Cognitive abilities; psychomotor abilities; physical abilities; and, sensory abilities	Oral comprehension; Perceptual speed; Stamina; Finger dexterity; Peripheral vision
	Work styles	Achievement orientation; social influence; interpersonal orientation; adjustment; conscientiousness; independence; and, practical intelligence	Initiative; Attention to detail; Self-control; Innovation
	Occupational interests	Occupational interests compatible with Holland's model of personality type	Realistic; Investigative; Artistic; Social; Enterprising; Conventional
	Occupational values	Work-related needs based on Dawis & Lofquist's Theory of Work Adjustment	Achievement; Recognition; Independence; Relationships; Support; Independence
Occupation-specific information	Tasks	19,612 tasks; average of 20 tasks per occupation	Record patients' medical information and vital signs; Review blueprints to determine work details and procedures; Audition and select performers for musical presentations
	Tools and technology	26,900+ equipment, tools, machines, software, and other information technology	Theodolites; Project management software; Calipers; Power saws
Workforce characteristics	Labor market information	Occupational statistics	Wages; employment statistics (from Bureau of Labor Statistics)
	Occupational outlook	Occupational projections	Future economic conditions (from Bureau of Labor Statistics)
Experience requirements	Experience and training	Related work experience; On-the-job training; Apprenticeship	Months/years of related work experience required; Months/years of required on-the-job training

In this sense, scholars and practitioners may need to augment O★NET data with other more detailed occupational information to enhance specificity and impact. In our experience, however, the nationally representative information in O★NET provides data that are both rigorous and rare. This nearly always makes O★NET a high-utility departure point for workforce applications (Morgeson & Dierdorff, 2011).

As clearly illustrated in this book, the scope of workforce readiness necessarily encompasses individuals, organizations, and the nation. Workforce readiness thus reflects an important feature of a country's or an organization's current level of human capital. For individuals, readiness reflects their own personal capital or competencies, which is the *sine qua non* of labor market participation and employability. In this sense, it is valuable to consider the ways in which O★NET information can inform the kinds of applications that seek to promote human capital development for these different stakeholder groups.

Perhaps the most obvious implications for O★NET involve promoting workforce readiness among individuals. Here, workforce readiness applications include helping people identify educational or training needs, supporting their initial job entries or job transitions, and facilitating their career explorations. It is interesting to note that many of the individual applications aided by O★NET can be either self-directed or facilitated by professionals such as career counselors or employment specialists. This is a valuable characteristic, as many have noted the growing importance of lifelong learning and self-management of one's expertise in the modern world of work (Bhattacharya, Gibson, & Doty, 2005; Manyika et al., 2017). Academic research has supported the effectiveness of many individual-level applications where O★NET has been used to better understand when and how job transitions affect well-being and wage growth over time (Monfort et al., 2015), improving the selection of specialties within specific occupations (Woods, Patterson, Wille, & Koczwara, 2016), enhancing career preparedness among college undergraduate students (Koys, 2017), as well as diagnosing person-occupation fit in terms of individual abilities (Converse, Oswald, Gillespie, Field, & Bizot, 2004).

O★NET links to several government-maintained resources, which further enhances its utility for individual-level workforce readiness applications. For example, occupations are cross-referenced with the *Occupational Outlook Handbook* (Bureau of Labor Statistics, 2018) that provides information relevant to education, credentialing, certifications, wages, and employment outlook. The taxonomic structure of O★NET allows users to locate "related occupations" that are aligned in terms of the types of work performed and KSAOs required. This feature is especially relevant for addressing issues of unemployment, underemployment, and job transitions, all of which necessitate a deeper understanding of the similarity and differences in the demands of particular occupations. With regard to career exploration, the O★NET database allows users to search a specific occupation, group of occupations by certain descriptors (e.g., key skills, technology used), and identify occupations with particular characteristics (e.g., industry type, high-growth employment). Such features provide essential information to individuals as they explore and learn about potential career choices. To further aid explorations, O*NET also provides an online assessment (mynextmove.org) that measures vocational fit based on profiles of individuals' interests and occupational environments, based on the work of Holland (1987, 1997).

Organizations must address the challenges associated with workforce readiness in areas such as talent identification and acquisition, talent management, and compensation. O*NET information can be applied to these issues in several ways. For example, large-scale research has shown that firms engaging more frequently in human resource planning outperform firms that do not, across a host of performance indicators (Combs, Liu, Hall, & Ketchen, 2006). Essential to human resource planning efforts is forecasting labor supply and demand relative to organizational strategy and the broader labor market. This entails not only forecasting "head counts" but also the types of expertise or skills that will be needed and where such competencies may be found externally. Here, O*NET information can be used to identify key worker requirements (KSAOs and education) for jobs that will be new to an organization. When seeking to fill openings in existing jobs, O*NET can facilitate the identification of related occupations with similar work and worker demands, which can indicate additional talent pools from which to recruit. Moreover, the employment growth rates and wage data that are cross-referenced in O*NET can further inform cost–benefit analyses for recruitment budgets in "tight" versus "loose" labor markets, as well as firms' compensation strategies that set wages above, below, or equal to market value.

When talent must be developed internally (see Guzzo chapter in this volume), O*NET can be used to facilitate talent management practices that rely on training needs assessments and developmental interventions. For example, academic research has supported the utility of O*NET where it has been used to build organization-specific tools for assessing training needs (Reiter-Palmon, Brown, Sandall, Buboltz, & Nimps, 2006), to identify the relevance of educational curricula to workforce needs (Thompson & Koys, 2010), as well as to facilitate internal placement and outplacement transitions (Reiter-Palmon, Brown, et al., 2006; Reiter-Palmon, Young, Strange, Manning, & James, 2006). Research by Taylor and colleagues (2008) has also demonstrated the transportability of several O*NET descriptors (activities, skills, and work styles) across four different national contexts: New Zealand, China, Hong Kong, and the United States. This research suggests the value of using O*NET in multinational firms as well as for managing workforce readiness of human capital inflows to the United States.

As a nationally representative database, O*NET holds several implications for examining and promoting the overall preparedness of the U.S. workforce.

Here, workforce readiness applications include strategic workforce management, economic development and policy, as well as financial, technological, and human capital investments. As we discussed earlier, one advantage of an occupational approach is that occupations can serve as an important link connecting different levels of workforce data that are pertinent to promoting readiness. For national-level applications, this linkage allows researchers and policymakers to better integrate the variety of macro-level data that are frequently used to gain insights into issues of workforce readiness, such as industry size and rates of change, concentrations of specialized businesses or infrastructures, as well as regional employment and labor market trends or characteristics. In fact, economists have long noted the need to better describe local or regional economies by distinguishing between what is made and what is performed, with occupations put forth as an important mechanism to connect broader industries with narrower regional capabilities for creating more effective and focused economic development strategies (Barbour & Markusen, 2007; Feser, 2003; Koo, 2005; Thompson & Thompson, 1987). On this point, Wolman and Hincapie (2015) recently noted, "economies are much better viewed as linked clusters of activity across various industrial sectors rather than as isolated sectors defined by the [industry] code at whatever level of specificity" (p. 147).

Researchers have also provided specific examples of how O*NET information can be used to identify clusters of occupations that then can be linked to industry-related data with implications for workforce readiness. For example, Nolan and colleagues (2011) used O*NET to derive 15 occupational clusters based on 33 knowledge requirements and linked these to both industry and geographic information to illuminate regional employment growth, industry concentrations, and investment and outputs related to innovation activities (see www.statsamerica.org/innovation). Such work has clear relevance for proactively managing job and career transitions by allowing people to not only assess a displaced worker's current competencies relative to employer needs but also identify and create the necessary pathways to reengage the worker in new opportunities within the regional economy. Thus, interventions can be focused on individuals and regions, which stands to benefit employers as well because they can focus on their regions of operation.

Other national-level applications of O*NET data to workforce readiness focus on shifts in the nature of work and the ensuing demands placed on workers. For example, the expansive research efforts by the McKinsey Global Institute (Manyika et al., 2017) integrated O*NET information to ascertain the types of occupations that would be most impacted by increasing automation of various work activities in order to then depict the various educational, wage, hours worked, and employment demand implications of these changes due to automation. This integration allowed further insight into where transitions out of existing occupations would be most likely to occur at the national level, which can be used to inform workforce strategy and policies. Another example of using O★NET information to identify changes in occupational employment and demands was conducted by Dierdorff and colleagues (2009, 2011). These authors investigated the effects of "green economy" activities and technologies (e.g., renewable energy technologies, construction) on occupational requirements with regard to whether such changes might lead to new or emerging occupational roles. Here, occupational information was used to derive three different effects due to the "greening" of occupations: (1) increases in employment demand for existing occupations; (2) changes in work and worker requirements needed for occupational performance; and (3) generating unique work and worker requirements leading to new occupational roles. These levels of greening were then used to identify emerging occupations, shifting occupational demands, increases in employment, as well as new occupational tasks associated with such changes.

It is clear that an occupational approach can provide substantial value for workforce readiness issues at multiple levels of research and practice. Further, there is a wealth of existing data that can be brought to bear to better study and facilitate workforce readiness. We describe O★NET as one such source, with several examples of how O★NET data inform questions concerning workforce readiness. We next provide a more in-depth example to illustrate how O★NET information can be used to gain further insights into workforce readiness.

Workforce Readiness, Rare Skills, and Occupations

Much has been written over the past 15 years about the kinds of skills that will be required by "21st-century work" and how such capabilities are substantially lacking among individuals set to enter the workforce as well as the failure of educational institutions in inculcating these capabilities (Casner-Lotto & Barrington, 2006; Chen, Donahue, & Klimoski, 2004; Oliveri, Lawless, & Molloy, 2017). Multiple large-scale surveys of employers, educators, and researchers point to a common set of these in-demand, but rare skills, which have been often described as "collaborative problem-solving" (Oliveri et al., 2017). More specifically, these in-demand attributes entail more discrete skills such as critical thinking, communication, coordination, cooperation, leadership, creativity, problem-solving, and adaptability (Hesse, Care, Buder, Sassenberg, & Griffin, 2015). The overarching conclusion of this scholarship is that developing these skills must be a priority for both individuals and organizations in order to ensure the nation's workforce readiness. This imperative is exemplified in a McKinsey Global Institute (Manyika et al., 2017) report:

> Moreover, we find that workers of the future will spend more time on activities that machines are less capable of, such as managing people, applying expertise, and communicating with others. They will spend less time on predictable physical activities, and on collecting and processing

data, where machines already exceed human performance. The skills and capabilities required will also shift, requiring more social and emotional skills, and more advanced cognitive capabilities, such as logical reasoning and creativity.

(p. 14)

With this literature in mind, we examined O⋆NET data to gain insight into the kinds of occupations that could be impacted by these workplace shifts. If the assumptions are correct that demand for such skills will increase, then one might expect occupations that currently have high requirements for these skills to likewise be those that are projected to have strong future growth in employment. From an occupational perspective, it may be than occupations will meaningfully cluster along these in-demand skills. Moreover, these occupational clusters could span multiple industries, entail different educational demands, or be associated with distinct wage brackets.

In order to identify occupational clusters, we applied latent profile analysis (LPA), a type of latent variable mixture modeling that is useful for identifying subpopulations based on selected indicator variables (McLachlan & Peel, 2000). More specifically, O⋆NET data on 20 specific skills and five work styles were used to create six composite scores representing the skill sets which have been identified as in-demand for workforce readiness (Hesse, Care, Buder, Sassenberg, & Griffin, 2015). The skill composites were as follows: critical thinking and problem-solving, communication, teamwork and collaboration, leadership, flexibility and adaptability, and creativity. We then used a three-step process to identify an interpretable occupational cluster solution, similar to the approach used by Pastor, Barron, Miller, and Davis (2007). In the first step, several LPAs were performed on the skill composite scores, estimating cluster solutions ranging from 3 to 10 latent profiles, and utilizing two different model parameterizations. The first parameterization included freely estimated means for indicators both within and between clusters and allowed variances to differ across indicators within clusters, but included fixed variances across clusters. The second parameterization included freely estimated means and variances both within and between clusters. In the second step, all of the cluster solutions were examined and compared with regard to model fit statistics (i.e., information criteria and likelihood ratio tests comparing k versus $k-1$ profile solutions), classification accuracy (i.e., entropy), and interpretability. Lastly, after a final cluster solution was chosen, we examined the relationships between cluster membership and several variables commonly examined in the economics literature: education/experience requirements, median wages, and projected occupation growth.

After examining the various occupational cluster profiles, the model with freely estimated means and variances, and eight clusters was chosen as the final cluster solution. This choice was based several factors. The information criteria were relatively lower than the models with fewer clusters, two of the likelihood ratio tests suggested that eight profiles provided a better fit than seven profiles, the accuracy of the classification of occupations into clusters was relatively high, and most importantly we believe that the eight-cluster model provided the most interpretable profiles with sufficient differentiation in terms of occupational groups. Table 7.2 provides a summary of each of the eight clusters, with regard to the dominant occupational group(s) within each profile, as well as sample occupations.

In examining the eight occupational profiles (see Figure 7.1), the primary distinction between the clusters was in the level of importance across the six in-demand skill composites (i.e., peaks and valleys tended to be parallel, with few crossovers). For example, cluster 8 (7% of occupations; primarily healthcare practitioners and technical occupations, and management occupations) included occupations that tended to be higher in importance on four of the six critical skills, and cluster 1 (9%; primarily production occupations) represented occupations that were lower across all of the skill composites. Approximately 45%

TABLE 7.2 Occupational Clusters from Latent Profile Analysis

Cluster	Prevalent Major Groups (Percent of Cluster)	Sample Occupations
1	Production occupations (28%)	Food servers, landscaping and grounds-keeping workers, agricultural equipment operators, farmworkers and laborers
2	Architecture and engineering occupations (15%)	Software developers, electrical engineering technologists, robotics technicians, web administrators
3	Education, training, and library occupations (74%)	Architecture teachers, biological science teachers, history teachers, library science teachers
4	Management occupations; Life, physical, and social science occupations (31%)	Biomass power plant managers, solar energy installation managers, food service managers, foresters
5	Installation, maintenance, and repair occupations (29%)	Industrial machinery mechanics, automotive master mechanics, plumbers, power plant operators
6	Production occupations; Construction and extraction occupations (70%)	Motorboat mechanics and service technicians, crane and tower operators, brickmasons and blockmasons, cabinetmakers and bench carpenters
7	Office and administrative support occupations (32%)	Counter and rental clerks, tellers, court clerks, insurance claims clerks
8	Healthcare practitioners and technical occupations; Management occupations (56%)	Chief executives, emergency management directors, preventive medicine physicians, clinical psychologists

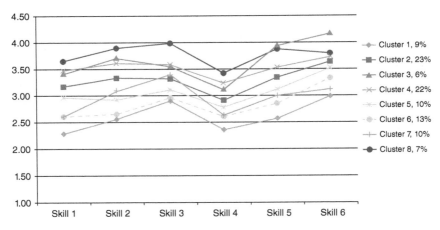

FIGURE 7.1 Skill 1 = critical thinking and problem-solving; Skill 2 = communication; Skill 3 = teamwork and collaboration; Skill 4 = leadership; Skill 5 = flexibility and adaptability; Skill 6 = creativity.

of the occupations analyzed were categorized into clusters 2 (23%; primarily architecture and engineering occupations) and 4 (22%; primarily management occupations and life, physical, and social science occupations), which both had above-average skill profiles (i.e., higher mean importance scores). There were some cases of greater variability across the skill indicators relative to other profiles (i.e., crossing over in importance on some skills). In particular, cluster 3 (6%; primarily education, training, and library occupations) was not the highest profile for several of the skills, but it had the highest importance for two particular skill composites related to learning/adaptability and innovation. And, cluster 7 (10%; primarily office and administrative support occupations) showed more variability in skill importance relative to the majority of the other occupational profiles.

In further interpreting and examining the eight occupational clusters, we also examined differences across the clusters with regard to other variables. Figure 7.2 depicts the variability in educational/experience requirements across the eight clusters, with clusters 3 and 8 requiring the highest levels of education/experience, and clusters 1, 6, and 7 requiring relatively lower levels of education/experience. Furthermore, an analysis of variance indicated significant differences in education/experience requirements across the clusters, $F(7,944) = 224.10$, $p = 0.000$, with post hoc analyses (Tukey's HSD and Bonferroni) indicating multiple significant comparisons across clusters. Figure 7.3 shows the variability in 2016 median wages by occupational cluster, with clusters 4 and 8 having the highest median wage (on average), and clusters 1 and 7 having the lowest median wage. Additional analysis indicated significant differences in

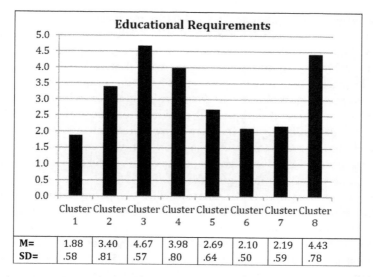

FIGURE 7.2   Requirements are job zones; Zone 1 = little or no preparation needed
(some may require high school diploma or GED); Zone 2 = some
preparation needed (usually require high school diploma); Zone 3 =
medium preparation needed (most require vocational training or associate's degree); Zone 4 = considerable preparation needed (most
require four-year bachelor's degree); Zone 5 = extensive preparation
needed (most require graduate-level degree).

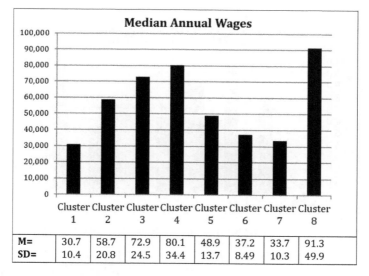

FIGURE 7.3   Means (M) and standard deviations (SD) in 1000s.

median wages across clusters, $F(7,944) = 84.75$, $p = 0.000$, with post hoc comparisons indicating multiple clusters differed significantly from one another. Finally, Figure 7.4 indicates the variability in projected occupation growth from 2016 to 2026 across occupational clusters, with clusters 3 and 8 projected to show the greatest percentage of positive growth, and clusters 1 and 6 projected to show negative growth. Again, an analysis of variance indicated significant differences in projected occupational growth across the clusters, $F(7,944) = 19.16$, $p < 0.001$. Though there were fewer significant differences between paired clusters as compared to the education and wage analyses, the post hoc comparisons revealed several significant disparities among the eight clusters on overall projected occupational growth.

Several consistent trends also emerged when comparing the results for the occupational cluster profiles we examined here to findings from the 2017 McKinsey Global Institute report that investigated the impact of automation on occupations. For example, several occupational groups that were projected to exhibit positive net growth due to automation (5%–49%) were also those found in clusters 4 and 8, which similarly showed higher project growth (e.g., nurses, pharmacists, executives, managers, medical doctors). Several occupational groups that were projected to exhibit negative net growth due to automation were also members of low-growth clusters 1 and 6 (e.g., production workers, food preparation workers, agricultural equipment operators, equipment cleaners). Interestingly, the McKinsey report noted that two occupational groups—construction workers and building or maintenance

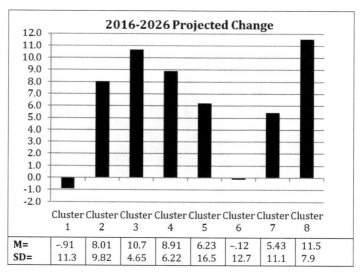

FIGURE 7.4 Rates of projected change in number of jobs.

engineers—would have strong growth (5%–24%). These occupations fell into cluster 6 in our analysis, which showed low requirements for the six skill composites. This result suggests that not all projected growth due to automation is necessarily aligned with in-demand "21st-century" skills. Along these lines, several high-growth occupational groups in the McKinsey report were members of cluster 2, which was a profile that was roughly in the middle with regard to demand for the six skills (e.g., childcare, engineers, health support, computer engineers). Cluster 2 also had encompassed several occupations that the McKinsey report indicated negative growth projections (e.g., information and record clerks, office support workers, machinery installation, and repair workers). This suggests some obvious variability in this cluster, demonstrating again that not all occupations with skills thought to be in-demand are poised for growth due to automation.

Challenges Ahead for an Occupational Approach to Workforce Readiness

In this chapter, we tried to articulate the value of an occupational approach to workforce readiness as well as provide an example of how O*NET information can be applied to research and practice for a variety of stakeholders. Yet, infusing an increased attention to occupations in future workforce readiness scholarship will likely entail several challenges. We discuss three of these concerns below.

We argued that occupations allow a flexible common language to use for capturing the changing nature of work and to link such changes across multiple levels of analysis and practical applications. The future utility of an occupational approach is contingent upon the extent to which "occupation" maintains an empirical distinctiveness; that is, the degree that occupations continue to create meaningful descriptive boundaries to delineate the world of work as we know it. Much scholarship has been dedicated to discussing the rapidity of technological change and increased fluidity with which human and intellectual capital passes across industries, economic sectors, and organizations (Cappelli, 1999; Hollister, 2011). It has even been suggested that nearly 18% of the current workforce is employed in jobs that did not exist in 1980 (Lin, 2011; Manyika et al., 2017). Further still, estimates indicate that approximately 20% of U.S. workers earn income through independent, nonstandard work arrangements (Cappelli & Keller, 2013). The rise of the "gig" economy adds to this dynamic, with some research suggesting that nearly 70% of individuals say they choose such work out of preference, not because they cannot find a traditional job (Manyika et al., 2016). It should also be pointed out that it would seem safe to assume that many of these individuals are simultaneously employed in traditional work arrangements (e.g., the Uber driver who also holds a traditional job). If these kinds of workforce changes render occupations as more longitudinally unstable or porous, an occupational approach becomes less valuable. We believe this is somewhat unlikely because, by definition, occupations reside at a level above individual jobs, which appear to be the location for much of the fluctuations often linked to these workplace changes. Nonetheless, a key challenge for workforce readiness is to focus on new and emerging occupations as well as addressing how to best prepare individuals for occupational roles that reflect rather evolving and nonstandard employment structures at the organizational and job levels.

A second challenge to workforce readiness in general, and to taking an occupational approach, in particular, pertains to the difficulties of effectively transitioning individuals into new occupations. This entails not only the identification of occupations and occupational incumbents most likely to be in need but also issues of reskilling for new occupational roles. Evidence for the efficacy of federal job retraining efforts has been mixed (Bloom et al., 1993; McConnell et al., 2016), and often individuals forego transitions even when their employment and focal occupation are clearly in decline. Indeed, there are several industries that continue to have labor supply issues for associated occupations despite high demand. For example, transportation industry occupations have long showed unmet labor demands despite significant investments in recruitment and training (Costello & Suarez, 2015; U.S. Department of Labor ETA, 2007).

Third, although we noted that an important benefit of an occupational approach coincides with its meso-level unit of analysis, there are times when the occupational level is still too broad to inform specific interventions for workforce readiness (Converse et al., 2004). This may be the case when considering individual-level applications, especially those that are derived from the results of occupational clustering. For example, our illustrative analyses showed that while occupations can be meaningfully grouped along profiles of six in-demand skills, within each occupational cluster there were a variety of occupational roles. Such variety could imply rather different occupational demands on other factors important to workforce readiness, such as educational requirements (Levine, 2013). Thus, it is likely that practitioners and policymakers will need to increase the specificity of evidence-based interpretations, examine multiple occupational clusters, or further link occupational clusters to other regional economic factors prior to taking action.

Finally, we described how taking an occupational approach holds the promise of integrating the various disciplines as well as varied data that contribute to workforce readiness scholarship and practice. We now live in a world where access to large-scale and expansive sources of information is available. The lure of "big data" is enticing and has been often lauded as a panacea for addressing a host of economic, business, and educational problems. Data-driven insight and decision-making is indeed a promising path forward for addressing concerns of workforce readiness. Yet, it is crucial to recognize the perils as well. Merely having access to expansive data does not guarantee valid insights, nor can quantitatively sophisticated data-mining techniques be expected to clearly illuminate *why* the observed relationships actually exist. So much of the debate around skill shortages, for example, comes from employer-associated sources and consulting groups rather than academic stakeholders and workers themselves. These circumstances constrain our ability to address workforce readiness in a robust and systematic manner, both empirically and for policy-making. Cappelli (2015) echoed this constraint by noting,

> It is difficult to think of another labor market issue for which academic research or even research using standard academic techniques has played such a small role, where parties with a material interest in the outcomes have so dominated the discussion, where the quality of evidence and discussion has been so poor, and where the stakes are potentially so large.
>
> *(p. 283)*

As we have discussed throughout this chapter, an increased emphasis and integration of occupations holds substantial value in helping to overcome the challenges associated with workforce readiness. Occupations provide an essential common language for promoting more effective communication between the many stakeholders involved in understanding and affecting workforce readiness. The flexibility of an occupational approach offers considerable utility for examining issues of workforce readiness, both within and across levels (individuals, jobs, organizations, regions, industries, etc.). Toward this end, we sought to articulate and illustrate the multiple ways that occupations can be brought to bear to inform research and practice. The fact that previous workforce readiness scholars and practitioners seem to recognize occupations as important elements is indeed promising. However, we believe that fulfilling this promise requires an increased infusion of an occupational approach in our empirical and practical efforts. Doing so will improve the formal processes and interventions that we create and, more importantly, will develop the essential human capital required for the betterment of individuals, organizations, and society.

References

Barbour, E., & Markusen, A. (2007). Regional occupational and industrial structure: Does one imply the other? *International Regional Science Review, 30*, 72–90.

Bhattacharya, M., Gibson, D. E., & Doty, D. H. (2005). The effects of flexibility in employee skills, employee behaviors, and human resource practices on firm performance. *Journal of Management, 31*, 622–640.

Bloom, H. S., Orr, L. L., Cave, G., Bell, S. H., & Doolittle, F. (1993). *The national JTPA study: Title IIA impacts on earnings and employment at 18 months.* Bethesda, MD: Project Report of Abt Associates Inc.

Bureau of Labor Statistics, U.S. Department of Labor. (2018). *Occupational outlook handbook.* Retrieved from https://www.bls.gov/ooh/home.htm

Cappelli, P. H. (1999). *The new deal at work: Managing the market-driven workplace.* Boston, MA: Harvard Business School Press.

Cappelli, P. H. (2015). Skill gaps, skill shortages, and skill mismatches: Evidence and arguments for the United States. *ILR Review, 68,* 251–290.

Cappelli, P., & Keller, J. R. (2013). Classifying work in the new economy. *Academy of Management Review, 38,* 575–596.

Casner-Lotto, J., & Barrington, L. (2006). *Are they really ready to work? Employers' perspectives on the basic knowledge and applied skills of new entrants to the 21st Century U.S. workforce.* Washington, DC: Partnership for 21st Century Skills.

Chen, G., Donahue, L. M., & Klimoski, R. J. (2004). Training undergraduates to work in organizational teams. *Academy of Management Learning and Education, 3,* 27–40.

Combs, J., Liu, Y., Hall, A., & Ketchen, D. (2006). How much do high-performance work practices matter? A meta-analysis of their effects on organizational performance. *Personnel Psychology, 59,* 501–528.

Converse, P. D., Oswald, F. L., Gillespie, M. A., Field, K. A., & Bizot, E. B. (2004). Matching individuals to occupations using abilities and the O⋆ NET: Issues and an application in career guidance. *Personnel Psychology, 57,* 451–487.

Costello, B., & Suarez, R. (2015). *Truck driver shortage analysis 2015.* Arlington, VA: The American Trucking Associations.

Dawis, R. V., & Lofquist, L. H. (1984). *A psychological theory of work adjustment: An individual-differences model and its applications.* Minneapolis: University of Minnesota Press.

Dierdorff, E. C., & Morgeson, F. P. (2007). Consensus in work role requirements: The influence of discrete occupational context on role expectations. *Journal of Applied Psychology, 92,* 1228–1241.

Dierdorff, E. C., & Morgeson, F. P. (2009). Effects of descriptor specificity and observability on incumbent work analysis ratings. *Personnel Psychology, 62,* 601–628.

Dierdorff, E. C., Norton, J. J., Drewes, D. W., Kroustalis, C. M., Rivkin, D., & Lewis, P. (2009). *Greening of the world of work: Implications for O⋆ NET-SOC and new and emerging occupations.* Raleigh, NC: National Center for O⋆NET Development.

Dierdorff, E. C., Norton, J. J., Gregory, C. M., Rivkin, D., & Lewis, P. (2011). *Greening of the world of work: Revisiting occupational consequences.* Raleigh, NC: National Center for O⋆NET Development.

Dierdorff, E. C., Rubin, R. S., & Morgeson, F. P. (2009). The milieu of managerial work: An integrative framework linking work context to role requirements. *Journal of Applied Psychology, 94,* 972–988.

Dye, D., & Silver, M. (1999). The origins of O⋆ NET. In N. Peterson, M., Mumford, W. Borman, P. Jeanneret, & E. Fleishman (Eds.), *An occupational information system for the 21st century: The development of O⋆ NET* (pp. 9–20). Washington, DC: American Psychological Association.

Feldman, D. C. (2002). When you come to a fork in the road, take it: Career indecision and vocational choices of teenagers and young adults. In D. C. Feldman (Ed.), *Work careers: A developmental perspective* (pp. 93–125). San Francisco, CA: Jossey-Bass.

Feser, E. (2003). What regions do rather than make: A proposed set of knowledge-based occupation clusters. *Urban Studies, 40,* 1937–1958.

Hesse, F., Care, E., Buder, J., Sassenberg, K., & Griffin, P. (2015). A framework for teachable collaborative problem solving skills. In P. Griffin & E. Care (Eds.), *Assessment and teaching of 21st century skills: Methods and approach.* Dordrecht, The Netherlands: Springer.

Holland, J. L. (1985). *Making vocational choices: A theory of vocational personalities and work environments.* Englewood Cliffs, NJ: Prentice-Hall.

Holland, J. L. (1987). Current status of Holland's theory of careers: Another perspective. *The Career Development Quarterly, 36,* 24–30.

Holland, J. L. (1997). *Making vocational choices: A theory of vocational personalities and work environments.* Odessa, FL: Psychological Assessment Resources.

Hollister, M. (2011). Employment stability in the U.S. labor market: Rhetoric versus reality. *Annual Review of Sociology, 37,* 305–324.

Koo, J. (2005). How to analyze the regional economy with occupation data. *Economic Development Quarterly, 19,* 356–372.

Koys, D. J. (2017). Using the department of labor's "My Next Move" to improve career preparedness. *Journal of Management Education, 41,* 94–117.

Kristof, A. L. (1996). Person-organization fit: An integrative review of its conceptualizations, measurement, and implications. *Personnel Psychology, 49,* 1–49.

Levine, M. V. (2013). *The skills gap and unemployment in Wisconsin: Separating fact from fiction.* University of Wisconsin at Milwaukee, Center for Economic Development.

Lin, J. (2011). Technological adaptation, cities, and new work. *Review of Economics and Statistics, 93,* 554–574.

Manyika, J., Lund, S., Bughin, J., Robinson, K., Mischke, J., & Mahajan, D. (2016, October). *Independent work: Choice, necessity, and the gig economy.* San Francisco, CA: McKinsey Global Institute.

Manyika, J., Lund, S., Chui, M., Bughin, J., Woetzel, J., Batra, P., …, & Sanghvi, S. (2017, December). *Jobs lost, jobs gained: Workforce transitions in a time of automation.* San Francisco, CA: McKinsey Global Institute.

McConnell, S., Fortson, K., Rotz, D., Schochet, P., Burkander, P., Rosenberg, L., …, & D'Amico, R. (2016). *Providing public workforce services to job seekers: 15-Month impact findings on the WIA adult and dislocated worker programs.* Washington, DC: Mathematica Policy Research.

McLachlan, G. J., & Peel, D. (2000). *Finite mixture models.* New York, NY: John Wiley & Sons.

Monfort, S. S., Howe, G. W., Nettles, C. D., & Weihs, K. L. (2015). A longitudinal examination of re-employment quality on internalizing symptoms and job-search intentions. *Journal of Occupational Health Psychology, 20,* 50–61.

Morgeson, F. P., & Dierdorff, E. C. (2011). Job and work analysis: From technique to theory. In S. Zedeck (Ed.), *APA handbook of industrial and organizational psychology* (pp. 3–41). Washington, DC: American Psychological Association.

Mumford, M. D., & Peterson, N. G. (1999). The O*NET content model: Structural considerations in describing jobs. In N. G. Peterson & M. D. Mumford (Eds.), *An occupational information system for the 21st century: The development of O*NET* (pp. 21–30). Washington, DC: American Psychological Association.

Nolan, C., Morrison, E., Kumar, I., Galloway, H., & Cordes, S. (2011). Linking industry and occupation clusters in regional economic development. *Economic Development Quarterly, 25,* 26–35.

Okhuysen, G. A., Lepak, D., Ashcraft, K. L., Labianca, G. J., Smith, V., & Steensma, H. K. (2013). Theories of work and working today. *Academy of Management Review, 38,* 491–502.

Oliveri, M. E., Lawless, R., & Molloy, H. (2017). A literature review on collaborative problem solving for college and workforce readiness. *ETS Research Report Series, 2017,* 1–27.

Pastor, D. A., Barron, K. E., Miller, B. J., & Davis, S. L. (2007). A latent profile analysis of college students' achievement goal orientation. *Contemporary Educational Psychology, 32*, 8–47.

Peterson, N. G., Mumford, M. D., Borman, W. C., Jeanneret, P. R., Fleishman, E. A., Levin, K. Y., ... Gowing, M. K. (2001). Understanding work using the Occupational Information Network (O* NET): Implications for practice and research. *Personnel Psychology, 54*, 451–492.

Reiter-Palmon, R., Brown, M., Sandall, D. L., Buboltz, C., & Nimps, T. (2006). Development of an O*NET web-based job analysis and its implementation in the U.S. Navy: Lessons learned. *Human Resource Management Review, 16*, 294–309.

Reiter-Palmon, R., Young, M., Strange, J., Manning, R., & James, J. (2006). Occupationally-specific skills: Using skills to define and understand jobs and their requirements. *Human Resource Management Review, 16*, 356–375.

Spokane, A. R. (1985). A review of research on person–environment congruence in Holland's theory of careers. *Journal of Vocational Behavior, 26*, 306–343.

Taylor, P. J., Li, W. D., Shi, K., & Borman, W. C. (2008). The transportability of job information across countries. *Personnel Psychology, 61*, 69–111.

Thompson, K. R., & Koys, D. J. (2010). The management curriculum and assessment journey: Use of Baldrige criteria and the occupational network database. *Journal of Leadership & Organizational Studies, 17*, 156–166.

Thompson, W. R., & Thompson, P. R. (1987). National industries and local occupational strengths: The cross-hairs of targeting. *Urban Studies, 24*, 547–560.

Tranberg, M., Slane, S., & Ekeberg, S. E. (1993). The relation between interest congruence and satisfaction: A meta-analysis. *Journal of Vocational Behavior, 42*, 253–264.

Trice, H. M. (1993). *Occupational subcultures in the workplace*. Ithaca, NY: Cornell University Press.

U.S. Department of Labor. (1991). *Dictionary of occupational titles* (4th ed.). Washington, DC: U.S. Government Printing Office.

U.S. Department of Labor Employment and Training Administration. (2007). *Identifying and addressing workforce challenges in America's transportation industry*. Retrieved from http://www.doleta.gov/BRG/pdf/Transportation Report_final.pdf

Vogel, R. M., & Feldman, D. C. (2009). Integrating the levels of person-environment fit: The roles of vocational fit and group fit. *Journal of Vocational Behavior, 75*, 68–81.

Wolman, H., & Hincapie, D. (2015). Clusters and cluster-based development policy. *Economic Development Quarterly, 29*, 135–149.

Woods, S. A., Patterson, F. C., Wille, B., & Koczwara, A. (2016). Personality and occupational specialty: An examination of medical specialties using Holland's RIASEC model. *Career Development International, 21*, 262–278.

PART III

Technology

8

TECHNOLOGY AND WORKFORCE READINESS

Implications for Skills Training and the Economy

Harry J. Holzer

Introduction

How will the growing use of robotics, and especially artificial intelligence (AI), affect the U.S. workforce in the next few decades? Will there be large-scale worker displacements from their jobs, as machines increasingly perform the tasks formerly done by workers? If so, how can we prepare for such a future? What can we learn from the analysis of technical change in the labor market to date? And how can we make our existing system of education and training for the labor market more effective at increasing worker readiness to join the labor market?

Worker fear of automation, and its potential for displacing workers, is not new. The Luddites in 19th-century Britain during the Industrial Revolution are the best known, but not the only, historical example of workers expressing such fears about machines taking all of their jobs. Much more recently, an "automation scare" occurred in the United States during the late 1950s and early 1960s, as awareness of the existence of computers spread through all strata of society. And fears that digital technology would allow enormous numbers of jobs to be offshored to China and India were very widespread about a decade ago (e.g., Blinder, 2006), though the panic surrounding offshoring seems to have diminished since then.

Yet massive displacement and unemployment in the aftermath of major technological breakthroughs have *never* occurred. Indeed, unemployment shows no long-term trend, and average worker earnings have continued to rise over time through all past episodes of growing industrialization and mechanization of the workplace. Even though millions of workers might be personally displaced by technologies over time, many of them and most other workers adapt to these new circumstances and are able to find new employment.

Why is this so? According to economists, the spread of new workplace technologies tends to reduce the costs of production and therefore the prices of goods and services produced; these falling prices tend to raise the real incomes of consumers, who in turn buy more of the cheaper products over time and more of other goods and services as well, creating new jobs in these and other sectors (Levy & Murnane, 2013). Workers might need to obtain new skills, to obtain these newly available jobs, but they have strong incentives to make these adjustments, and generally do so over time.

At the same time, it would be foolish to be completely sanguine about future worker prospects in the United States as automation spreads. For one thing, some workers are permanently displaced by new technologies, and their future employment prospects tend to be dim. Furthermore, many workers do not adapt to new labor market realities by obtaining the requisite education and training for new jobs, or at least well-paying ones. Indeed, since the spread of new digital technologies throughout the economy that began in the 1980s, less-educated workers and especially less-educated men overall have suffered from stagnant or declining wages as well as declining employment (Autor & Wasserman, 2013). Our ability to help workers gain the skills they need to succeed in a "knowledge-based" economy clearly leaves much to be desired.

Finally, there remains an open question regarding robotics and AI going forward: *Is this time different?* In other words, will the economic adjustment processes that have enabled workers of the past to adjust to automation be sufficiently strong to handle what is potentially a much greater wave of workplace innovation—and one that might lead to wholesale displacements of professionals in health care, education, finance, the law, and many other industries as well as those in manufacturing and some services? Might the greater "humanness" of machines with AI—including its ability to learn over time—threaten many more workers, and overwhelm the adjustment processes I've outlined above? How should education and training policy respond to these developments?

I try to answer some of these questions below. In the next section, I review the effects of technological change on the labor market, and how they have led to rising labor market inequality since about 1980. Specifically, I discuss how new technologies often change the *demand* for labor—in other words, the types of workers and their mixes of skills by employers, and what they are willing to pay to hire them. Workers on the *supply side* of the labor market then have new incentives to invest in obtaining the skills that the labor market now rewards. But this process can be slow and very incomplete, especially if public policies do not address the many hurdles students and workers face in higher education or the labor market.

In the following section, I specifically address the question of how future automation might change the mix of skills needed for success in the labor market, and the kinds of additional policies and practices that might be needed to help students and workers adapt to a labor market where machines with AI become increasingly common. I also argue that another type of policy that has been frequently advocated to deal with widespread displacement—the notion of a "universal basic income"—is ill-advised and should not be implemented.

Finally, I conclude with a summary of labor market issues and policy implications in the final section.

Skill-Biased Technical Change: Labor Demand Shifts and Supply Adjustments[1]

Skill-Biased Technical Change and the Demand for Labor

The introduction and diffusion of new technologies in workplaces often change the mix of skills that are needed in those workplaces, along with how different skill groups are rewarded in the labor market. This type of technological change is known to economists as "skill-biased" technical change (SBTC), as opposed to "skill-neutral" changes in which all groups of workers by skill category are equally affected by the changes.

The reason for the frequent "skill bias" of technical change is that new technologies *substitute* for some kinds of workers but *complement* other types. For instance, digital technologies introduced into the workplace since about 1980s have often substituted for workers performing quite routine tasks on the job, such as those on assembly lines in manufacturing or clerical workers in offices. At the same time, the need for engineers and technicians to develop, operate, and maintain the new machines has grown; and the need for workers who engage in tasks requiring social/communication skills (e.g., childcare and eldercare) as well as those requiring more complex and abstract analyses (e.g., many professions and managerial jobs) have also risen. Accordingly, the demand for college-educated workers—especially those with technical or analytical skills—has grown while demand for those with high school or less education has shrunken.

The effects of these forces can be illustrated in Figure 8.1. In part A, we see that SBTC shifts out the demand for college-educated labor, causing wages for such labor to rise. At the same time, the demand for high school–educated labor shifts inward, causing wages for these workers to decline. As a result, earnings inequality between more- and less-educated workers rises. In addition, employment rates among the high school–educated workers decline, as their market wages decline and make the labor market less attractive relative to alternative uses of their time.

Indeed, these outcomes are exactly what we've observed in labor markets over the past 35–40 years. Specifically, the gap in earnings between those with high school vs. college (four-year) education has roughly doubled since 1980s. Autor (2014) argues that SBTC, along with the rising penetration of imported

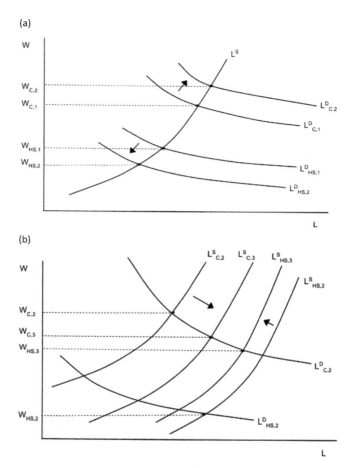

FIGURE 8.1 Labor demand shifts and supply responses for college and high school graduates. (a) Effects of labor demand shifts toward college graduates. (b) Labor supply responses.

Note: To simplify these diagrams, we assume a joint labor supply curve between high school and college graduates in part A, but separate ones in part B. W and L denote wages and employment respectively, while C and HS denote workers with college and high school education, respectively. 1, 2, and 3 refer to initial and subsequent time periods.

goods into the United States, accounts for much of the rising inequality in U.S. labor markets within the bottom 99% of workers.[2]

In other words, SBTC plus globalization have led to rising inequality in the U.S. labor market. These two forces have particularly reduced the demand for unskilled workers in manufacturing—an industry where less-educated people (typically men) have enjoyed strong earnings premia in earlier decades. More broadly, their wages and employment rates have fallen as well, while their dependence on disability policies and opioids has risen (Krueger, 2017).

But demand has not declined uniformly for all low-wage workers and jobs. Autor (2010) has argued that we have growing "polarization" in the U.S. labor market. Labor demand—measured both by employment rates and wages—has risen in both the top and bottom deciles of the U.S. wage distribution. In the top two or three deciles, earnings among professional and managerial employees who perform more complex analytical tasks which cannot be automated or offshored (at least not yet) have risen; while, in the bottom few deciles, both earnings and employment have also risen a bit as demand for workers performing social and communicative tasks in the low-wage service sectors has increased as well. In contrast, earnings and employment in the middle of the wage distribution have declined, as routine tasks previously performed by relatively less-educated workers in production and clerical jobs have increasingly been done by digital technologies or workers abroad.

Two important caveats must be mentioned at this point. First, not all middle-skill or middle-wage jobs have shrunken in number. Holzer (2015), in particular, has argued that a new set of middle-skill jobs in health care, advanced manufacturing, information technology (IT), transportation/logistics, and parts of the service sector have grown in recent years, especially where technical skills are necessary. Their growth has been more than offset by the decline we have observed in production and clerical jobs, though employers seem to have some difficulty finding and retaining workers with the needed skills to perform this work.[3]

Second, SBTC and globalization are not the only factors that account for rising labor market inequality. In addition to those factors, weakening labor market institutions like collective bargaining and minimum wage laws have reinforced the decline in wages among less-educated workers (Card & Dinardo, 2008). While economists continue to debate the exact magnitudes of the contributions to rising inequality accounted for by each of these forces, there can be no question that SBTC has contributed importantly to these developments, changing the numbers and quality of millions of jobs in the labor market, and the compensation earned by workers filling those different jobs.

Skill Acquisition and the Supply of Labor

The changes in labor demand and also wages by SBTC and other forces raise not only the earnings gaps between more- and less-educated workers but also the incentives of workers to acquire the skills that now draw higher earnings in the labor market.

The rising earnings premia associated with college degrees, caused by SBTC and other forces, will encourage more Americans to invest in higher education, thereby increasing the supply of college-educated labor, while the supply of high school graduates declines, as shown in Figure 8.1b. These forces, in turn, should reduce the gaps in wages between college and high school graduates, reducing at least some (if not all) of the inequality that arose as a result of SBTC and other forces discussed above.[4]

It is important to note that the high returns to college appear not only in the earnings of those with bachelor's or graduate degrees but also in many credentials earned in the "sub-BA" postsecondary market. These credentials include the associate degree in arts (AA), science (AS), and applied science (AAS) like health care. They also include a range of certificates offered at public two-year as well as for-profit colleges and universities—some of which are "for credit" and some which are not. The certificates are a mix of longer term (up to a year) or shorter term credentials. Individuals who gain multiple for-credit certificates can "stack" them in many states to generate associate degrees, as part of "career pathways" built in those states.

Not all credentials earned in the sub-BA market offer strong earnings (relative to those with high school only). For instance, earnings for those with terminal AA degrees, especially in the humanities, lag substantially behind those with AS and AAS degrees. And earnings rewards for the certificate programs vary as well, with longer term ones or those in more technical areas and in high-demand industries (like health care, advanced manufacturing, IT, etc.) generating the greatest rewards (e.g., Backes, Holzer, & Velez, 2015).

It is often on the not-for-credit and the shorter term certificates that state-level workforce development policies focus, though these efforts can include for-credit certificate and associate programs as well. Many adults returning to college for additional education or training enroll in these programs, though youth can do so too.[5]

Increasingly, "sector-based partnerships" between employer groups, training providers (usually community colleges), and intermediaries help train more workers for jobs and careers in the high-demand sectors where employers have difficulty hiring and training workers on their own. Rigorous research indicates that the best of these programs generates strong earnings improvements for disadvantaged workers. In addition, the earnings gains can last for many years, despite fears among some policy analysts that individuals who leave the sectors for which they have been trained will see the returns to their credentials fade over time.[6]

Sub-BA credentials like these are also being rewarded to individuals engaging in "work-based learning" programs, like apprenticeship. Interest in such programs has grown in the past decade as a vehicle for training workers for the jobs that many employers have the most trouble filling. For that reason, employers tend to value them, while workers are more highly motivated to learn when they are paid to do so. Apprenticeships generate strong earnings for workers in evaluation studies, which do not necessarily fade when employees leave the firm or even the sector in which they have been trained. Increasingly, apprentices earn sub-BA credentials like certificates or AS degrees while they train, which further improves the portability of their skills over time (Lerman, 2014).

Yet, for all of these potential credentials generating strong earnings for those with BAs and higher and even for those with sub-BA credentials, the outcomes observed for students in higher education have been quite mixed over the past few decades. As a result, earnings inequality has stayed very high. And many students and workers also fail to gain the sub-BA credentials in high-demand fields that could also improve their earnings quite substantially. Indeed, just under half of all Americans earn a postsecondary credential from a higher education institution—and earnings without one remain quite weak in most cases (Holzer, 2017).

In an era where the monetary rewards for postsecondary education remain so high, why do too few Americans attain them? For one thing, though college *enrollments* have risen dramatically in the past few decades—especially among minorities or disadvantaged students—*completion* rates have fallen, especially among the disadvantaged. Indeed, associate degree completion rates out of students who enroll in community colleges are about 20%. If one includes those who transfer to four-year institutions and obtain a bachelor's degree, as well as those who attain a certificate, completion rates are still only about 35%. They are also quite low in the for-profit institutions, though certificate completion rates there are higher (Holzer & Baum, 2017).

In addition, many students earn credentials with relatively little labor market reward. At public two-year colleges in at least some states, as many as 40% of students earn AA degrees in the humanities—including fields such as "general studies" or "liberal studies"—which earn virtually no return in the labor market. Those who fail to earn a credential often have accumulated too few credits (or the wrong ones) to gain much labor market reward, on top of their failure to earn what economists call the "sheepskin" effect—in other words, the income boost received purely from attaining the actual degree. These liberal arts concentrations and degrees would not be so bad if these students ultimately obtain BA or BS degrees; but only about 12%–14% of community college students do so. And, in the meantime, many students rack up significant debt while pursuing their degrees, although they fail to achieve a credential that raises their earnings. As a result, defaults on student loans have risen substantially as well among these students (Baum, 2016).

What accounts for these dismal outcomes? A number of factors can be cited—some of which reflect the characteristics and circumstances of *students*, while others are functions of the *institutions*—public community colleges, low-ranked four-year colleges, and the for-profit schools—where most disadvantaged or first-generation college students tend to concentrate (Holzer & Baum, 2017). *Employer* characteristics can also contribute to weak labor market outcomes, as we note below.[7]

On the student side, many attend open-access colleges where they are admitted despite very weak academic preparation in the K-12 years. At the community colleges, many are required to take "developmental education" classes until they can pass math (usually at the level of Algebra I) and English tests before they can enroll in classes for academic credit. But most remedial programs are not effective at improving college completion rates (Bettinger, Boatman, & Long, 2013), and some are even harmful (Clotfelter, Ladd, Muschkin, & Vigdor, 2013).

In addition, students from disadvantaged families often need financial aid that is too complex to fully understand or too limited in what it covers. For instance, Pell grants and other financial aid provided through Title IV of the federal Higher Education Act (HEA) can only be used to finance students in for-credit programs of at least 600 hours per year; shorter term or noncredit workforce development classes cannot be paid for this way. And many students attend for-profit institutions—which very successfully market to low-income individuals—where they pile up very large debts while pursuing programs that may or may not be of higher quality and labor market value and which they often do not complete.

Furthermore, first-generation college students often lack information or "social capital" about where to go and how to succeed once they get there. They often do not know what to study or where to obtain help—especially at the community colleges, where they get very little guidance from counselors. Finally, many youth and even more adults or parents who need to work part time or full time to support their families, making it difficult to attend college full time and complete their programs of study.

On the institutional side, too many disadvantaged students attend institutions—like public community colleges—where both resources and incentives to respond to the labor market are low. For one thing, community colleges receive well under half of the funds per full-time student that the average public four-year colleges obtain, with funding declining over time (in inflation-adjusted dollars) in both places. They receive relatively low funding even though their students often arrive with greater need for counseling and other supports, which the institutions cannot afford to provide.

But, in addition, incentives to respond to market forces are weak. The schools get the same tuition or dollars or state subsidies regardless of whether students finish or what they study; and the costs of instructors as well as equipment in technical, high-demand fields are usually very high. It is little wonder, then, that teaching capacity is often limited in these fields—especially health care—where students have difficulty gaining access to the courses they need to complete credentials in high-demand fields. Adjuncts are often hired to teach in these areas—even in certificate programs—which make them hard to scale up.

Of course, with so little counseling provided about the labor market as well as academics, many students do not know what labor markets reward and often choose to study in nontechnical areas (where many also prefer the material and are not affected by weak math or science training). The One-Stop offices funded by the Department of Labor to provide such information are usually not located at or near the colleges students attend to gain workforce preparation, generating a fragmentation between labor market information and training that exacerbates these problems.

Furthermore, Thomas Bailey of Columbia University and his colleagues have described many community colleges as "cafeterias" where students wander aimlessly and pick courses randomly, while also staying in fields where they have little chance of completion (Bailey, Jaggars, & Jenkins, 2015). Vastly higher numbers of students take liberal arts classes because they intend to transfer to four-year colleges and obtain BAs than those who successfully do so. Many of these students would be better served in strong associate or certificate programs. On the other hand, at the for-profit colleges, students obtain more guidance but are not protected from predatory practices that leave many without credentials and with much debt.

Finally, we note that employers might also contribute to insufficient skill formation by failing to provide their workers with opportunities for work-based learning and on-the-job training. These failures could be caused by a range of factors such as imperfect employer information about the benefits of training, liquidity constraints on these employers (especially in public companies that face short-term pressure to generate profits), or inability of employers to coordinate with one another and thereby address the fixed costs of setting up such programs (Holzer, 2016).

A wide range of policy efforts is needed to seriously deal with these problems, and we outline them in the concluding section below.

Future Automation: How Should It Change Workforce Preparation Efforts?

SBTC has been a form of technical change which has already created incentives for workers to invest in skills that complement the new technologies, rather than remaining substitutes for them. Yet, as the above discussion indicates, the ability of many workers to do so, and to attain postsecondary credentials that are in high demand in the labor market, remains limited.

What does all of this imply for automation and AI moving forward, given that the displacements they cause in the future could potentially be much greater than what we've seen to date?

One potential implication of AI, and our uncertainty about who will be displaced in the future, is that workers should not invest much in credentials and skills *specific* to occupations or industries that are in high demand today but might not remain so tomorrow. For instance, if one believes that *all* young workers face high-displacement risks in the future, then they should not invest heavily today in high-demand sectors and fields—since there is no way to know whether today's good-paying, sub-BA jobs in health care, advanced manufacturing, IT, transportation/logistics, and the like will remain in high demand tomorrow.

Instead, many analysts argue that we should focus only on the *general* skill development of these workers, rather than those specific to high-demand occupations and industries. This would make them more adaptable to different occupations and sectors over time where high demand might exist only temporarily. Indeed, scholars focus on "21st-century skills," such as communication, teamwork, and critical thinking (or problem-solving), that would make them trainable in specific contexts.

While I think providing students these skills in the K-12 years and even in college is very important, I find the argument against expanding specific training in currently high-demand fields unpersuasive. Providing the relevant postsecondary education and training to enable disadvantaged workers to obtain good-paying jobs today makes sense while such demand still exists. If the specificity of the skills they obtain puts them at some greater risk of displacement tomorrow, then we should consider ways of minimizing their exposure to such risks, while maximizing their abilities to adjust if/when these displacements occurs.

Then how should we proceed? As I suggest above, a solid foundation in general skills in the K-12 years is critical. Even when students take career and technical education classes and programs—which I support when they are high in quality and closely related to labor market skill needs, and when they create good "pathways" into college or careers—they should still be given strong analytical and communication skills, with heavy emphasis on critical thinking and problem-solving as well (Gormley, 2017).

When workers gain sector-specific training through sector partnerships and apprenticeships, it is important for them to also attain somewhat broader credentials that have portability beyond their current job. Combining apprenticeships or sector-based training with AS or AAS attainment is one important way of doing this.

In addition, an important recent report by McKinsey (2017) suggests that automation is not likely to completely eliminate many jobs in the future; instead, it will enable machines to be responsible for more but not all tasks that workers usually perform on their jobs. Accordingly, it will make sense for workers to pivot toward more of the tasks that the machines cannot do—in other words, those that complement the robots as much as possible (Kirby & Davenport, 2016). It will sometimes be in the interests of employers to help them do so—in other words, to help them retrain for other duties on the job, rather than undertaking the costs of recruiting, hiring, and training completely new employees. But, since the avoidance of displacement, whenever possible, constitutes something of a public good, it might also make sense for public efforts to help employers do so, perhaps through tax credits or technical assistance for such training.

In addition, if we believe the frequency and seriousness of worker displacements will rise over time, we should begin now to create "lifelong learning" systems to help workers more easily retrain under those circumstances. For instance, how will workers finance such new education or training? The states of Maine and Washington have created Lifelong Learning Accounts for each worker where a small percentage is deducted from their payrolls each period and added to the fund for such eventual training. We might consider reforms in programs like Unemployment Insurance to encourage more such training. And making such training more accessible to adults with family responsibilities—perhaps through greater use of online education plus workplace learning—will be important as well.

Of course, some analysts fear that there will be too few jobs remaining in the future, relative to workers, and that we will therefore need to plan for "universal basic income" support for the millions who will not be able to find work (e.g., Avent, 2016). I do not share this point of view. I think the adjustment processes that economists have always stressed regarding automation—wherein lower costs and prices of goods and services generate higher real incomes and spending that will, in turn, create new jobs—will continue to create new jobs. Not all of them will be of the same quality as those eliminated, and we might need to supplement low worker earnings with expansions of tax credits (like the Earned Income Tax Credit) and subsidized health insurance or childcare.

But a program of universal basic income would encourage many workers not to accept available jobs, and it will be extremely hard to finance—especially in a world where we already face daunting challenges funding the Social Security and Medicare needed by Baby Boomers as they retire. Creating one more very expensive income transfer program should therefore not be high on our current list of priorities.

Conclusion

The discussion above indicates that major changes have occurred on the demand side of the labor market (i.e., among employers), partly induced by automation and technical change, but also reflecting growing globalization and weakening institutions and policies (like unions or minimum wages). We also note the sluggish responses to the changes noted above on the supply side of the market (i.e., among students and workers), where low college completion rates among enrollees and pursuit of credentials without labor market value impede worker readiness to adjust to the demand changes. These problems especially plague disadvantaged or first-generation college students.

And future automation, embodying AI and other characteristics of "smart" machines, could potentially generate a much larger wave of displacements of workers and jobs, if we do not find a way to enhance worker responses to these developments. In the past, most workers have been able to adjust to these developments, by developing skills enabling them to be complements to the new technology rather than substitutes; whether workers will be able to do so in the future remains to be seen.

All of this suggests a broad policy agenda is needed, to help reduce labor market inequality, of which workforce policy is a key component.[8] Changes in higher education and workforce programs and policy should occur at federal, state, and local levels; they should target both students and the institutions they attend; and they should involve employers and take labor demand into account, whenever possible.

Regarding workforce policy, the Workforce Innovation and Opportunity Act (WIOA) was reauthorized in 2014; large additional changes in the federal law, or its implementation at the state and local levels, will not take place in the foreseeable future. In addition, its funding levels are too low, reflecting decades of declines, to greatly affect the market.[9] Workforce efforts appear in several other federal programs, primarily in income support programs for the poor (like Temporary Assistance to Needy Families and Supplemental Nutrition Assistance Programs), but these are also not where broader workforce and education programs will be reformed.

Instead, I focus here on higher education programs at the federal level—including the HEA, and in particular Title IV funding (for Pell and other grants, loans, and work-study programs) for students—which has grown dramatically over time and dwarfs all other federal sources of support for both academic and workforce education. Federal regulations and oversight, especially of the growing for-profit college sector, are important too. And state subsidies of public colleges and universities remain very important as well and will be discussed below.

For Students: Improve Supports and Services for the Disadvantaged

Students who struggle to complete degree or certificate programs in higher education—and also to choose the right schools to attend and programs to study—could benefit from a range of better supports and services.

More and better academic and labor market counseling are sorely needed. This should begin before students first arrive in college. For high school students, these could be available through their guidance counselors; but for the many adults and independent students who now return to college for workforce as well as higher education, that option is not available. One possibility is to improve student access to the One-Stop offices (now called American Job Centers) funded by WIOA and to locate more of them (or at least satellite offices) on or near college campuses.

But, once there, students should receive a range of such supports and services that extend beyond counseling. A few models of student supports have shown strong impacts on completion rates in rigorous evaluation: Accelerated Studies in Associate Programs (ASAP) and Stay the Course. Cost-effective ways of delivering these services should be further explored.[10]

Two other crucial areas where reforms in supports and services are needed are developmental education and financial aid.

As noted earlier, completion rates in developmental education for underperforming students are very low, and evidence suggests such programs are mostly ineffective (or even harmful) in their current form. A number of colleges and states are now implementing reforms. For instance, much of the remediation is becoming "co-requisite" rather than prerequisite, so students are not prevented from taking for-credit classes before passing the required tests. Many colleges are moving away from traditional tests that have been stumbling blocks and are putting more weight on more fundamental numerical and statistical skills rather than more abstract ones like algebra and calculus.[11] And some states are learning to embed remediation within skills training classes—as done in the I-BEST program in the state of Washington—so that remediation is provided directly when students need it to understand a concept in the applied courses they are taking.[12] In addition, some states are seeking to identify gaps in basic readiness among like college students while they are still in high school, or at least before they arrive on campus, and to provide remediation well before students arrive on campus.[13]

Reforms in financial aid should be (and are) being considered at a number of levels. It is widely recognized that Pell grants and student loans need to become more accessible to students, with simplified application processes wherever possible, but also need to have stronger academic performance standards and incentives. Income-based loan repayment options need to be expanded and strengthened, though it is not clear that all reform proposals will do so (Blagg, 2017).

One important issue that is currently under much discussion is whether Title IV funding requirements under HEA should be loosened, so that more students in short-term or not-for-credit workforce programs with labor market value become eligible for assistance. I tend to support some movement in this direction, though slowly and carefully, as we explore ways to enforce quality control and labor market value.[14]

For Institutions: Strengthen Resources, Incentives, and Accountability

As noted above, many colleges that prepare students for the labor market—particularly public two-year colleges and the lower tiers of the four-year system—are both under-resourced and underincentivized to raise completion rates and respond to the labor market. In addition, the for-profit colleges tend to not always protect the financial interests of low-income students, whom they heavily recruit.

I thus believe that these colleges need both more resources, stronger performance incentives, and more regulation and accountability.

Regarding resources, I favor very carefully targeted injections of new federal or state funds into community (and perhaps the lower-tier four-year) colleges.

I believe such funds should pay only for expanding teaching capacity in high-demand degree and certificate programs, plus whatever supports and services students need to more frequently complete these programs (Holzer, 2018).

But I also believe that state funding for higher education should be more closely tied to performance. Indeed, most states are already moving toward "performance-based funding" of public higher education, though in very different ways (National Conference of State Legislatures, 2017). States need to be very careful in generating such performance incentives, so as not to create negative unanticipated consequences (like raising the selectivity bar for students in the admissions process, or lowering standards for program completion). My own view is that states should put more weight on subsequent student earnings and not just credit attainment and program completion—and to especially emphasize these outcomes for disadvantaged, minority, and/or first-generation students. Special care must be taken to "risk-adjust" any such performance measures, so as not to encourage colleges to diminish the presence of at-risk students on their campuses.

With both stronger funding and stronger incentives, colleges would presumably be more interested in expanding sector-based training, career pathway, and stackable credential programs. Indeed, a major challenge facing these institutions is how to replicate and scale the best models noted by researchers without sacrificing quality. Other innovations that would strengthen attainment of credentials with labor market value—such as competency-based credential awards—would likely be expanded as well. And experimentation with new models of community college structure and curriculum delivery—such as Tom Bailey's "guided pathways" (Bailey et al., 2015)—would be encouraged as well.

One new approach about which I am not too enthused is the recent move toward making community college completely free, supported by President Obama and now being implemented by at least a few states (such as Tennessee, Oregon, and New York). While free community college might improve student access, too many resources will likely be squandered on middle-class students who do not need financial assistance, and some student outcomes could actually worsen.[15]

Regarding the for-profit colleges, I strongly believe they need to be publicly regulated. Whether the current "gainful employment" federal regulations are the best way to do so can be debated; but I strongly oppose efforts by the Trump Administration and others to dilute and eliminate any such approaches.

A Few More Issues

A few more issues on workforce development merit more comment. Though space is not available here to go into any of these in depth, at least a few words on each is appropriate in any treatment of workforce readiness among workers.

There is currently a great deal of interest in apprenticeship and other models of work-based learning.[16] But the question remains about how to encourage more employers to offer them. States differ greatly in their efforts to promote apprenticeship; South Carolina, for instance, offers employers a $1,000 tax credit for every new apprentice, and the state markets these very heavily to individual employers. In states such as Georgia and Wisconsin, public schools play a greater role in recruiting students and connecting them to apprenticeships. In Kentucky, the Federation for Advanced Manufacturing Education has developed an apprenticeship system by private companies with some encouragement from the state.

In addition, some employers feel that "registered" apprenticeship, in its current form, is too heavily regulated and too costly for small firms to undertake. These costs are sometimes exaggerated, by rumors that each apprentice costs the firm $100,000 or more—a notion that is widely off the mark.[17] Many employers associate registered apprenticeship with unions whom they strongly oppose, especially in construction. Still, it is worth exploring whether a more lightly regulated model of apprenticeship should be developed and evaluated, alongside other evaluations of the registered model, as we consider which approach best serves employers as well as students over time.

How to encourage employers more broadly to create well-paying jobs, and to invest more in skills training to fill such jobs, remains an important question beyond just the creation of apprenticeships. Encouraging more employers to engage in sector partnerships and at larger scale would be valuable. Small- and medium-sized employers, in particular, may know too little about how to set up training, and their startup costs may be high. Exploring a variety of ways of engaging with such employers, and encouraging them to join partnerships with training providers like community colleges, should be high on the research and policy agenda.

Finally, given the likely but unknown effects of automation in future years and decades, it would be worthwhile for more states to set up Lifelong Learning Accounts, as Maine and Washington have done. Some encouragement and maybe assistance from the federal government would be valuable here, along with other reform efforts to encourage more currently (or soon-to-be) unemployed workers to participating.[18] Encouraging and assisting employers to help more potentially displaced workers retrain for newer responsibilities after new technology is implemented, and making such training as accessible as possible, should also be high on the policy agenda in this realm for years to come.[19] And more research from better data on exactly who becomes displaced over time, and what kinds of retraining are cost-effective for which groups of displaced workers, will be needed as well.[20]

Notes

1 The discussion below borrows heavily from the important work of Goldin and Katz (2008).
2 Inequality associated with the top 1% reflects additional factors, such as executive compensation trends and enormous rewards to financial managers.

3 Economists continue to debate whether a "skills mismatch" exists in the labor market, and why it might persist. Many argue that such mismatch, and key shortages of workers, should generate more wage growth than we have seen to date (Holzer, 2016).

4 If the academic quality of students attending college declines as enrollments rise, this could also lower the average earnings of college graduates, assuming they complete their programs and attain degrees. The absolute and relative wages of high school graduates might also adjust in this scenario, depending on the average skills of the marginal students now enrolling in college versus those who remain high school graduates only.

5 A range of other industry-based certificates, micro-credentials and badges, are also growing in number. The number of these credentials is growing so large that some new efforts to document and describe them all, such as Credential Engine, are beginning to emerge.

6 While most evaluations of sector-based training measure impact only two years after training begins, Schaberg (2017) and Elliott and Roder (2017) find large impacts three and six years later, respectively.

7 The weak responses to labor market incentives reflect a mix of *market failures*, such as imperfect information and institutional barriers, as well as *inequities* that limit responses among disadvantaged students and workers even in well-functioning markets.

8 Much of the discussion below appears in more extensive form in Holzer and Baum (2017).

9 By several estimates (e.g., Holzer, 2009), public funding of WIOA has declined by over 80%, relative to its earliest predecessor—the Comprehensive Employment and Training Act—in 1980.

10 See Gupta (2017) and Evans, Kearney, Perry, and Sullivan (2017). Per student costs of ASAP in New York averaged about $14,000 and about $9,000 in Ohio. In contrast, Stay the Course has cost only about $5,000 per student.

11 As Bailey et al. (2015) note, promising remedial math programs like Quantway and Statway emphasize such practical numerical and statistical skills.

12 Other states are also implementing the Accelerated Opportunity model of career pathways that begin with embedded remediation into other skills training classes.

13 The Florida College and Career Readiness Initiative is an effort to identify major shortfalls in academic skills needed for college by the 11th grade, while the LaGuardia Bridge program in New York is an example of an effective program to begin remediating skill gaps after high school but before students attend college.

14 Since there are some clear advantages to certificates with credit—like the facts that credits generally earn labor market rewards, and for-credit certificates can be stacked to obtain associate degrees—we should limit any potential movements from for-credit to not-for-credit certificates.

15 Some students will now attend two-year colleges with hopes of transfer, instead of going straight to the four-year colleges, but will fail to transfer successfully. Also, due to capacity constraints in the community colleges, many students might now be squeezed out of courses and programs that they badly need to be successful.

16 High-quality career and technical education and "pathways" from high school to college are more broadly discussed in Hoffman and Schwartz (2017). See also Rosenbaum, Ahearn, Rosenbaum, and Rosenbaum (2017) for a good discussion of effective CTE programs in community colleges.

17 These high-cost figures include wages paid to workers over three years or more, in return for worker provision of goods and services to the firm. If firms cannot recoup all of their wage costs in this time period, then they can pay apprentices submarket wages until they are productive enough to justify full wage payments.

18 "Rapid response" efforts by the U.S. Department of Labor in response to displacements that have been announced could initiate some such training processes, though they could also begin much earlier when employers know they are about to introduce major new automation into production.

19 Indeed, Helper, Martins, and Seamans (2017) argue that employers can choose different modes of implementation that will allow their workers to complement the new technologies to greater or lesser degrees.

20 Andersson, Holzer, Lane, Rosenblum, and Smith (2013), among others, find that dislocated worker training is generally not very cost-effective when funded through existing federal programs. But Jacobson, LaLonde, and Sullivan (2005) find stronger results among those training at community colleges, especially in high-demand or technical fields.

References

Andersson, F., Holzer, H. J., Lane, J. I., Rosenblum, D., & Smith, J. (2013). *Does federally funded job training work? Nonexperimental estimates of WIA training impacts using longitudinal data on workers and firms.* National Bureau of Economic Research Working Paper No. 19446.

Autor, D. (2010). *The polarization of job opportunities in the us labor market.* Washington, DC: Center for American Progress.

Autor, D. (2014). Skills, inequality and the rise of earnings inequality among the other 99 percent. *Science, 344*(6186), 843–851.

Autor, D., & Wasserman, M. (2013). *Wayward sons: The emerging gender gap in labor markets and education.* Washington, DC: The Third Way.

Avent, R. (2016). *The wealth of humans: Work, power and status in the 21st century.* New York, NY: Macmillan.

Backes, B., Holzer, H. J., & Velez, E. D. (2015). Is it worth it? Postsecondary education and labor market outcomes for the disadvantaged. *IZA Journal of Labor Policy, 4*(1).

Bailey, T. R., Jaggars, S. S., & Jenkins, D. (2015). *Redesigning America's community colleges.* Cambridge, MA: Harvard University Press.

Baum, S. (2016). *Student debt: Rhetoric and realities in higher education financing.* Washington, DC: Urban Institute Press.

Bettinger, E. P., Boatman, A., & Long, B. T. (2013). Student supports: Development education and other academic programs. *The Future of Children, 23*(1), 93–115.

Blagg, K. (2017). *The PROSPER act changes the math for student loan borrowers.* Washington, DC: Urban Institute.

Blinder, A. (2006, March/April). Offshoring: The next industrial revolution? *Foreign Affairs,* March/April issue.

Card, D., & Jonathan, D. (2008). The impact of technological change on low-wage workers: A review. In R. Blank, S. Danziger, & R. F. Schoeni (Eds.), *Working and poor: How economic and policy changes are affecting low-wage workers.* New York, NY: Russell Sage Foundation.

Clotfelter, C. T., Ladd, H. F., Muschkin, C., & Vigdor, J. L. (2013). Developmental education in North Carolina community colleges. CALDER Working Paper, American Institutes for Research, Washington, DC.

Elliott, M., & Anne Roder. (2017). *Escalating gains: Project quest's sectoral strategy pays off.* New York, NY: Economic Mobility Corporation.

Evans, W., Kearney, M.S., Perry, B., & Sullivan, J. X. (2017). *Stay the course: Improving persistence and graduation rates in America's community colleges.* Boston, MA: JPAL.

Goldin, C., & Lawrence, K. (2008). *The race between education and technology.* Cambridge, MA: Harvard University Press.

Gormley, W. (2017). *The critical advantage: Developing critical thinking skills in school.* Cambridge, MA: Harvard Education Press.

Gupta, H. (2017). *The power of fully supporting community college students.* New York, NY: MDRC.

Helper, S., Martins, R., & Seamans, R. (2017). *Value migration and industry 4.0: Theory, field evidence and propositions.* Cleveland, OH: Case Western Reserve University. Unpublished.

Hoffman, N. & Schwartz, R. (2017). *Learning for careers: The pathways to prosperity network.* Cambridge, MA: Harvard Education Press.

Holzer, H. (2009). Workforce development policy: What do we know? What should we do? In M. Cancian & S. Danziger (Eds.), *Changing poverty.* New York, NY: Russell Sage Foundation.

Holzer, H. (2015). *Job market polarization and worker skills: A tale of two middles.* Washington, DC: Brookings Institution.

Holzer, H. (2016). Worker skills and the US labor market: What role should policy play? In M. Strain (Ed.), *The US labor market: Questions and challenges for public policy.* Washington, DC: American Enterprise Institute.

Holzer, H. (2017). *Building a new middle class in the knowledge economy.* Washington, DC: Progressive Policy Institute.

Holzer, H. (2018). A 'Race to the Top' in public higher education to improve education and employment outcomes of the poor. *RSF: The Russell Sage Journal of the Social Sciences, 4*(3).

Holzer, H. & Baum, S. (2017). *Making college work: Pathways to success for disadvantaged workers.* Washington, DC: Brookings Press.

Jacobson, L., LaLonde, R. J., & Sullivan, D. (2005). The impact of community college retraining on older displaced workers: Should we teach old dogs new tricks? *Industrial and Labor Relations Review, 58*(3), 215–398.

Kirby, J., & Davenport, T. (2016). *Only humans need apply: Winners and losers in the age of smart machines.* New York, NY: Harper-Collins.

Krueger, A. (2017). *Where have all the workers gone? An inquiry into the decline in labor force participation.* Washington, DC: Brookings Institution.

Lerman, R. (2014). Expanding apprenticeship opportunities in the United States. In M. Kearney & B. Harris (Eds.), *Policies to address poverty in America.* Washington, DC: The Hamilton Project, Brookings Institution.

Levy, F., & Murnane, R. (2013). *Dancing with robots: Human skills for computerized work.* The Third Way, Washington, DC.

McKinsey and Company. (2017). *A future that works: Automation, employment and productivity.* New York, NY.

National Conference of State Legislatures. (2017). Performance-based funding for higher education. http://www.ncsl.org/research/education/performance-funding.aspx.

Rosenbaum, J. E., Ahearn, C. E., Rosenbaum, J. E., & Rosenbaum, J. (2017). *Bridging the gaps: College pathways to career success.* New York, NY: Russell Sage Foundation.

Schaberg, K. (2017). *Can sector strategies provide long-term effects?* New York, NY: MDRC.

9

DATA AND TECHNOLOGY FOR IMPACT HIRING

Two Early Experiments

Darko Lovric, Shanti Nayak, Abigail Carlton, and Mark McCoy

Introduction

Although experts agree that data and technology are radically transforming the labor market, its impacts on the future of the economy and of society itself are far from certain. Futurists and the popular press deal in the currency of long-term predictions or binary conclusions—yet both modes are situated comfortably far from today's reality, where real and more nuanced insights are required. In this moment, much can in fact be learned from the nuanced ways information and innovation are known to shape firm behavior and worker outcomes. Better understanding of how people and organizations adapt and respond to data and technology can lead to creating stronger rules and norms that point disruptive effects toward social good.

This chapter presents two experiments that explored private sector applications of data and technology to drive positive outcomes for "opportunity youth"—a term used to describe the nearly six million young Americans between the ages of 16 and 24 who are out of work and out of school. The Rockefeller Foundation partnered with boutique consulting firm, Incandescent, to conduct both experiments as part of its work to advance "impact hiring"—business-driven talent practices that incent companies to hire and develop individuals facing barriers to economic opportunity.[1] These experiments demonstrate the promise and limitations of data and technology. Firms can apply these tools to improve both social and business outcomes associated with recruitment, job matching, skill development, and retention; however, human capital continues to be critical.

Experiment 1 describes a partnership between The Rockefeller Foundation, Incandescent, and HMSHost to analyze retention data and increase tenure for young, entry-level workers that include opportunity youth. Experiment 2 describes a partnership between The Rockefeller Foundation, Incandescent, and Knack to use gamified assessments as a recruitment tool for entry-level hiring.

These experiments can be framed within a more central role of modern philanthropy, whose risk capital can prove out solutions that can later be further validated by the academia and, if results hold, scaled by the government. This chapter presents two such early experiments.

Experiment 1—Increasing Retention of Young Employees

Entry-level customer service jobs represent one of the key entry points for unemployed youth without a college degree into the labor market. The high attrition rate endemic in frontline work is one of the greatest practical challenges for employers today. Think-tank studies suggest that the cost of turnover ranges from $3,000[2] to $8,000[3] per frontline associate, accumulating to millions of dollars lost over time for large organizations. From a social impact perspective, too, an entry-level job creates value for employees only if they persist long enough to build a sense of agency, skills in navigating the workplace environment, and credibility for advancement at the same employer or elsewhere.

Early conversations among employers in the 100,000 Opportunities Coalition[4] revealed a hypothesis that the frontline manager behavior can positively impact retention in young employees by increasing their engagement and skill development. Employers felt ill-equipped, however, to put this intuition to use to move the needle on their shared concern regarding frontline retention.

The Rockefeller Foundation, consulting firm Incandescent, and food operator HMSHost came together to test and develop an approach to improve associate engagement and, by extension, retention. In this work, the Foundation agreed to support and fund the development of an innovative approach; the consulting team was charged with translating a hypothesis into a set of testable interventions; and HMSHost offered the context for the experiment, with the aim of creating a proof point internally, as well as for the other employers in the coalition.

This intervention was designed to identify specific manager behaviors that improve associate engagement and retention, support managers to change their behavior, and measure the effectiveness of these efforts.

Building a Deep Understanding of Retention Challenges at HMSHost

In 2016, the CEO of HMSHost, which operates quick service and full-service restaurants in airports and travel plazas, identified associate retention as a strategic priority. Frontline associates (e.g., cooks, servers, and cashiers) are the vast majority of the company's workforce. In recent years, three out of four associates leave within the first year, and young associates (<24 years old), which comprise 57% of their hires, are retained at even lower rates. Of their younger workers, 78% leave in the first year, compared with 64% for associates aged 25 years and older.

Additionally, HMSHost was finding that high turnover was perpetuating the problem, as managers had to divert their already scarce available time away from supporting and engaging existing employees to driving necessary recruiting efforts.

Our analysis of retention and exit survey data isolated the factors that most significantly influence retention: manager behaviors, staffing levels and employee workload, employee age (young employees were retained at lower rates), and whether employees work in tipped or nontipped roles. In parallel, this analysis also ruled out the variables that made no difference to retention (e.g., unionization, full-time or part-time status), and decisively cut through some powerful, long-standing retention "myths" (e.g., that wages were a primary reason for attrition, and that the 90-day mark represented a significant point after which employee retention got easier).

To help build the business case for focusing on engagement and retention, we completed a multivariate regression analysis of HMSHost data. The analysis attempted to empirically distinguish the impact of associate tenure and associate turnover from the influence of the other factors (e.g., manager tenure, seasonal variation, and location or other fixed differences among establishments). In doing so, we found the following strong indications:

- Reduced associate overtime hours are associated with reduced turnover;
- Associates productivity is associated with job tenure, and this benefit is gained within the first two years;
- Customer complaints are associated with reduced turnover and increased job tenure.

Identifying Key Manager Behaviors

Frontline interviews and observations at locations with average and above-average retention outcomes helped us identify the manager behaviors that matter most for associate engagement. Through nearly 100 conversations with HMSHost employees (associates, managers, and HQ staff), 7 manager behaviors emerged as consistent drivers of employee engagement and retention:

Creating an environment where associates can succeed:

1. **Setting up the team to work effectively**—Having the necessary tools and resources (e.g., mops, fry scoopers) was foundational to engagement. Conversely, not having tools at the ready frustrated associates who wanted to do good work.

2. **Upholding consistent standards**—Accountability and follow-through attracts and retains the right people. Being fair and firm, rather than nice, mattered to associates.

Painting a Vivid Picture of Associates' Value and Purpose:

1. **Recognizing performance authentically**—Many associates' proudest moments were instances when their manager directly recognized their work. Recognition that was provided verbally, sincerely and with specific examples was most potent (e.g., "you did a great job serving customers today, especially on such a busy day—I was impressed with how you were able to help customers quickly while being friendly and courteous with everyone") and was even more impactful following moments when employees were/had been challenged.
2. **Connecting the job to purpose**—Managers who genuinely believed and communicated to associates the importance of their jobs (e.g., describing a utility team at a motorway as critical to delivering positive customer experience) drove higher employee engagement.

Empowering Associates to be Problem Solvers:

3. **Listening to and solving frontline challenges**—Conversations probing "what's working and what's not" and mutually exploring solutions were more effective at driving retention than ascribing blame.
4. **Creating feedback touchpoints**—Managers who encouraged informal, regular two-way communication about how to succeed in the job fostered associate pride and comfort in sharing ideas, which seemed particularly empowering for youth hires-and often improved operations.

Mobilizing Associates for Growth:

5. **Laying out a career path**—Workforces in which employees believed that development and promotion opportunities were available to them (e.g., seeing colleagues get promoted, or feeling that they were developing specific skills that would lead to a new or expanded role), experienced higher retention.

The importance of these behaviors, although universally valuable for employees both young and old, is amplified for opportunity youth who often lack experience in navigating challenges in the workplace. Field research on support programs for opportunity youth consistently shows that one of the most important drivers of youth success is a connection to a caring adult in their lives. For many opportunity youth, what they lack is not ambition or accountability—77% believe that getting a good education and job is their own responsibility and depends on their own effort—but appropriate guidance and support.[5]

Our frontline observations were designed to spend time with managers who were driving average retention outcomes, along with their managerial peers who were driving exemplary retention outcomes while working under similar conditions and facing similar constraints. Our comparisons revealed that even managers who drove average associate engagement demonstrated these behaviors; but that exemplary managers brought to life these behaviors in different and more powerful ways.

For example, many managers said "thank you" to their associates at the end of the shift, but exemplary managers gave specific, story-based recognition to associates that drew attention to the impact of the associate's actions and built authentic pride (e.g., "Great job serving customers today, especially on such a busy day! You kept the line short while being friendly and courteous with everyone").

Exemplary managers were often more creative in helping their people, for example, by creating learning moments with their associates. One manager had a night shift barista who wanted employees on the morning shift to restock, rather than owning that responsibility on her shift. The manager rotated this barista onto a morning shift, so the associate could experience that shift firsthand. Since then, the associate has made sure the store was in top shape for the morning shift. Another manager initiated customer walk-throughs, asking associates to "be the customer" and walk the floor with him to share their observations and brainstorm improvements.

We believe every company, like HMSHost, has exemplary managers who deliver distinctive employee experiences and retention outcomes. Building a vivid and specific description of "what good looks like here" is an important step in understanding how to improve frontline retention. In addition to uncovering the value of specific manager behaviors, field conversations shed light on the reality that frontline managers lacked access to robust associate engagement and retention data and any clear sense of how their behavior, in turn, influenced retention.

We subsequently designed a pilot with the following two goals:

1. To help managers adopt behaviors that are correlated with strong associate retention (focused on those behaviors that would require a relatively light lift from managers, while producing quick associate feedback)
2. To introduce associate engagement and retention data to frontline managers as target variables

Pilot Design and Rollout

We launched an 11-week pilot in two airports, focused exclusively on improving managers' skills at practicing three specific behaviors: (1) recognizing associates' performance authentically, (2) listening to and solving frontline challenges, and (3) creating feedback touchpoints with associates.

To accelerate real behavior change over the short time frame, managers went through a four-stage test-and-learn feedback loop driven by biweekly roundtable discussions and reinforced by regular survey data:

- **Stage 1—Galvanize to action:** Managers learned about the three behaviors (using real examples of "what good looks like" drawn from their peers—other frontline managers who are driving significantly better retention outcomes among their associates), often through curated "aha moments" in roundtables designed with a "show not tell" approach.
- **Stage 2—Prioritize specific actions:** At the end of each roundtable, managers individually made specific commitments related to target behaviors (e.g., "before the next roundtable, I will try recognizing three associates on my team in a new way").
- **Stage 3—Take action:** Managers put what they learned into practice, and they followed through on their commitments.
- **Stage 4—Debrief:** During each roundtable, managers debriefed lessons learned from following through on their commitments.

As the pilot got underway, many managers were skeptical or even indifferent about changing their behavior, driven by two beliefs: (1) that they were already effectively recognizing, listening, and giving feedback to their associates and (2) that structural issues—namely, insufficient associate training and chronic short-staffing—were the primary or even sole cause of low associate engagement.

Early in the process, we've exposed the need to explore potential gaps between managers' self-perception and their associates' perceptions, which was crucial to kick-starting the process of manager buy-in. Sometimes these gaps were discovered to be yawning. Managers anonymously evaluated their own performance, rating themselves particularly favorably on associate recognition and on making associates feel their ideas and suggestions matter. Their associates, by contrast, rated both behaviors as among their managers' weakest points. Managers were genuinely surprised—even moved—to see these differences revealed to them.

When managers began following through on their commitments, they were often surprised to see how associates responded, creating a positive learning loop:

- An associate who had worked 2+ years at HMSHost had a busy Memorial Day Weekend day where she prepared 20 pizzas for the display window. At the end of the day, her manager sought her out, shook her hand, and told her she had done a "really good job." She described this interaction as her proudest moment working at HMSHost.
- A manager told us "I used to think that saying thank you or giving a gift card was recognition, but there was a big difference when I sat them down

and specifically told them how great a job they did by keeping a smile on their face as they worked to move a long line of customers through the register as quickly as possible. They were beaming after that."

The 11-week pilot—notably conducted during one of the busiest times in HMSHost's business cycle—improved every associate engagement metric related to the behaviors in focus by an average of 17%, with signs of reduced turnover. In addition, we noted a clear "halo" effect—the pilot study boosted associates' engagement metrics related to behaviors *not* central to the pilot study (by 9% on average, with the strongest improvement being associates' perception of feeling "cared about as a person" which improved by nearly 14%). We found that young associates exhibited far greater responsiveness or sensitivity to manager treatment than older workers. Perceptions of bad treatment from their managers make young people especially unhappy, while perceptions of good treatment make them especially happy. In particular, feeling cared about and having their questions, concerns, and issues addressed impact happiness significantly more for younger workers than their older counterparts. Every manager on the frontline has the power to change a young person's outlook on work and thus improve their engagement in the workplace. Over time, such changes can significantly impact the whole workforce.

Takeaways—Improving Frontline Manager Behavior

Two takeaways stand out from the pilot. Across the locations we observed, frontline managers did not have access to clear and accurate retention data—as a result, they weren't able to concretely and correctly identify the leverage points for influencing engagement and retention. Although the company understood and regularly tracked operational metrics such as overtime hours and peak transactions, they lacked a data-driven assessment of the root causes of attrition and how those root causes might differ across job type and employee populations. In analyzing retention through the pilot, we shifted our focus away from the often-used turnover ratios (how many associates depart relative to the total number of active associates), toward retention data—how long do associates stay with the company, and when are the significant "drop-off points" when associates voluntarily or involuntarily leave. It is well known that organizational data on turnover do not usually point to the root causes for turnover, despite how "objective" turnover data appear to be. Data on engagement and retention efforts and outcomes tend to be more useful for understanding and addressing the motivation of the employee as it relates to turnover (or lack thereof, it is often hoped).

Finally, while this pilot was driven with external support, the majority of the behaviors managers learned and practiced through the pilot were drawn entirely from existing bright spots within the company. Without question, all companies have exemplars to draw on and learn from—the more companies can draw out "what's already working" from individuals who are getting distinctively good outcomes (both people and business outcomes), the better.

Experiment 2—Game-Based Assessments as a Tool to Increase Job Access

Innovations in employment technologies have abounded in recent years, leveraging the joint power of gamification and data science in the attempt to improve crucial labor market functions, such as job access and matching, with the desired goal of providing a more realistic and meritocratic way to appeal to a broad job applicant population and select those most skilled for the particular job.

Today, companies are:

- Identifying talent requirements by making solid inferences on the basis of performance data of current employees—rigorously determining which combinations of traits and abilities at the point of employee selection will help drive practical results on the job;
- Leveraging technology in an effective, timely, and ethical manner to evaluate candidates in ways that deliver valid signals for the characteristics most critical to job performance; and
- Measuring performance on the job in a granular, repeatable, and systematic way—and feeding these data into both job design and the predictive signals that drive hiring systems.

Game-based talent analytics can do what is all too rare in the recruiting process: establish a quantifiable predictor of workplace performance that can complement and perhaps substitute for an organization's traditional qualifications in screening and hiring. Knack's games are designed to elicit a wide variety of individual responses to different stimuli, which are mapped to a range of cognitive skills, personality traits, emotional and social abilities, and mindsets and aptitudes. These data are then mapped to what the company refers to as *knacks* (e.g., logical reasoning, social intelligence, motivation, resilience, creativity, action orientation)—a specific trait or aptitude relevant to an aspect of a job. By using independent, validated measures of these *knacks*, Knack builds models that turn gameplay data into trait and ability scores. These "knacks" can be combined into a basket of skills ("ultraknacks")—an overall measure of a large class of job-relevant behaviors and aptitudes (e.g., customer service).

With these trait and ability scores, Knack then builds quantitative models to predict job performance in a broad range of occupations. One of the ways in which Knack builds these models is through working directly with employers: employees play the games, then Knack uses the data from a part of the employee sample to develop a custom predictive model. This model correlates gameplay data with the company's own performance ratings (e.g., an overall performance rating or specific measures of productivity). Then the model is tested against the rest of the employee sample to evaluate its power to predict performance. These predictive models, called *ultraknacks*, are used to assign any individual who plays the games a score that predicts their level of performance in the role, based on the specific footprint of traits and abilities that individual demonstrates through gameplay. The hope is that the range of traits that predict performance on the job correspond with the range of traits that can be measured and selected on (via ultraknacks) in a pool of job applicants.

Knack's game-based technology has been used to predict on-the-job performance in a wide range of applications—from finding entry-level workers for retail, operations, sales, and business management roles, to identifying high-potential scientists for Shell's R&D Innovation program and surgery residents for NYU Medical Center. Working with 18 youth service providers that serve low-income young adults not currently employed or enrolled in school, Incandescent enlisted over 600 participants, ages 18 to 24, to play the Knack mobile games. Results indicated that a number of key attributes differentiated high performers from low performers in each of a spectrum of entry-level roles.

More specifically, among our sample of 600 youth, we used Knack to score youth in terms of their potential to perform successfully in four separate jobs: (1) entry-level customer service role at a financial institution, (2) claims processing role, (3) restaurant service role in a restaurant chain, and (4) highly skilled financial analyst role in a large insurance firm. In each case, Knack had already developed the ultraknacks (predictive models) for these roles using the employer's own workforce, so we were able to identify youth talent using these validated predictive models.

It is important to note that the Knack scores—like any scores gathered and used for personnel selection—should be viewed as indicative of the *potential* for youths to perform successfully on the job, all else being equal, rather than as an estimate of what the youths' performance would actually be. For instance, all the individuals in the financial analyst role have training and experience in finance. One would certainly expect that anyone who entered into this job without that training and experience would struggle to deliver on the basic requirements, regardless of the individual's other aptitudes. However, Knack's predictive models show us how an individual would be most likely to perform given equivalent training.

Five Myths Debunked

Myth #1

REALITY: A large number of "opportunity youth" off the radar of most employers demonstrate the quantifiable attributes predictive of success in high-quality entry-level jobs. Many of them outscore the individuals working in these jobs today.

This reality debunks a first commonly-held myth: that only a few "opportunity youth" have what it takes to outperform the more experienced and educated people companies are recruiting into high-quality entry-level roles. The customer service ultraknack we used in this study was built using data from employees in a customer service role in a large financial institution—a high-quality entry-level job in terms of skill level, working conditions, pay and potential for advancement. As a predictive model, this ultraknack is based on more than enough data to ensure that it makes stable and consistent predictions. In contrast with interviews and resumes, where information is gathered used in a subjective manner by most employers to guide hiring decisions, this model produces a clear, quantifiable, and pronounced difference between higher and lower job performers.

Comparing the customer service ultraknack scores with the 600 youth in our study showed that

- 39% score higher than the average of current customer service employees at the company
- 28% score higher than the average of current, company-identified, high-performing employees in this role at the company

In other words, two in five of the youth in these 18 programs, which focus specifically on young people who face significant obstacles to gaining employment, score higher on Knack's predictive model than the average employee already working in this high-quality entry-level job—and one in four perform better on the predictive model than the employees who have been identified as the company's top performers.

This striking result was not limited to the customer service role. In fact, the data showed similar results for the three other roles we included in this study. Specifically, 32% of the youth in our sample score above the average among high performers in an entry-level claims processing role at a large employer in this space, and 29% score higher than the average among high performers in a restaurant service role at a California restaurant chain operator. Even for a highly skilled entry-level financial analyst role at a global health insurer, 32% of the youth in our sample score at the level of the average current employees in this role, and 11% score as high as the top quintile of star financial analysts working at this firm.

Myth #2

REALITY: "Opportunity youth" have a distribution of traits, abilities, and aptitudes no different from that of the general population.

This debunks a second commonly-held myth: that the aptitudes of "opportunity youth" differ systematically and significantly from those of the broader population (e.g., scoring lower on traits that are generally viewed as positive).

Take a moment to review the six alphabetically listed knacks below.

Digital Mindset
Planning
Resilience
Seeking Adventure
Staying Focused
Teamwork

For three of these knacks, the 600 youth in our sample were at least 10% *more* likely than the general population to score above a threshold—a level identified through Knack's analysis—that represents a given knack as an area of strength for the assessment taker. And for the other three knacks, these 600 youth were at least 15% *less* likely than the general population to score above that threshold.

These results support arguments suggesting that youth bring particular strengths to the workforce that employers should seek out. Digital Mindset, Resilience, and Seeking Adventure echo themes one frequently hears in these kinds of discussions. Opportunity youth can bring tech savvy, a sense of daring to try new things, and the resilience that comes from tackling hard life circumstances. In our experiment, however, these are three knacks on which our opportunity youth are somewhat **less likely** to excel than the general population. Planning, teamwork, and staying focused are all areas in which these youth are **more likely** to excel than the general population, dismantling stereotypes that youth today are more easily distracted, less disciplined and more in it for themselves than their older counterparts.

Although these six results are all statistically significant, the fact remains that the overall similarities between youth and the general population far outweigh the differences. When looking at how the youth and general population score on different knacks, which is visually represented in Figure 9.1, the overwhelming similarity is readily apparent by the large amount of overlap represented by blue shading. If the data had supported the myth that youth differ significantly and systematically from the general population, we would expect to see far less overlap in the distributions of scores on far more knacks.

What matters from an employment perspective isn't that youth, as a cohort, are different from other age groups in the talent market. What matters is that youth are different from one another and have a wide range of aptitudes that suit different individuals for distinct types of jobs, and that is what we witness here.

Myth #3

REALITY: "Employability" isn't a single sort of assessment that can be applied across the board to whole cohorts of youth. Different youth excel at the aptitudes that predict success in different roles, and most of the youth in our sample fit the success profile for at least one of the four target roles well.

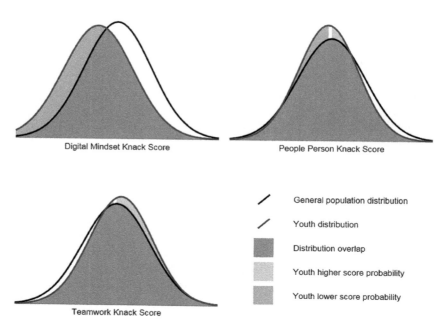

FIGURE 9.1 The Youth Sample is Broadly Similar to the General Population.
Note: Youth (black line) and general population (dotted line) distributions of scores on the Digital Mindset knack (top left), People Person knack (top right), and Teamwork knack (bottom left). Shaded areas indicate overlap of youth and general population scores (light grey), where youth score below the general population (dark grey), or where youth score above the general population (black).

This debunks a third commonly-held myth: that some youth are simply more "employable" than others and have greater aptitude across the spectrum of entry-level roles.

One might intuitively picture "employability" as a kind of cocktail of attributes that would apply in very similar ways to different kinds of entry-level work. For instance, many people believe a combination of ability to understand people, self-discipline, and communication—or some set of traits like these—form a "soft skills" core that determines whether people will perform well, acceptably, or poorly in any of the four entry-level jobs we focus on in this study. According to that view, if Knack or another talent analytics company is able to predict who will perform how well, one would assume they must be testing for something like that core group of soft skills. This view implies an expectation that youth who score high on the core group of soft skills, as measured by the games, would be predicted to excel across a range of jobs—and those youth who score low on this core skill set would be predicted to perform poorly across a similarly wide range of jobs that have similar determinants of success.

Intuitive as such a picture might seem, it is absolutely at odds with the data from our study. Even looking at just four jobs, and comparing their respective ultraknack scores with youth in our study, we found:

- Only 6% of the youth were "all-around super athletes" who scored at least at the average of the company's designated high performers for at least three of the four jobs...
- ... but 65% of the youth scored at least at the average of the company's designated high performer for one or more of the four jobs...
- ... and 83% scored at least at the level of the company's average performers among their current employee base for at least one job

If one expanded the range and diversity of the jobs considered, one would undoubtedly see an even stronger version of this result. The aptitudes relevant for work in construction, for example, do not likely match particularly closely the aptitudes relevant for restaurant service or claims processing.

The reason we see this result is that different knacks are in fact positively— and negatively—associated with success in these four jobs. For example, Knack has identified that high-performing customer service representatives show strong resourcefulness, self-confidence, and inspirational leadership abilities while also being more introverted and spontaneous; whereas high-performing financial analysts are optimistic, pragmatic, risk averse, and able to regulate their negative reactions. Although a tiny number of people might embody both profiles, these two jobs in fact require attributes that pull in different directions. As a larger number of employers get more granular and more accurate about exactly what attributes matter, the net effect is that a wider range of candidates shine to employers who value their particular, distinctive mix of abilities. Just as employers choose among a range of candidates with their talents, youth choose among a range of employers who have these different granular needs. Ultimately, good person-job fit is the ideal outcome for all parties involved.

This is a deeply encouraging result for the field of youth employment. If employability were more single-faceted and broadly consistent across most entry-level jobs, it would be difficult and expensive to move the needle for those youth who are currently less employable. The Knack data indicate that employability is a not a single thing, but a diverse, heterogeneous set of factors that vary significantly across different entry-level jobs. This points to an opportunity to strengthen the focus of the youth employment field on matching: helping employers identify youth who already have the aptitudes associated with success in a particular job, and enabling youth to identify opportunities that are the best match for them.

Myth #4

REALITY: Although skills and knowledge gained in the classroom may be directly relevant for certain jobs, education is not a proxy for abilities and skills relevant to job performance.

This debunks a fourth commonly-held myth: that education alone can be used as a proxy for a job candidate's ability to perform.

Employers routinely use educational level as a proxy for performance when making hiring decisions. They may, for instance, not care particularly about any specific material that a college graduate learns in the university classroom, but believe that college graduates will be more likely have certain general abilities that will help them to succeed: better problem-solving skills, perhaps, or better ability to use data to inform decisions.

These generalizations can be hazardous to both employers and jobseekers. Research conducted by Innovate+Educate, an organization that employs research-based strategies to address the national "skills gap," found that while only 1% of unemployed New Mexican young adults meet the criteria for jobs that require a college degree, 33% meet the qualifications when their aptitude is instead measured by skills. Employers in New Mexico who partnered with Innovate+Educate to leverage a skills-based hiring approach experienced 25%–75% reductions in turnover, time to hire, cost to hire, and a reduction in training.

Similarly, our study of youth underscores the lack of close connection between educational attainment and the aptitudes that distinguish high performers in entry-level roles. Given the nature of our sample, we could not contrast college graduates with high school graduates, but we were able to compare the ultraknack scores of the 155 youth with some college to those of the 430 youth with no college. In no case was the percentage of youth scoring above the average of the employees currently in one of our four roles, or above the average of the employer's designated high performers, significantly different between the "some college" and "no college" subgroups in the sample.

Take, for instance, the financial analyst role—the role one would most naturally associate with the kinds of aptitudes that might be prevalent in a college-educated population, and for which an undergraduate degree is indeed a prerequisite. Thirty-four percent of the "no college" youth score at least as high as the average of the employees currently in the analyst role, versus 29% of the youth with some college, a difference that does not reach the 5% threshold of statistical significance. Eleven percent of both groups score at the same level as those analysts the employer called out as the highest performers.

This result does not preclude the possibility that education could be associated with superior performance on the job in the kinds of roles we used in our study. For instance, completing an undergraduate major in accounting almost certainly confers skills and knowledge to some degree relevant to success in the financial analyst role. Knack's predictive talent analytics wouldn't pick up this effect, both because all of the financial analyst employees who played the games had a college education and because Knack's games don't measure accounting expertise.

The trap to avoid, which these results underscore, is looking at education beyond its direct relevance to the work as an indirect proxy for other aptitudes. By identifying and measuring aptitudes more directly instead, we can begin to see "hidden talents" that employers could easily miss as they implement protocols for resume screening that build in incorrect assumptions, not driven by data, with regard to education or experiences being proxies for desired qualities.

Myth #5

REALITY: "Opportunity youth" score as strongly on attributes associated with the potential to advance into higher level roles as other demographic groups. "Potential" is a useful notion only when it can be translated into specific attributes that can be measured; once this translation is made, youth are as likely to excel at those attributes as others. This debunks a fifth commonly-held myth: that youth may be able to perform well in entry-level roles, but many do not have the aptitudes associated with advancement into higher level roles.

The best employers focus not only on hiring individuals able to perform in the immediate job at hand but on hiring and nurturing individuals who can stay committed and capably advance into higher value roles in the company over the longer term. For example, Starbucks grows baristas into some of the industry's best store, district, and regional managers. P.F. Chang's looks at the dishwasher role as a point of entry to test and grow talent that they then rotate into increasingly high-value roles in their restaurants.

Hiring for potential makes logical business sense, although it can easily lead to bias if the factors associated with potential for job promotion are left undefined. Hiring managers can, consciously or unconsciously, default to seeing potential as "someone like me," and hire on the basis of factors irrelevant to the long-term capacity to perform and advance. If, however, potential can be pinned down to specific, measurable qualities, it becomes a powerful basis for data-driven hiring.

To take an example from our study, let's take a look at the matches for the customer service role. Within this sample, one can map the knacks of resourcefulness—an important foundation for day-to-day performance in this job—and logical reasoning, which we could hypothesize, is an important factor in the potential to advance into supervisory roles involving greater focus on process design and operational decision-making. Figure 9.2 is a scatterplot of the youth who matched the customer service role showing where they score on these two knacks. A company focused just on ensuring good performance in the current job might select candidates based on resourcefulness (the pink

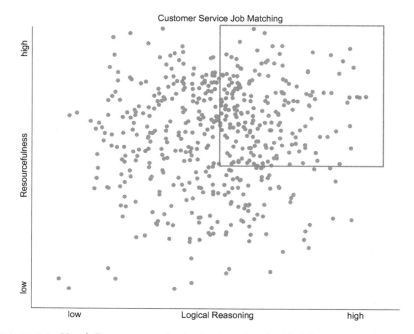

FIGURE 9.2 Youth Demonstrate Aptitudes Associated with Advancement Potential.
Note: Youth Logical Reasoning (horizontal axis) and Resourcefulness (vertical axis) knack
scores are shown for each individual. Pink shaded area indicates candidates an employer
might consider for near-term performance potential based on their high resourcefulness.
Square indicates candidates who score well for near-term performance potential as well as
advancement potential based on their logical reasoning ability.

shaded section of the plot). Given the larger number of individuals who fulfill
these less stringent criteria, the employer could look to drive excellence on operating metrics such as low time-to-fill open positions. A company balancing
focus on long-term potential with performance in the immediate job at hand
might draw from the smaller set of candidates in the red square, who are strong
both in resourcefulness and logical reasoning.

As described in the discussion of the "second myth" above, opportunity
youth have a similar distribution of knacks to the general population. For any
given target group of aptitudes (e.g., people person + planning + logical reasoning), we see about the same numbers who score high in our group as we'd
see in the general population, and the same kinds of interrelationships among
aptitudes (e.g., a positive correlation among certain cognitive abilities) that
one would expect based on the broader research literature. When an employer
commits to the path of delineating what potential really means and to measuring the relevant underlying pattern of talent markers as objectively as possible,
that opens the door to finding talent beyond their traditional recruiting sources
to those who have the aptitudes relevant for long-term advancement.

Takeaways: Data-Driven Hiring for Entry-Level Jobs

There are more tools and better practices available today than ever before to identify human potential and to manage human capital. Often, the limiting factor is the institutional will for companies to make a commitment to data-driven hiring, build the relevant accountabilities into their line management and human resource organizations, and shift the day-to-day basis for decision-making from intuition to data.

Individual employers have a great deal to gain from the application of talent analytics. The gains from infusing predictive talent data into talent markets are even greater when we look at the broader social consequences. Talent markets exchange our most valuable resources, but they are often compromised by severe systematic failures: bias, information gaps, and unreliable and idiosyncratic decision-making stand in the way of hiring individuals who could be strong performers. These market failures most greatly affect the disadvantaged: individuals who are disconnected, vulnerable to discrimination, and lacking in the markers that employers traditionally value (e.g., experience and education). Youth are particularly likely to be hurt by such market failures. Not only are their strengths often invisible to those employers who have not put tools in place to see them, but also these youth often don't have insight into the nature of their own true potential and what undreamt-of opportunities that potential could allow them to access.

Solving our nation's youth employment challenge will require advancing the ways that talent markets work to identify young people with the specific aptitudes that drive success on the dimensions employers value. In order to promote timely and technical innovation that works to bridge these gaps, the social sector must work closely with employers while ensuring that the resulting tools successfully reach the populations most in need. Data-driven hiring will solve one critical part of a systemic problem. A range of other supports will be required to address the specific gaps in job readiness and challenging life circumstances that distinct segments of opportunity youth face. The more that provision of these supports can also be informed by data and analysis, the better we will be able to move the ecosystem of youth employment from a cottage industry of local programs to a scalable, market-driven effort. From both the perspective of human need and the perspective of economic value, this is an opportunity from which we cannot turn away.

Notes

1 Although we believe these experiments were well designed, they are foremost a pragmatic exploration of a solution and not rigorous academic research—they are best viewed as an early indicator rather than a settled empirical result.
2 Bouchey, H., & Glynn, S. J. (2012). *There are significant business costs to replacing employees*. Washington, DC: Center for American Progress.

3 Workforce Institute. (2008). *Retaining your best hourly workers.* Lowell, MA; Kronos Institute

4 Launched in August 2015, the 100,000 Opportunities Initiative is the largest employer-led coalition focused on hiring opportunity youth.

5 Hossain, F., & Bloom, D. (February 2015). *Toward a better future: Evidence on improving employment outcomes for disadvantaged youth in the United States.* Washington, DC: MDRC.

10

IDENTIFYING AND MANAGING TALENT IN THE AGE OF ARTIFICIAL INTELLIGENCE

Reece Akhtar, Dave Winsborough, Darko Lovric, and Tomas Chamorro-Premuzic

The Talent Economy: Present State and Future Prospects

Twenty years have now passed since McKinsey declared the beginning of the *war for talent*, postulating that people, in particular high-performing employees, would become a key asset to organizations, just like their products, services, IP, or brands. In line with this notion, organizations are immersed in what might be described as a war to attract, engage, and retain top talent, and this people-imperative is a critical driver of organizational effectiveness across all types of industries and sectors. The rise of talent management divisions within human resources (HR) departments during the past two decades illustrates the notable impact that McKinsey's premise has had on organizations. In fact, most of the traditional and process-based elements of HR have been automated by technology, making talent management the key strategic initiative of HR, as well as many organizations' formal attempt to win the war for talent.

Despite unprecedented investment in talent and the near-unanimous acceptance of McKinsey's idea during the past two decades, there is no indication that organizations have mastered the art of attracting and retaining talented people, or that they are even getting better at it. Of course, *some* organizations may feel justifiably pleased with their ability to appeal to highly sought-after employees—for example, top Ivy league students, quantitative Wunderkinds, and high-potential leaders. But for every Google, Goldman Sachs, and Amazon, there are thousands of organizations struggling to fill pivotal roles with strong candidates, and even among top Silicon Valley and Wall Street firms, the demand for top talent surpasses supply, at least in the eyes of their talent management departments. And if the most successful organizations in the world have big problems with talent, the situation is even more problematic for the majority of employers, as data from global employee surveys suggest.

For example, surveys that monitor employee engagement levels around the world have consistently reported that as much as 87% of the global workforce is not engaged (Mann & Harter, 2016). In the United States alone, it has been estimated that disengagement results in a productivity loss of around $500-billion a year, a figure that is calculated by extrapolating typical performance differences between engaged and disengaged employees (Sorenson & Garman, 2016). However, given that disengagement is also a cause of counterproductive work behaviors, such as bullying, harassment, theft, and corporate fraud, there are probably bigger financial consequences to it. Thus, although engagement is positively associated with individual, team, and organizational performance, even in organizations that understand the return on investment of engagement and invest unprecedented resources on boosting it, only about 30% of the workforce appears to be reasonably engaged.

Other than being a predictor of critical organizational outcomes, disengagement is also an important diagnostic of leadership effectiveness. Indeed, around 30% of the variability in team- and organization-level engagement can be attributed to the manager or leader, which suggests that even the most successful organizations are experiencing leadership problems (Kim, Kolb, & Kim, 2012). Academic reviews estimate that the baseline for leadership failure is around 50% (Hogan, Curphy, & Hogan, 1994), and opinion polls report a strong negative correlation between the amount of money spent on leadership selection and development interventions, and people's confidence in their leaders (Kaiser & Curphy, 2013). One only has to search "my boss is" or "my manager is" to get a sense of the typical experience employees have of their bosses. As the saying goes, people join companies but quit their bosses.

At times, people don't just quit their bosses, but traditional employment altogether. Indeed, a third salient indicator of organizations' struggle with the war for talent is the growing appeal of self-employment, even in strong economic circumstances where job opportunities abound. According to estimates, by 2020, 40% of the U.S. workforce will have been self-employed at some point in their career (Neuner, 2013), and throughout the 35 counties belonging to The Organisation for Economic Co-operation and Development (OECD) self-employment levels are at historically high rates relative to unemployment levels (OECD, 2017). Although people will generally increase their job satisfaction when they transition from traditional to self-employment, they will typically work more to earn less and contribute less to the overall economy than when they are employed by someone else. By the same token, there has been a recent surge in start-up activity even in low unemployment areas, with a growing number of people fantasizing of being the next Steve Jobs or Elon Musk, though the odds of attaining such levels of success are rather dismal. Failure rates have historically been very high for new ventures, with only 30% of businesses growing beyond a one-man venture and 70% dying during the first decade.

Given these circumstances, it is easy to be optimistic about the future of the talent economy, but only because in some ways, it is hard for things to get worse. More specifically, the war for talent resembles a war *on* talent, with organizations repelling, alienating, and mismanaging the majority of their employees, including top talent. To be sure, the essence of talent is unlikely to change so long as humans inhabit the workplace. In line with Chamorro-Premuzic, Akhtar, Winsborough, and Sherman (2017), we argue that talent will always be understood in terms of four basic heuristics, namely:

1. *The rule of the vital few:* As illustrated by Pareto's principle, in any group or collective of individuals, a relatively small proportion of members will account for a disproportionately large amount of group output or performance. These "vital few" may be considered an organization's "top talent."
2. *The maximal performance rule:* There is a well-known premise within I-O Psychology that stipulates that the best way to test a person's ability is by evaluating the best they *can do*. Regardless of the talent domain, this so-called *maximal performance* rule will always be useful to identify systematic individual differences in talent or competence. Importantly, people must want to do their best in order to display their talents, so there is no reason to expect individuals to perform to the best of their capabilities at all points in time (Sackett, 2007).
3. *The effortless performance rule:* Another classic I-O tenet essentially defines performance as talent + effort. Simple algebra then suggests that, talent = performance—effort. In other words, talented people will generally require less effort to achieve a certain level of performance than their less talented counterparts will. In other words, when individuals exert the same level of effort, performance differences between them will remain, unless they have the exact same level of talent. By the same token, early manifestations of talent, such as precocious talent, stand out because of their effortless performance: for example, Messi in football, Mozart in music, and Marie Curie in science. With limited training and practice, they are able to surpass more seasoned and experienced, but less talented, counterparts.
4. *Personality in the right place:* A final heuristic that will remain in place for understanding talent in the future is that talent emerges from personality being in the right place. That is, when there is a strong match between people's default predispositions and the characteristics of their respective jobs or roles, their talent emerges as result, which fuels future career development. In line with this idea, all talent management interventions can ultimately be seen as an attempt to enhance person-job fit, and in turn job performance.

It is also important to acknowledge that despite the rapidly changing circumstances of work, the essential ingredients of talent are unlikely to change any time soon, at least when it comes to human talent. Thus in any domain of competence or expertise, an individual's probability to be designated as "talented" will increase if he/she is more able, socially skilled, and driven (Hogan, Chamorro-Premuzic, & Kaiser, 2013). Ability includes both general intelligence and domain-specific expertise, encompassing what a person can learn and has learned. Social skills concern empathy, intra- and interpersonal competence, and likability. Drive concerns ambition and conscientiousness, which can accelerate or inhibit any degree of talent. In an age when organizations devote an enormous amount of time to creating their own extensive competency models, often to reinvent the wheel or introduce an unnecessary level of complexity, talent management practitioners would be well advised to remain focused on these general ingredients of talent in order to identify their most valuable employees, as well as those who will likely add more value in the future. That is, even if the jobs of the future are hard to define, it is a safe bet to expect individuals who are more rather than less able, socially skilled, and driven, to excel in them.

The Old World: Current Talent Management Tools

Science and practice rarely move in tandem, with one often lagging behind the other. This is true for talent management. Although HR departments are becoming more evidence based, the past 100 years in the field of personnel psychology have seen significant developments and innovations. Using theory, data, and statistical modeling, a great deal is now known about how to identify those individuals who have the potential to perform and create value for their organizations. In order to understand where talent management is going, it is important to understand where it has been and where we currently are. In this section, we review three popular practices, highlighting their strengths and limitations.

Interviews

It seems almost inconceivable that any form of selection task and decision is not informed by one, indeed many, job interviews. In fact, it is estimated that 90% of employment selection decisions involve interviews (Cook, 2004) and have been used in selection for over two centuries (e.g., the Royal Navy used job interviews as early as 1800). Whether it comes at the beginning or end of the selection process, the selection interview is thought to be a crucial and central part of the process, whereby the employer and applicant can help achieve a mutual understanding of one another and make inferences about the suitability of the applicant. Of all the selection methods, they are rated as the most acceptable method (Cook, 2004). Given their ubiquity, are interviews sufficient to identify talented employees?

A seminal meta-analysis by Cook (2004) investigated the predictive validity of interviews on job performance from over 500 studies and found that the validity coefficient for unstructured interviews as predictors of job performance is $r = .15$, whereas the validity for structured interviews is around $r = .28$. There may be rather different reactions to this validity coefficient. An optimist might point out that overall, the validity is impressively high, given the many differences in interview technique—some are psychological, some situational, some job related—and the fact that they were attempting to assess very different traits from creativity to conscientiousness. Indeed, compared to various other job selection methods, this result is impressive. The pessimist, however, may point out that a value of $r = .25$ means in effect an interview is accounting for a paltry 5%–6% in of the variance in later work behavior. That is, it is not accounting for about 95% of the variance.

Whether one is an optimist or a pessimist in terms of validity, there are other important issues associated with interviews. First, they are costly and demand a significant amount of time from both the interviewer and the candidate. Not only does this create scalability issues when trying to identify talent at volume, interviews are unlikely to deliver a return on investment when compared to the cost, delivery, and validity of other methods and tools. Second, the interview process and the subsequent decision might be influenced by implicit cognitive biases and heuristics. Implicit biases and heuristics shape the way interviewers view the world, process information, make decisions, and form judgments of others, all happening because of our cognitive load is made easier, interviewers are operating under time and social pressures, and so on. Biases and heuristics can sometimes be useful and efficient, but they can also be prone to inaccuracies, overgeneralizations, and stereotypes. Given the interpersonal nature of interviews, implicit heuristics have shown some evidence for adversely impacting the success of minority groups in interview contexts (Purkiss, Perrewé, Gillespie, Mayes, & Ferris, 2006). Conversely, interviewers are more likely to form favorable judgments of others who are of a similar demographic, background, and life history. Together, these points raise the question whether interviews cause more organizational and personal harm than good.

It is unlikely that interviews will ever disappear, nor should they. That said, how can we make them better? Cook (2004) offers evidence-based recommendations for improving interview reliability and validity:

1. Select talented interviewers. Many studies have demonstrated considerable interviewer variability, meaning some people are better interviewers than others. It is, therefore, important to identify and train those people.
2. Be consistent using the same interviewers for all interviews or use panel interviewers as they are more reliable and avoids unwanted variance due to the idiosyncrasies of any individual interviewer.
3. Have planned, structured interviews with clarity about precisely what questions to ask (Chamorro-Premuzic & Furnham, 2010).

Biodata

Biodata measures have informed selection decisions for many years and are still widely used in certain areas of employment, such as sales and insurance. In broad terms, biodata measures include information about a person's background and life history (e.g., civil status, previous education, and employment), ranging from objectively determined dates—date of first job, time in last job, years of higher education—to subjective preferences, such as those encompassed by personality traits. Biodata are most commonly collected through resumes and job application forms.

The main assumption underlying the use of biodata is that the "best predictor of future performance is past performance" (Wernimont & Campbell, 1968), though biodata focus as much on the *predictors* of past performance as on past performance itself. Indeed, it has been argued that one of the greatest potential routes for understanding and improving the prediction of work performance is the relationship between individuals' life history and their performance at work (Flieshman, 1988), a question directly related to biodata. Is there evidence to support this assumption?

A meta-analysis by Bliesener (1996) involving over 100 samples found that, when correcting for methodological artefacts and statistical errors, the overall validity for biodata inventories was $r = .22$. Interestingly, Bliesener's results showed that biodata were a more valid predictor of occupational success for women ($r = .51$) than for men ($r = .27$). Thus, Bliesener concluded that "Biographical data are a valid predictor of an applicant's suitability. This, combined with their high economy, their universal applicability and the ease of combining them with other predictive procedures, makes them a valuable instrument in personnel selection" (1996, p. 118).

Given that biodata measures are able to exceed the validity and limitations of interviews, what are its drawbacks? First, for biodata to be a valid, they must be first scored correctly. In practice, this is often not the case, such as when resumes and application forms are judged subjectively as a check for basic requirements and to inform an interview discussion. Applying a sound scoring methodology is preferred to human judgments that are subject to the aforementioned biases, heuristics, idiosyncrasies, and inconsistencies. Fortunately, there are multiple methodologies practitioners can choose when scoring biodata, with different advantages and disadvantages, such as *empirical keying* (which weights responses according to their correlations with the criterion) or *factorial keying* (items statistically reduced to a handful of general factors). Secondly, although biodata are prone to faking, as recruiters rarely invest the time to follow up with references and do appropriate investigative work because of time restrictions. Similarly, research has shown that when comparing biodata between applicants and incumbents, and when scored correctly, the former have inflated scores (Harold, McFarland, & Weekley, 2006). This demonstrates that just like interviews, biodata measures are susceptible to impression management and faking-good.

Psychometric Assessments

The scientific study of individual differences adopts a perspective whereby dispositions in thought, feelings, and behavior are continuous, roughly normally distributed, and can be accurately measured through data-driven practices called psychometrics. Psychometric assessments are survey-like tools that seek to measure relevant psychological constructs. Not only do they overcome the limitations of both interviews and biodata; psychometrically developed assessments have the potential to offer superior predictive validity. Two psychological constructs that have received the most attention and practical use are personality and cognitive ability.

There are many models and taxonomies of personality (i.e., temporally and situationally stable behavioral tendencies and characteristics), yet the most influential and empirically supported framework is the "Five Factor Model" (McCrae & Costa, 1987). According to this model, personality can be organized around five broad, distinct, and continuous dimensions: openness, conscientiousness, extroversion, agreeableness, and emotional stability. Each of the five dimensions has been found to predict critical work outcomes. For example, conscientiousness and job performance ($r = .22$; Barrick & Mount, 1991), extraversion and leadership effectiveness ($r = .19$; Bono & Judge, 2004), openness and innovation ($r = .49$; Batey, Chamorro-Premuzic, & Furnham, 2010), agreeableness and organizational citizenship ($r = .36$; Ilies, Scott, & Judge, 2006), and emotional stability and job burnout ($r = .36$; Bakker, Van Der Zee, Lewig, & Dollard, 2006).

Intelligence describes the extent to which people can solve complex problems, understand abstract patterns, and engage in critical thought (Chamorro-Premuzic & Furnham, 2010). Of all the psychological constructs and tools to identify talent, intelligence remains the single most predictive construct of positive work outcomes. A meta-analysis by (Hunter & Hunter, 1984) found that intelligence consistently predicted job performance across multiple levels of job complexity, with validity coefficients ranging between .23 and .58. Similarly, another meta-analysis by Bertua, Anderson, and Salgado (2005) found intelligence to predict job and training performance ($r = .48$; $r = .50$). In fact, when intelligence tests are combined with other selection tools such as interviews or personality assessment, the predictive validity can increase to over .60, which is likely near the ceiling of the predictive power of selection tests.

Despite their evidence in support of predictive validity, psychometric assessments are not without their limitations. First, they can be cumbersome and lengthy to complete, resulting in a poor user experience. Second, they may lack face validity and therefore be treated with suspicion by the test taker. Third, they rely on self-assessment and therefore raising concerns around faking-good. Although this is not an issue with intelligence tests, as there is a right or wrong answer, this final point has created much debate within the field given mixed evidence that faking does or does not harm their utility and validity (Schmitt, 2013). Fortunately, the next generation of assessments are quickly providing solutions to these limitations.

The New World: Artificial Intelligence and Deep Data

As William Gibson once said, the future is already here, just not very evenly distributed. This is the case with the use of innovative methodologies and tools for talent identification: some organizations are experimenting with novel approaches, but their use is patchy and inconsistent. For the most part, anyone who went through an employment interview or assessment center 50 years ago would recognize the modern version is more or less unchanged, except that paper questionnaires are now completed on a smartphone or computer, and interviews may be done over Skype. The technologies of the last 75 years have merely been computerized.

On the other hand, the unprecedented growth of digital records is emerging as a resource for those seeking to identify or understand how best to manage talented individuals. Unprecedented is exactly the right word: Facebook counts nearly one third of all human beings as active users (2.07 billion people or 27% of the world's population) and has achieved this growth in less than a decade. Other platforms (LinkedIn, Instagram, Twitter, Snapchat, WeChat, VKontakte, WhatsApp, and so on) have similarly accumulated hundreds of millions of users. LinkedIn, for example, has nearly half a billion workers who have willingly provided it with their work histories, aspirations, skills qualifications, endorsements, and most important business connections.

This mass of data has created the conditions for two significant shifts in HR practice. First, it has made public, and easily searchable, detailed information about employees and candidates in a way that has never previously been possible (Slovensky & Ross, 2012; Van Iddekinge, Lanivich, Roth, & Junco, 2016). Correspondingly, these platforms have begun to play an important role in HR recruitment and hiring, founded on the belief that people are more open and revealing online or share information that would otherwise be withheld from job applications. A recent survey found that in the United States, 84% of firms use social media sites for recruitment and *cybervetting* is growing; 44% use candidate social media profiles to screen candidates; and 36% have disqualified candidates on the basis of information found (Society for Human Resource Management, 2017). To place these figures in context, social media as a predictor in hiring decisions are as prevalent as the existing use of behavioral interviews (26% of employers), situational judgment tests (23%), cognitive ability test use (16%–20%), and growing to the levels of aptitude test use (42% of employers; Davison, Bing, Kluemper, & Roth, 2016; Rogelberg, 2006).

The second shift is the transformation of these digital records and data into descriptions and predictions of behavior, potentiating a range of tools and insights that are genuinely novel. It is our firm belief that the effects of digitization, although significant, are not yet profound and will grow ever more impactful. We coined the phrase "talent signals" to describe how individuals' online behavior (encompassing dynamic activity as texts posts, updates, tweets, photos, videos, likes, hashtags, browser use, browser history, settings, and other technical arcana; and static information such as user's provide in profiles) represent identity claims and reliable individual differences (Chamorro-Premuzic, Winsborough, Sherman, Hogan, 2013; Winsborough & Chamorro-Premuzic, 2016). A corpus of research findings is steadily accumulating and showing not just that talent signals can be identified, but used to make meaningful predictions about future behavior.

The original work in this area was done by Dr. Michal Kosinski. In a series of studies, Kosinski showed that a computer algorithm could be trained to interpret the pattern of "likes" on Facebook and produce startlingly accurate classifications of users personality, gender, voting preferences, and even sexual orientation (Kosinski, Stillwell, & Graepel, 2013; Lambiotte & Kosinski, 2014; Schwartz et al., 2013). Others have replicated this work, extending the findings to relationships between the images people post, their language, and even dark side personality traits — unconscious traits which negatively affect performance at work and interpersonal relationships (Akhtar, Winsborough, Ort, Johnson, & Chamorro-Premuzic, 2018; Liu, Preot, & Ungar, 2016; Ortigosa, Carro, & Quiroga, 2014).

There are three reasons that we believe this work represents a powerful new approach to talent identification. First, online behavior is not significantly different from off-line behavior. Although people may attempt to project themselves differently online, the cross-situational effects of personality "leak" and ultimately reflect the underlying self. Mitja Back and colleagues compared personality ratings gleaned from social media profiles against self-report personality scores and ideal self-ratings for 236 people. They found that the social media profiles were more closely aligned with user's actual vs. their descriptions of their "best selves," suggesting that online presence is an extension of real-world presence (Back et al., 2010). Other findings confirm that raters can accurately determine user personality from examination of their Facebook profiles (Gosling, Gaddis, & Vazire, 2007; Tskhay & Rule, 2014) or their LinkedIn profiles (van de Ven, Bogaert, Serlie, Brandt, & Denissen, 2017).

Second, algorithmic analysis of digital data sources has the distinct advantage of a wider set of behavioral samples and consistent approaches. Research shows that machine-learning algorithms are better judges of personality than friends and family because they can process much wider range of behavioral signals (Bachrach, Kosinski, Graepel, Kohli, & Stillwell, 2012; Youyou, Kosinski, & Stillwell, 2015).

Finally, as long as organizations have robust criteria, their ability to identify novel signals will increase, even if those signals are unusual or counterintuitive. Since talent signals lsuch asike, personality have long been shown to be highly predictive of a range of work-relevant outcomes (Hogan & Holland, 2003; Kuncel, Ones, & Sackett, 2010), and it has been shown that personality can be reliably inferred from social media data; so therefore, it is reasonable to hypothesize that signals obtained from thin slices of digital data should be predictive of work behavior. Early work looks promising: Kluemper found Facebook-rated personality traits correlate with supervisor ratings and academic success (Kluemper, Rosen, & Mossholder, 2012). Or consider that at least at present, job applicants who use Firefox or Chrome as their web browsers are likely to stay in their jobs longer and perform better than those who use Internet Explorer or Safari (Dubner & Werth 2015). Knowing which browser candidates submitted their online applications through may turn out to be a weak but still useful talent signal, because browser usage, performance, and employment longevity appears to be associated with the initiative required to download a non-native browser (Dubner & Werth 2015). In other contexts, digital signals of personality have been shown to predict purchasing activity: matching advertisements to people's extraversion or openness level resulted in up to 40% more clicks and up to 50% more purchases than mismatching or unpersonalized appeals (Matz, Kosinski, Nave, & Stillwell, 2017; Matz & Netzer, 2017).

The outworking of the talent signals approach is beginning to appear in real-world applications used by companies hiring and developing talent. For example, the ubiquitous interview is being supplanted (or augmented) by digital interviews that rely on consumer grade equipment to translate candidates vocal and facial behaviors into a psychological profile or an estimate of their potential fit for a role, based on the prediction of their future job performance or employee engagement level. Firms such as Precire in Germany or Hirevue in the United States are providing platforms that allow candidates to be interviewed online, at any time convenient to them; then they subject the interview to analysis by human judges from the hiring organization, or purely by algorithm. The promise of such approach is the standardization of the interview process, making it more objective and cost-efficient, while reducing the impact of interviewer biases. Research within this field has found verbal and nonverbal channels of communication (i.e., vocal characteristics, facial expressions, and body movements) to be valid predictors of personality traits (Biel, Tsiminaki, Dines, & Gatica-Perez, 2013; Bombari, Schmid Mast, Canadas, & Bachmann, 2015; Nguyen, Frauendorfer, Mast, & Gatica-Perez, 2014). Nguyen found that social sensing technology could explain 29% of the variance in hiring decisions, over and above survey measures of the Big Five and cognitive ability (Nguyen & Gatica-Perez, 2016).

More dramatically, gamification is beginning to emerge in a variety of talent applications, although few of these are yet mainstream. Efforts to make assessments more game-like (e.g., engaging, competitive, visually appealing) are based on three observations. First, similarities exist between playing online role-playing games and the situations in the workplace, like discussing plans, cooperating in teams, and giving each other feedback (Yee, 2006). Second, there is considerable overlap between the mental processes needed to win at video games and those that define work-relevant abilities such as intelligence, integrity, and curiosity (Ewell, Guadagno, Jones, & Dunn, 2016; Foroughi, Serraino, Parasuraman, & Boehm-Davis, 2016; Unsworth et al., 2015). RedBull, for example, has gamified aspects of its online assessment tool, which is designed to provide career-relevant feedback for the candidate, encourage competition and connection with peers, and to identify good talent for the company (Leutner, Yearsley, Codreanu, Borenstein, & Ahmetoglu, 2017).

Looking out further, we can imagine applications extending the range of inputs that they utilize to create more detailed insights and understanding of the people working in a company. Blockchains might one day store all the data scattered across Facebook, LinkedIn, company databases, wearables, and smartphones, allowing algorithms to interpret it and help individuals and managers determine best fit with roles, particular projects, or even team mates. Although this may seem creepy or intrusive, if users are provided with effective controls and the ability to grant or rescind permission to access the data, the result could be a much more engaging and rewarding workplace that better fits individual talents, preferences, and abilities. Managers could be coached by their own digital assistant to change their behavior to get the best from employees; staff could review their actions and choices to learn how to address problems and mitigate potential biases.

On the other hand, problems accessing and using these data bring real concerns. For example, many social media sites include information that may identify users as members of a protected class (Jeanneret, 2007), rendering the data unusable. A recent study found that profiling by human judges from social media revealed evidence of group differences in favor of whites (Van Iddekinge, Lanivich, Roth, & Junco, 2016) which raises the specter of discrimination. Then too, ethnic differences exist in the use of various social media sites (Duggan, 2015), as does differential use by personality types (Correa, Hinsley, & de Zúñiga, 2010). Although advocates of machine learning argue that human bias is endemic, idiosyncratic, and hard to detect, and that algorithms can *correct* for bias, concerns remain that the training sets required to produce fair assessments are hard to accumulate.

Then too, some applicants feel that their privacy had been invaded (Stoughton, Thompson, & Meade, 2013) by data scraping, and a successful/unsuccessful hiring decision did not moderate that sense. Berkelaar suggests that transparency—in that organizations declare to candidates what they will access and why—should become the currency of screening for job selection (which applies as much to traditional methods and novel ones).

Getting Ready for the Brave New World

Talent is vital to a well-functioning economy and society—properly deployed, it drives progress for all, while offering a chance to pursue excellence and meaning to the large portion of the workforce. A society with talented leaders and professionals is a society on its way to a better tomorrow. At the very least, this is the vision of what drives many expert practitioners and researchers to engage in the topic of improved talent assessment.

While the notion of meritocracy can be critically examined (Young, 1958), it is hard to argue with the logic that society needs to assess talents of its workforce and that accomplishing this task more accurately is both instrumentally and morally beneficial.

Increasingly accurate assessment of talent entails freedom from bias and prejudice, and capability of identifying more nuanced talent differences as well as latent talents that may blossom with the right exposure.

In this chapter, we explored how new digital talent signals may increase both the validity and reliability of the talent assessments, providing vastly improved tools for talent management.

Powerful new technologies frequently lead to ethical dilemmas and unintended consequences, especially in the field of artificial intelligence (Wallach, 2015).

Although organizations that will leverage these new tools will likely turn to select few providers, ultimate responsibility for how these novel assessments will be effectively deployed will not rest with the providers, but with their own legal and HR departments. To accomplish this task effectively and realize the promise of more accurate talent assessments while minimizing unintended consequences, organizations must develop four new capabilities in their HR departments:

1 **Data literacy** can be defined as the ability to interpret collected data and reach valid inferences, based on the understanding of mathematical tools of statistics and basic algebra applied to those data (Schield, 2004). In other words, data literacy turns data into information, and information into knowledge. Organizations, teams, and employees differ in the quantity and quality of data habitually used to reach business decisions, and the depth of the analysis used—data literacy is heterogeneous within each organization. Talent departments in most organizations rely on relatively simple structured data based on human judgment (e.g., scores on a structured interview of performance score sheet) that do not require high levels of data literacy. Therefore, the bottleneck to new more nuanced talent signals in most organizations is not the theoretical availability of the data or new solutions, but the lack of inclination and knowledge to collect, use, interpret, and trust these data to reach better talent decisions.

2 **Algorithmic bias** occurs when the data used to develop and refine algorithms reflect implicit values of the society in ways that are judged as irrational or unfavorable. To take a simple fictional example, a recruiting algorithm could identify that recruits from a certain college are more likely to rapidly advance in an organization and therefore assign a favorable rating to new applicants from that college, even if such rating were the result of an organizational bias favoring an "Ivy League network" rather than a reflection of talent. Detecting and dealing with algorithmic bias requires significantly

more advanced data literacy, especially as new talent frameworks are being selected and calibrated. These skills need to exist to select the right providers and the right data for the new talent signals—such judgment obviously can't be outsourced to the providers. Inability to critically evaluate the context of data collection and therefore assuming that the data collected are objective and valid, even though its design and the underlying data capture may reflect inherent biases of designers or human systems, is a key risk in use of these systems (Kitchin, 2016). To make this distinction clearer, we can use Drucker's (2011) distinction between "data," which is assumed to be objective/given, and "capta," which is assumed to be actively selected/taken. The field of talent analytics is especially prone to the risks of algorithmic biases, because these algorithms explicitly deal with "capta" reflecting the human judgment of other human beings, an arena where many of our collective biases and assumptions are particularly salient.

3 **Maintaining privacy** is crucial if new talent signals are going to be widely adopted and accepted, as well as lead to individual and social improvements we hope for. Recent news events regarding social media data clearly point to the critical societal need for data privacy. The majority of organizations are aware of their obligation to maintain employee privacy, safety, and security and to provide transparency on how their data are collected and used. However, new talent signals are significantly more intrusive, tracking a wide range of employee behaviors out of which one could potentially infer a range of personal characteristics (e.g., health status). Therefore, data standards associated with new talent signals often need to go beyond existing company data standards, and a systematic approach of opting-in and developing trust will be required to ensure adoption. This includes offering assurances that the individual data collected will be used only for the specific purpose for which it is gathered, and that the other data will be used only in sufficiently aggregated way to ensure individual anonymity, as is reflected in international perspectives on these issues (World Economic Forum, 2011).

4 **Measuring business impact** is key to ensure that the talent signals are indeed reflecting job effectiveness. To increase the validity of talent signals, it is important to precisely and accurately attribute job output to individuals—a feat that is often difficult to accomplish outside of sports and other games, where the rules for behaving, scoring, and winning are well understood and agreed upon. Indeed, most likely applications of new types of talent analytics are in areas where direct link between behavior and output can be precisely established, such as trading, sales, or call center environments. In other areas, the precision of new tools to track behavior will be limited by the precision to measure the actual job output of individuals.

Promise of novel talent analytics techniques will only be realized within the context of accurate data literacy, careful de-biasing of data, user trust, and accurate attribution of performance. Neglecting any of these four key components may lead not only failing to achieve a promise of a more accurate talent assessment, but actually underperforming the existing methods of talent evaluation. However, if these conditions are realized, we can look forward to the world in which talent assessments will be more accurate, and our collective talents better deployed to the benefit of us all.

References

Akhtar, R., Winsborough, D., Ort, U., Johnson, A., & Chamorro-Premuzic, T. (2018). Detecting the dark side of personality using social media status updates. *Personality and Individual Differences, 132*, 90–97.

Bachrach, Y., Kosinski, M., Graepel, T., Kohli, P., & Stillwell, D. (2012). Personality and patterns of facebook usage. *Proceedings of the 3rd Annual ACM Web Science Conference*, 24–32. Evanston, IL.

Back, M. D., Stopfer, J. M., Vazire, S., Gaddis, S., Schmukle, S. C., Egloff, B., & Gosling, S. D. (2010). Facebook profiles reflect actual personality not self-idealization. *Psychological Science, 21*(3), 372–374.

Bakker, A. B., Van Der Zee, K. I., Lewig, K. A., & Dollard, M. F. (2006). The relationship between the big five personality factors and burnout: A study among volunteer counselors. *Journal of Social Psychology, 146*(1), 31–50.

Barrick, M. R., & Mount, M. K. (1991). The big five personality dimensions and job performance : A meta analysis. *Personnel Psychology, 44*(1), 1–26.

Batey, M., Chamorro-Premuzic, T., & Furnham, A. (2010). Individual differences in ideational behavior: Can the big five and psychometric intelligence predict creativity scores? *Creativity Research Journal, 22*(1), 90–97.

Bertua, C., Anderson, N., & Salgado, J. F. (2005). The predictive validity of cognitive ability tests: A UK meta-analysis. *Journal of Occupational and Organizational Psychology, 78*(3), 387–409.

Biel, J.-I., Tsiminaki, V., Dines, J., & Gatica-Perez, D. (2013). Hi YouTube! Personality impressions and verbal content in social video. *Proceedings of the 15th ACM on International Conference on Multimodal Interaction*, 119–126. Sydney, Australia.

Bliesener, T. (1996). Methodological moderators in validating biographical data in personnel selection. *Journal of Occupational and Organizational Psychology, 69*(1), 107–120.

Bombari, D., Mast, M., Canadas, E., & Bachmann, M. (2015). Studying social interactions through immersive virtual environment technology: virtues, pitfalls, and future challenges. *Frontiers in Psychology, 6*, 869–880.

Bono, J. E., & Judge, T. A. (2004). Personality and transformational and transactional leadership. *A Metaanalysis Journal of Applied Psychology, 89*, 901–910.

Chamorro-Premuzic, T., & Furnham, A. (2010). *The psychology of personnel selection.* Cambridge, UK: Cambridge University Press.

Chamorro-Premuzic, T., Akhtar, R., Winsborough, D., & Sherman, R. A. (2017). The datafication of talent: How technology is advancing the science of human potential at work. *Current Opinion in Behavioral Sciences, 18*, 13–16.

Chamorro-Premuzic, T., Winsborough, D., Sherman, R. A., & Hogan, R. (2013). New talent signals: Shiny new objects or a brave new world. *Industrial and Organizational Psychology: Perspectives on Science and Practice, 53*(9), 1689–1699.

Cook, M. (2004). *Personnel selection: Adding value through people* (5th ed.). West Sussex, UK: Wiley Blackwell.

Correa, T., Hinsley, A. W., & de Zúñiga, H. G. (2010). Who interacts on the web?: The intersection of users' personality and social media use. *Computers in Human Behavior, 26*(2), 247–253.

Davison, K. K., Bing, M. N., Kluemper, D. H., & Roth, P. L. (2016). Social media as a personnel selection and hiring resource: Reservations and recommendations. In R. Landers and G. Schmidt (Eds.), *Social media in employee selection and recruitment: Theory, practice, and current challenges* (pp. 15–42). Cham, Switzerland: Springer.

Drucker, J. (2011). Humanities approaches to graphical display. *Humanities, 5*(1), 1–23.

Dubner, S. J., & Werth, C. (2015). The maddest men of all: A new freakonomics radio podcast. Freakonomics. Retrieved November 26, 2018, from http://freakonomics. com/podcast/the-maddest-men-of-all-a-new-freakonomics-radio-podcast/

Duggan, M. (2015). *The demographics of social media users.* Washington, DC: Pew Research Center

Ewell, P. J., Guadagno, R. E., Jones, M., & Dunn, R. A. (2016). Good person or bad character? Personality predictors of morality and ethics in avatar selection for video game play. *Cyberpsychology, Behavior, and Social Networking, 19*(7), 435–440.

Flieshman, E. A. (1988). Some new frontiers in personnel selection research. *Personnel Psychology, 41*(4), 679–701.

Foroughi, C. K., Serraino, C., Parasuraman, R., & Boehm-Davis, D. A. (2016). Can we create a measure of fluid intelligence using puzzle creator within portal 2? *Intelligence, 56*, 58–64.

Gosling, S. D. S. D., Gaddis, S., & Vazire, S. (2007). Personality impressions based on facebook profiles. *Proceedings of the International Conference on Weblogs and Social Media 2007*, 1–4. Boulder, Colorado.

Harold, C. M., McFarland, L. A., & Weekley, J. A. (2006). The validity of verifiable and non-verifiable biodata items: An examination across applicants and incumbents. *International Journal of Selection and Assessment, 14*(4), 336–346.

Hogan, J., & Holland, B. (2003). Using theory to evaluate personality and job-performance relations: A socioanalytic perspective. *Journal of Applied Psychology, 88*(1), 100–112.

Hogan, R., Chamorro-Premuzic, T., & Kaiser, R. B. (2013). Employability and career success: Bridging the gap between theory and reality. *Industrial and Organizational Psychology, 6*(1), 3–16.

Hogan, R. T., Curphy, G. J., & Hogan, J. (1994). What do we know about personality: Leadership and effectiveness. *American Psychologist, 49*, 493–504.

Hunter, J. E., & Hunter, R. F. (1984). Validity and utility of alternative predictors of job performance. *Psychological Bulletin, 96*(1), 72–98.

Ilies, R., Scott, B. A., & Judge, T. A. (2006). The interactive effects of personal traits and experienced states on intraindividual patterns of citizenship behavior. *Academy of Management Journal, 49*(3), 561–575.

Jeanneret, P. R. (2007). Professional and technical authorities and guidelines. *Employment Discrimination Litigation: Behavioral, Quantitative, and Legal Perspectives, 248*, 47–101.

Kaiser, R. B., & Curphy, G. (2013). Leadership development: The failure of an industry and the opportunity for consulting psychologists. *Consulting Psychology Journal: Practice and Research, 65*(4), 294–302.

Kim, W., Kolb, J. A., & Kim, T. (2012). The relationship between work engagement and performance: A review of empirical literature and a proposed research agenda. *Human Resource Development Review, 12*(3), 248–276.

Kitchin, R. (2016). Thinking critically about researching algorithms. *Information, Communication & Society, 20*(1), 14–29.

Kluemper, D. H., Rosen, P. A., & Mossholder, K. W. (2012). Social networking websites, personality ratings, and the organizational context: More than meets the eye? *Journal of Applied Social Psychology, 42*(5), 1143–1172.

Kosinski, M., Stillwell, D., & Graepel, T. (2013). Private traits and attributes are predictable from digital records of human behavior. *Proceedings of the National Academy of Sciences of the United States of America, 110*(15), 5802–5805.

Kuncel, N. R., Ones, D. S., & Sackett, P. R. (2010). Individual differences as predictors of work, educational, and broad life outcomes. *Personality and Individual Differences, 49*(4), 331–336.

Lambiotte, R., & Kosinski, M. (2014). Tracking the digital footprints of personality. *Proceedings of the IEEE, 102*(12), 1934–1939.

Leutner, F., Yearsley, A., Codreanu, S.-C., Borenstein, Y., & Ahmetoglu, G. (2017). From Likert scales to images: Validating a novel creativity measure with image based response scales. *Personality and Individual Differences, 106*, 36–40.

Liu, L., Preot, D., & Ungar, L. (2016). Analyzing personality through social media profile picture choice. *Proceedings of the Tenth International AAAI Conference on Web and Social Media*, 211–220. Cologne, Germany

Mann, A., & Harter, J. (2016). *The worldwide employee engagement crisis.* Retrieved May 15, 2018, from http://news.gallup.com/businessjournal/188033/worldwide-employee-engagement-crisis.aspx

Matz, S. C., & Netzer, O. (2017). Using big data as a window into consumers' psychology. *Current Opinion in Behavioral Sciences, 18*, 7–12.

Matz, S. C., Kosinski, M., Nave, G., & Stillwell, D. J. (2017). Psychological targeting as an effective approach to digital mass persuasion. *Proceedings of the National Academy of Sciences, 14*(48), 12714–12719.

McCrae, R. R., & Costa, P. T. (1987). Validation of the five-factor model of personality across instruments and observers. *Journal of Personality and Social Psychology, 52*(2), 81–90.

Neuner, J. (2013). 40% of America's workforce will be freelancers by 2020. Retrieved May 15, 2018, from https://qz.com/65279/40-of-americas-workforce-will-be-freelancers-by-2020/

Nguyen, L. S., & Gatica-Perez, D. (2016). Hirability in the wild: Analysis of online conversational video resumes. *IEEE Transactions on Multimedia, 18*(7), 1422–1437.

Nguyen, L. S., Frauendorfer, D., Mast, M. S., & Gatica-Perez, D. (2014). Hire me: Computational inference of hirability in employment interviews based on nonverbal behavior. *IEEE Transactions on Multimedia, 16*(4), 1018–1031.

OECD. (2017). *OECD Employment Outlook 2017.* The Organisation for Economic Co-operation and Development. Paris, France: OECD Publishing.

Ortigosa, A., Carro, R. M., & Quiroga, J. I. (2014). Predicting user personality by mining social interactions in Facebook. *Journal of Computer and System Sciences, 80*(1), 57–71.

Rogelberg, S. (2006). *Encyclopaedia of industrial and organizational psychology.* Thousand Oaks, CA: Sage.

Sackett, P. R. (2007). Revisiting the origins of the typical-maximum performance distinction. *Human Performance, 20*(3), 179–185.

Schield, M. (2004). Information literacy, statistical literacy and data literacy. *IASSIST Quarterly, 28*, (3), 6–11.

Schmitt, N. (2013). Personality and cognitive ability as predictors of effective performance at work. *Annual Review of Organizational Psychology and Organizational Behavior, 1*(1), 45–65.

Schwartz, H. A., Eichstaedt, J. C., Kern, M. L., Dziurzynski, L., Ramones, S. M., Agrawal, M., ... Ungar, L. H. (2013). Personality, gender, and age in the language of social media: The open-vocabulary approach. *PLoS ONE, 8*(9), e73791.

Purkiss, S. L., Perrewé, P. L., Gillespie, T. L., Mayes, B. T., & Ferris, G. R. (2006). Implicit sources of bias in employment interview judgments and decisions. *Organizational Behavior and Human Decision Processes, 101*(2), 152–167.

Society for Human Resource Management. (2017). Using social media for talent acquisition. Retrieved May 24, 2018, from https://www.shrm.org/hr-today/trends-and-forecasting/research-and-surveys/pages/social-media-recruiting-screening-2015.aspx

Slovensky, R., & Ross, W. H. (2012). Should human resource managers use social media to screen job applicants? Managerial and legal issues in the USA. *Info, 14*(1), 55–69.

Sorenson, S., & Garman, K. (2016). *How to tackle U.S. employees' stagnating engagement.* Retrieved May 15, 2018, from http://news.gallup.com/businessjournal/162953/tackle-employees-stagnating-engagement.aspx

Stoughton, J. W., Thompson, L. F., & Meade, A. W. (2015). Examining applicant reactions to the use of social networking websites in pre-employment screening. *Journal of Business and Psychology, 30*(1), 73–88.

Tskhay, K. O., & Rule, N. O. (2014). Perceptions of personality in text-based media and OSN: A meta-analysis. *Journal of Research in Personality, 49*(1), 25–30.

Unsworth, N., Redick, T. S., McMillan, B. D., Hambrick, D. Z., Kane, M. J., & Engle, R. W. (2015). Is playing video games related to cognitive abilities? *Psychological Science, 26*(6), 759–774.

van de Ven, N., Bogaert, A., Serlie, A., Brandt, M. J., & Denissen, J. J. A. (2017). Personality perception based on LinkedIn profiles. *Journal of Managerial Psychology, 32*(6), 418–429.

Van Iddekinge, C. H., Lanivich, S. E., Roth, P. L., & Junco, E. (2016). Social media for selection? Validity and adverse impact potential of a facebook-based assessment. *Journal of Management, 42*(7), 1811–1835.

Wallach, W. (2015). *A dangerous master: How to keep technology from slipping beyond our control.* New York, NY: Basic Books.

Wernimont, P. F., & Campbell, J. P. (1968). Signs, samples, and criteria. *Journal of Applied Psychology, 52*(5), 372–376.

Winsborough, D., & Chamorro-Premuzic, T. (2016). Talent identification in the digital world: New talent signals and the future of HR assessment. *People & Strategy, 39*(2), 28–31.

World Economic Forum. (2011). *Personal data : The emergence of a new asset class. Forum American Bar Association.* Retrieved from http://www.weforum.org/reports/personal-data-emergence-new-asset-class

Yee, N. (2006). The labor of fun: How video games blur the boundaries of work and play. *Games and Culture, 1*(1), 68–71.

Young, M. D. (1958). *The rise of the meritocracy.* New York, NY: Routledge.

Youyou, W., Kosinski, M., & Stillwell, D. (2015). Computer-based personality judgments are more accurate than those made by humans. *Proceedings of the National Academy of Sciences of the United States of America, 112*(4), 1036–1040.

PART IV
Policy

11

EDUCATION FOR WORKFORCE READINESS

Findings from Reports of the National Academies of Sciences, Engineering, and Medicine[1]

Margaret Hilton

Introduction

Employers and policymakers are concerned that the current national education system (including elementary, secondary, and higher education) is not fostering workforce readiness. They view the pool of graduates entering the workforce as weak in several domains of knowledge and skill. First, some U.S. high school and even college graduates are weak in basic reading, writing, and mathematics. An Organization for Economic Cooperation and Development (OECD) survey (2013) of youth and adults, aged 16–65, found that the U.S. average proficiency in both literacy and numeracy was below average compared to that in other advanced economies. Second, some graduates lack the understanding of science, technology, engineering, and mathematics (STEM) needed to deploy rapidly evolving workplace technologies effectively. Third, some graduates lack the so-called "21st-century skills," such as effective communication, complex problem-solving, and self-management. For over a decade, employers have consistently called for more workers with these skills (Casner-Lotto & Barrington, 2006; Hart Research Associates, 2010, 2015). They view the content students are exposed to in K-12 and higher education as highly abstract, academic, and not relevant to workplace needs.

This chapter draws on three recent reports of the National Academies of Sciences, Engineering, and Medicine (hereafter referred to as "the Academies") to argue that these concerns can be addressed by improving educational and performance *processes*, based on research into how people learn and apply knowledge. It identifies "21st-century skills" related to persistence and success in higher education and summarizes research on teaching, learning, and applying teamwork—an important element of workforce readiness.

Deeper Learning for Transfer of Knowledge and Skills

Current concerns about gaps in workforce readiness reflect a long-standing challenge in education—how to develop knowledge that individuals can transfer to new situations. Transfer is especially challenging in today's workplaces, as jobs become increasingly complex and tasks frequently change. With automation, jobs involving routine tasks are disappearing, and more complex jobs are growing. The most rapidly growing jobs require a mix of cognitive and social skills, including the capability to solve nonroutine problems; such skills are sometimes referred to as "21st-century skills" (Autor, Levy, & Murnane, 2003; Deming, 2015; Weinberger, 2014). Although interest in these skills is growing, a wide range of different and poorly defined terms are used to describe and discuss them, slowing large-scale coordinated efforts to teach them in K-12 or higher education.

To address this challenge, a National Research Council[2] (NRC) committee (2012b) was charged to more clearly define "deeper learning" and "21st-century skills." The committee organized various lists of 21st-century skills into three domains of competence: cognitive (thinking abilities, including memory, reasoning skills); interpersonal (expressing information to others and responding to others' communications); and intrapersonal (emotions and feelings, including self-regulation; see the figure on pg 202). The three domains are closely related within the individual; for example, interpersonal competencies require cognitive reflection and reasoning to interpret another's message accurately and formulate and express an appropriate response.

The NRC committee defined "deeper learning" as the process through which an individual becomes capable of taking what was learned in one situation and applying it to new situations (i.e., transfer; National Research Council, 2012b, p. 5). It proposed that the product of deeper learning was "transferable knowledge, including content knowledge in a domain and knowledge of how, why, and when to apply this knowledge to answer questions and solve problems" and referred to this blend of both knowledge and skills as "21st-century competencies." A person with these competencies structures his or her knowledge around fundamental principles of the domain, rather than recall of disparate or superficial facts and procedures, supporting transfer to new settings. When faced with a particular task, the person can more quickly recall relevant knowledge and decide how best to share and/or apply this knowledge to address the task, either individually or with others.

Developing Cognitive Competencies

Deeper learning in K-12 and higher education would begin to address the employer concerns identified above, helping students develop both knowledge and skills in the core subjects of reading and writing, mathematics, and science (National Research Council, 2012b). At the K-12 level, educational standards in English language arts, mathematics, and science include goals for deeper learning, along with a cluster of cognitive competencies—critical thinking, nonroutine problem-solving, and constructing and evaluating evidence-based arguments.

How can teachers and faculty support the deeper learning that develops transferable knowledge and skills? Over a century, research has been dedicated toward answering this critical question. An important first step is to clarify the learning goals and develop assessments to measure learners' progress toward the goals. In addition, deeper learning is supported by the following principles of instructional design:

- Focus on increasing students' understanding of the fundamental principles of a content domain, rather than rote memorization of specific problem-solving procedures;
- Represent concepts and tasks in various ways (e.g., diagrams, mathematical representations) and help students map across these varied representations;
- Encourage learners to elaborate, question, or explain material to themselves or their peers;
- Present challenging tasks, while also providing guidance, feedback, and encouragement;
- Use examples and cases, such as modeling the steps to solve a problem;
- Motivate learners by engaging them in collaborative problem-solving and focusing on the concepts and skills they are developing, rather than on grades or scores; and
- Use formative assessment[3] to monitor and provide feedback on learners' progress toward learning goals, and engage learners in assessing their own learning progress and that of their peers.

"Seeds of Science/Roots of Reading," a research-based reading and science curriculum for middle school students, is an example of the application of these principles (see http://www.scienceandliteracy.org/). Students work in small groups to conduct hands-on investigations, read, write, and discuss science topics. For example, in a unit focusing on sand, students investigate unknown, "mystery" sand, use models to understand the formation of sand on a beach, and read the biography of a sand scientist, describing how he or she studies sand to determine its origin. Students also write daily entries in their science journals and meet in small groups to debate scientific issues arising from the investigations and reading. These activities reflect the instructional design principles listed above (e.g., encouraging learners to elaborate, question, or explain material). In a study of 94 fourth-grade classrooms, half of the teachers were randomly assigned to use the integrated curriculum, while the other half taught science and English language arts separately. Students in the classrooms receiving the integrated curriculum showed significantly higher levels of science understanding, science vocabulary, and science writing than control group students who received the traditional, separate science and English lessons (Cervetti, Barber, Dorph, Pearson, & Goldschmidt, 2012).

The Limits of Transfer

Although instruction aligned with these principles has been shown to support students' development of transferable competencies *within* a specific domain of knowledge, research to date suggests that this learning and expertise is difficult to transfer into different domains. Based on early experiments over a century ago, Thorndike and Woodworth (1901) proposed that transfer depends on the extent to which elements of the training environment are identical to elements of the performance environment. Thorndike later refuted the idea that mastering Latin developed general "mental muscle" that could be transferred to another subject, such as English (Thorndike, 1923). Subsequently, de Groot (1965) and then Ericsson and colleagues (2006) found that experts who can easily solve problems in a particular domain, such as chess, are not able to transfer their problem-solving skills to other domains. Cognitive scientists have also found that problem-solving skills that are *not* specific to a domain of knowledge are usually slow and inefficient relative to domain-specific approaches (Newell & Simon, 1972). The NRC committee concluded that "research to date provides little guidance about how to help learners aggregate transferable competencies beyond disciplines" (p. 7). This is indeed a challenge to employers, who seek domain-general skills (e.g., critical thinking, problem-solving, creativity) that can be applied to constantly changing problems and tasks in today's dynamic workplaces.

Developing Intra- and Interpersonal Competencies

The body of research on intra- and interpersonal competencies is younger, less extensive, and less rigorous than the literature on deeper learning and acquisition of cognitive competencies. Nevertheless, the cognitive science-based principles of instructional design listed above could potentially be applied to support students' deeper learning of intra- and interpersonal competencies (National Research Council, 2012b). However, a lack of common definitions and high-quality assessments of these competencies would make it challenging to clarify the learning goals and assess students' learning progress. To address this gap, the NRC (2012b) recommended that funders "provide sustained support for the development of valid, reliable, and fair assessments of intrapersonal and interpersonal competencies" (p. 13).

The Importance of Competencies and Education

The NRC committee reviewed research linking various cognitive, interpersonal, and intrapersonal competencies to desired economic, societal, and personal outcomes, such as employment and earnings, civic engagement, and health. It concluded that the available research was limited and primarily correlational in nature. Most research has focused on cognitive competencies, showing consistent, positive (but modest) correlations with desired outcomes (National Research Council, 2012b). Among inter- and intrapersonal competencies, conscientiousness is most highly correlated with desired educational and career outcomes, while antisocial behavior is negatively correlated with these outcomes (pp. 4–5).

The committee noted that a separate and stronger body of research has found that educational attainment (years of completed schooling) is related to higher adult earnings, as well as greater health and civic participation. Since the 1960s, economists have consistently estimated beneficial returns to years of schooling, even as they applied more sophisticated research methods to eliminate sources of bias (e.g., the possibility that more motivated people self-select into higher education). In one example, Barrow and Rouse (2005) estimate that each additional year of schooling generates about 10% increase in annual earnings.

It appears that employers—despite their stated concern that schools and colleges are not adequately developing 21st-century skills—continue to value years of completed education and reward increased educational attainment with higher wages.

21st-Century Competencies Supporting Higher Education

To build on the conclusion about the importance of educational attainment and begin carrying out the recommendation for development of stronger assessments of intra- and interpersonal competencies, the National Science Foundation (NSF) asked the Academies to conduct a follow-on study. NSF charged the Academies to examine how to assess intra- and interpersonal competencies of undergraduate students and to identify a range of competencies that may be related to success in undergraduate education and that can be enhanced through intervention.

To frame its work, the new Academies committee focused on research linking various competencies to success *during* college, using measures such as persistence from year to year, grade point average (GPA), test scores, and, ultimately, graduation. In addition, the committee gave special attention to intervention studies as it sought to identify competencies that were malleable in response to intervention. Applying these lenses to the literature, the committee concluded that there are major gaps in the research. Little research is available on the potential relationships between (a) interpersonal competencies and students' college success; (b) intra- and interpersonal competencies and community college students' success; and (c) intra- and interpersonal competencies and success in STEM fields (National Academies of Sciences, Engineering, and Medicine, 2017).

Competencies Related to College Success

Despite the limited research base, the NAS committee was able to identify eight intrapersonal competencies that show evidence of a relationship to college success.[4] The evidence was most promising for the malleable competencies of sense of belonging, growth mindset, and utility goals and values. There is more modest evidence that five other competencies are both malleable and related to college success, yielding a total of eight identified competencies (National Academies of Sciences, Engineering, and Medicine, 2017):

- **Behaviors related to conscientiousness**—behaviors related to self-control, hard work, persistence, and achievement orientation;
- **Sense of belonging**—a student's sense that he or she belongs at a college, fits in well, and is socially integrated;
- **Academic self-efficacy**—a student's belief that he or she can succeed in academic tasks;
- **Growth mindset**—a student's belief that his or her own intelligence is not a fixed entity, but a malleable quality that can grow and improve;
- **Utility goals and values**—personal goals and values that a student perceives to be directly linked to the achievement of a future, desired end;
- **Intrinsic goals and interest**—personal goals that a student experiences as rewarding in and of themselves, linked to strong interest;
- **Prosocial goals and values**—the desire to promote the well-being or development of other people or of domains that transcend the self; and
- **Positive future self**—a positive image or personal narrative constructed by a student to represent what kind of person he or she will be in the future (pp. 5–6).

These competencies are often embedded within particular contexts or domains of knowledge, reflecting the earlier study's finding that "21st-century competencies" comprise closely intertwined content knowledge and skills in a domain (National Research Council, 2012b). For example, a sense of belonging has been defined in terms of feelings about a particular institution (e.g., Walton & Cohen, 2011) and/or a field of study (e.g., engineering, in Walton, Peach, Logel, Spencer, & Zanna, 2015). Utility value has been conceptualized as the perceived usefulness of certain courses or topics (e.g., high school science and mathematics courses, in Harackiewicz, Rozek, Hulleman, & Hyde, 2012).

Brief, low-cost interventions to develop these competencies sometimes resulted in the largest effects for student groups that historically have had lower college completion rates than other student groups. For example, first-year students participating in a sense of belonging intervention received survey information showing that upperclassmen at their institution had initially worried about being accepted by others at the institution, but that those concerns had lessened with time. The first-year students then wrote an essay and gave a speech on this same theme of belongingness (Walton & Cohen, 2011). Black students in the treatment group received significantly higher grades than Black students in the control group, and impressively, this effect lasted over a period of three years (through their senior year). In another example, introductory biology students participating in a utility-value intervention completed three brief essays explaining why specific course material was directly relevant or useful to their own lives (Harackiewicz, Canning, Tibbetts, Priniski, & Hyde, 2015). Relative to the control group, all students who received the intervention showed improvement in course grades, and the largest improvement was for underrepresented minority students who were also first-generation students.

Assessing Intra- and Interpersonal Competencies

The committee reviewed the nature and quality of existing assessments of intra- and interpersonal competencies. Its evaluation of assessment quality relied largely on the *Standards for Educational and Psychological Testing (Standards)*, sponsored jointly by the American Educational Research Association, American Psychological Association, and National Council of Measurement in Education (2014). The *Standards* define a trinity of principles—validity, reliability/precision, and fairness—as the foundation for sound measurement. In its review, the committee found that the assessments used in the intervention studies to develop the eight identified competencies relied primarily on self-report methods and sometimes reported on their psychometric reliability, but rarely reported evidence of validity or fairness (National Academies of Sciences, Engineering, and Medicine, 2017). Examining a small sample of more established assessment instruments, the committee found that those developed with sustained research funding provided evidence on reliability as well as validity, but still lacked evidence on fairness (see Box 12.1).

BOX 12.1: AN EXAMPLE OF SUSTAINED ASSESSMENT DEVELOPMENT

The Motivated Strategies for Learning Questionnaire (MSLQ) was developed, refined, and validated over a 10-year period with funding from the U.S. Department of Education (Pintrich, Smith, García, & McKeachie, 1991). This self-report instrument includes a motivation section with six rating scales and a learning strategies section with nine rating scales. Among these 15 total scales, the six that measure constructs overlapping with six of the eight competencies identified by the committee show moderate to good reliability.

The validity of the MSLQ derives partly from its basis in a strong theoretical model of college students' motivation and self-regulated learning strategies (Duncan & McKeachie, 2005). Confirmatory factor analysis and structural modeling, aligned with this theoretical model and using data from nearly 400 college students, provided empirical support for the validity of the measure (Pintrich, Smith, García, & McKeachie, 1993). Moreover, the developers found a relationship between students' scores on the 15 scales and course grades, providing modest evidence of predictive validity. Ideally, continued research and development of the instrument would examine and provide evidence related to the fairness of the instrument when used to measure motivation and learning strategies among different student subgroups (e.g., groups differing in race/ethnicity).

Based on its review, the committee concluded that current assessments of the eight identified competencies were uneven in quality, providing only limited evidence of validity, reliability, and fairness (National Academies of Sciences, Engineering, and Medicine, 2017, p. 8). Supporting this latter point, in a subsequent meta-analysis of 273 correlations between growth mindset and academic achievement, Sisk and colleagues (forthcoming) were unable to correct individual effect sizes for measurement unreliability, because very few of the studies had reported a reliability estimate for the growth mindset assessments used.

The committee examined the measurement methods currently used to assess intra- and interpersonal competencies generally (not only the eight identified competencies), finding that self-report measures with well-documented limitations were frequently used (National Academies of Sciences, Engineering, and Medicine, 2017). When responding to self-report questions, individuals may be motivated to present themselves in a favorable light and may tend to respond in habitual ways, such as marking the extremes (e.g., "strongly agree" or "strongly disagree") or responding positively regardless of the question. Noting that recent research has developed new methods that might overcome some of these limitations (e.g., forced-choice questions in place of rating scales), the committee echoed the earlier report's call for improved assessments. It recommended that "federal agencies and foundations support additional research, development, and validation of new intra- and interpersonal competency assessments that address the shortcomings of existing measures" (p. 11). Improved assessments require real investments in measure development, psychometric evaluation of reliability, outcomes data collection to support validity, and studies examining fairness between demographic groups taking the assessment.

Developing Team Readiness

The boundaries between jobs are blurring, as individuals across a range of industries and organizational types more frequently work in and across teams. Recognizing this trend, the NSF commissioned the Academies to conduct a study of how to enhance the effectiveness of collaborative research in science teams, research centers, and institutes. This study committee found that team-based research was growing: the fraction of all science and engineering publications written by teams of two or more authors grew from about 55% in 1960 to 90% in 2013, and the average number of authors also grew (National Research Council, 2015). At the same time, it found that science and engineering teams, as well as teams working in other industries, often encounter challenges related to communicating effectively, coordinating tasks, and understanding team goals (National Research Council, 2015). Recognizing the need for individuals who can overcome such challenges, employers often rank teamwork at or near the top of the 21st-century skills they seek (e.g., Casner-Lotto & Barrington, 2006). Employers responding to a recent survey by the National Association of Colleges and Employers (2017) indicated that, beyond GPA, they most valued—and viewed as equally important—problem-solving skills and the ability to work in teams.

Concomitant with this development, or perhaps because of it, both K-12 and higher education students increasingly participate in group and team learning activities. Research has shown that carefully designed group learning activities support students' mastery of concepts and skills in STEM (National Research Council, 2012a) and other subjects (National Research Council, 2012b). Although students gain experience working as part of a team, the instruction and assessment components focus on the mastery of subject matter—with no attention to teamwork or other interpersonal competencies. For example, in the study of the "Seeds of Science/Roots of Reading" curriculum described above, investigators assessed only students' cognitive competencies. Students may develop interpersonal competencies through the team investigations and small-group discussions, but those competencies were not assessed.

Learning in student teams is often assessed based on the team's product, such as a paper, presentation, or video (Britton, Simper, Leger, & Stephenson, 2015; Hughes & Jones, 2011), with little or no attention to the team *process*. The lack of attention to team processes can hinder students' learning. For example, in a review of 104 articles about student teams in undergraduate engineering and computer science, Borrego and colleagues (2013) found that the teams often encountered challenges, especially "social loafing" (a team member sits back and lets other team members carry out tasks). The articles reported that faculty tried to address these challenges and build trust among team members, but only a few discussed the relevant research from industrial/ organizational psychology on how to avoid social loafing and address other team challenges.

With the growth of online education, students may work in virtual teams. Although this can make it even more difficult for instructors to understand team processes and reinforce their tendency to focus only on the team's product or cognitive learning, students' use of technology can also facilitate assessment of teamwork, as discussed further below.

Challenges of Assessing and Developing Teamwork

Earlier, this chapter proposed that principles of instructional design drawn from cognitive research could plausibly be applied to design instruction that would support deeper learning of intra- and interpersonal competencies (National Research Council, 2012b). These design principles begin by clarifying learning goals and also include using formative assessment to monitor and provide feedback on students' learning progress. However, assessing teamwork competencies is challenging for conceptual and technical reasons.

A team has been defined as a complex, multilevel phenomenon composed of individual-, team-, and higher-level influences that unfold over time (Kozlowski & Klein, 2000). With this definition in mind, it is understandable why clarifying teamwork learning goals—which includes defining the knowledge and skills to be learned and assessed—is challenging. Just as research has illuminated the importance of the *learning process* (e.g., deeper learning) to support transfer and application of individual knowledge, research on teams has illuminated the importance of *team processes* for supporting transfer of knowledge and skills to perform tasks and achieve team goals (National Research Council, 2015). Team effectiveness includes not only a team's performance but also its capacity for future performance and outcomes for individual team members (e.g., satisfaction, willingness to engage in future team tasks). The effectiveness of any given team is influenced by team processes including "shared mental models" (a common understanding of goals, procedures, and roles; Cannon-Bowers, Salas, & Converse, 1993) and "transactive memory" (knowledge of who knows what within the team; Lewis, Lange, & Gillis, 2005; Wegner, Giuliano, & Hertel, 1985). In a meta-analysis, DeChurch and colleagues (2010) found that both of these processes are positively related to (and thus may facilitate) team effectiveness.

Research on teams echoes the previously mentioned findings from cognitive science about the limits of transfer. Team researchers propose that competencies for teamwork include the knowledge, skills, and attitudes of individual team members and the team as a whole, many of which are specific to a particular team's task and context (National Research Council, 2015). For example, Cannon-Bowers and colleagues (1995) identified three specific team competencies:

- Context-driven (specific to a particular task and a particular team)
- Task-contingent (specific to a particular task)
- Team-contingent (specific to a particular team)

The authors also identified a fourth, more general type of team competency, which they referred to as "transportable" (Cannon-Bowers, Tannenbaum, Salas, & Volpe, 1995).

Cannon-Bowers and colleagues (1995) proposed that, to facilitate transfer (see Box 12.2), the first three types of competencies be developed through training of intact teams (the specific team context) in their real-work contexts (the specific tasks) or simulations of their work contexts. The authors suggested that only the fourth type of teamwork competency be developed through general education. Thus, there may be value in developing specific teamwork competencies at the team level through team training in the workplace, in addition to developing individual teamwork competencies in K–12 and higher education.

BOX 12.2: TEAM TRAINING FOR TRANSFER

Echoing the early research on transfer (e.g., Thorndike & Woodworth, 1901), organizational scientists have found that transfer of training to job performance is more likely when the training environment and tasks are very similar to the work environment and tasks (e.g., working on a simulated car engine in training and a real car engine in the garage) and less likely when the training and work environments are quite different (e.g., learning abstract principles of computer networking in the classroom and troubleshooting a network failure under time pressure; Royer, 1979). Similarities between the familiar training environments and the new work environments allow people to recall what they learned and perform tasks appropriately (Bass & Vaughan, 1966).

Based on this research, Cannon-Bowers and colleagues (1995) proposed that transfer of team competencies specific to a task and/or a team can best be supported through training of intact teams. The team itself, with its unique tasks and membership, forms a key element of the training environment that remains unchanged in the transfer environment. Team training has been defined as "training administered to an entire team, aimed at enhancing the performance of the team as a unit" (Delise, Gorman, & Brooks, 2010, p. 55). Research has shown that team training enhances team effectiveness. For example, Salas, Cooke, and Rosen (2008) found that team training had significant, positive effects on team processes and performance. And, in a meta-analysis of 21 studies of factors related to team effectiveness, Delise, Gorman, and Brooks (2010) concluded that team training had significant, positive effects on overall team effectiveness and on five dimensions of team effectiveness (affective, cognitive, subjective, task-based skill, objective task-based skill, and teamwork skill).

Approaches shown to increase team effectiveness in organizations could fruitfully be investigated, adapted, and applied to improve the functioning of student teams that operate in the context of K-12 and higher education. For example, Borrego and colleagues (2013) identified five constructs related to team effectiveness and proposed teaching approaches to avoid or promote each construct within engineering and computer science student teams. They proposed that, to avoid social loafing, faculty should assign a compelling project with inherent value, ask peers to evaluate individual effort, include complex tasks, and keep teams small. To promote shared mental models, faculty should clarify the project assignment, engage the team in shared goal setting, and encourage the team members to reflect on their interactions and how to improve them.

Progress in Assessing Teamwork

Defining teamwork in terms of individual-level, transportable competencies, researchers are making progress in assessing teamwork. In an early study, Stevens and Campion (1994) reviewed the research on teams and proposed a comprehensive taxonomy of teamwork knowledge, skills, and attitudes. Later, Stevens and Campion (1999) developed a test to measure these constructs, presenting hypothetical teamwork scenarios along with alternative responses for selection by the test-taker. This test has been widely used for employee selection and has also informed research in higher education.

More recently, researchers have begun to define teamwork competencies in terms of the different ways individuals can contribute to the team, and to assess these competencies using team member ratings, which may reduce biases associated with self-reports. Studies of business students have found that, when students rate their peers as well as themselves, they are less likely to engage in social loafing, more likely to perceive their grades as fair, and have more positive attitudes toward teamwork (Aggarwal & O'Brien, 2008; Chapman & van Auken, 2001; Erez, LePine, & Elms, 2002, cited in Ohland et al., 2012). At the same time, self- and peer-ratings face challenges, including some students' resistance to such ratings, and the potential for various forms of bias to influence the ratings (e.g., impression management in self-ratings, opportunity to observe in peer-ratings). Haynes and Heilman (2013) report on a series of laboratory studies examining how female and male team members allocated credit for the team's successful performance of performing a task. They found that women who were working in gender-diverse teams tended to devalue their contributions, whereas men did not.

Recent assessments tap the potential of technology to collect, analyze, and synthesize multiple self- and peer-ratings from student teams. For example, CATME-B, a web-based instrument, collects and analyzes self- and peer-ratings of three levels of performance across five categories of team member contributions (i.e., contributing to the team's work; interacting with teammates; keeping the team on track; expecting quality; and having relevant knowledge, skills, and abilities). The instrument demonstrated strong reliability as well as support for validity in terms of a statistically significant relationship with final course grades in a course requiring a high level of team interaction (Ohland et al., 2012). SPARK—the Self and Peer Assessment Resource Kit (Freeman & McKenzie, 2002)—another system for peer and self-evaluations of teamwork competencies reflects Cannon-Bowers and colleagues' (1995) proposal that many teamwork competencies are specific to particular teams or tasks. SPARK provides a template that allows faculty members to customize the evaluation criteria according to specific disciplines or project goals. Another recent system—the Peer Evaluation and Assessment Resource (Kulterel-Konak, Konak, Kremer, Esparragoza, & Yoder, 2014)—aims to measure students' progress in developing professional teamwork competencies over the course of the undergraduate years.

The OECD measured both cognitive and interpersonal competencies in a new section on collaborative problem-solving of the 2015 Program for International Student Assessment (PISA) online test. Drawing on prior theory, research, and assessment development, the assessment framework included four dimensions of problem-solving (exploring and understanding, representing and formulating, planning and executing, and monitoring and reflecting), along with three dimensions of collaboration (OECD, 2017a, p. 50):

- Establishing and maintaining shared understanding
- Taking appropriate action to solve the problem
- Establishing and maintaining team organization (e.g., understanding one's own role and others' roles)

The collaborative problem-solving section presented 15-year-old students with problem scenarios and related questions. The students collaborated with online intelligent agents, rather than other students, to address the scenarios. They were assigned different roles (e.g., team member, team leader) and worked with one or more agents having different characteristics (e.g., cooperative, negligent, error-prone); these variations were designed to obtain reliable measurement of all dimensions of collaborative problem-solving. The computer automatically scored the student's physical actions (e.g., clicking on a location on a map or selecting an object) and chats (selected from 3 to 4 alternative messages in a chat menu; OECD, 2017b).

Analysis of data from field trials provides encouraging evidence of the reliability of this new PISA module, as well as its validity in terms of correlations with external assessments (Graesser et al., 2016). Validity findings are supported and organized by the strong grounding of the assessment framework in relevant theory and research (OECD, 2017a).

Such progress in assessing individual teamwork competencies promises to support deeper learning of teamwork in K-12 and higher education. Whether these transportable teamwork skills learned in school will enhance the effectiveness of later team training to develop team- and task-specific teamwork competencies is an important empirical research question that remains to be answered.

Conclusion and Policy Implications

The research reviewed in this chapter suggests that educational policymakers and practitioners can improve workforce readiness by designing K-12 and higher education instruction for deeper learning and transfer. In the cognitive domain, deeper learning supports students' development of basic literacy and numeracy, as well as understanding of key concepts and skills in STEM and other academic subjects. Instructional design principles based on cognitive research could also support students' development of transferable intrapersonal competencies (e.g., sense of belonging) and interpersonal competencies (e.g., teamwork) that are of critical concern and value in higher education and the workplace.

Refocusing K-12 and higher education on teaching and learning for transfer will require federal, state, and local investments to develop curriculum materials, along with extensive, practice-based professional development for teachers and faculty (National Research Council, 2012b). It will also require sustained public and private investments in research and development of assessments, particularly new assessment instruments that can accurately measure teamwork and other intra- and interpersonal competencies. For example, further development of forced-choice assessments can address some of the limitations of self-report rating scales, and technology-based methods show promise for accurately measuring interpersonal competencies (for further discussion, see National Academies of Sciences, Engineering, and Medicine, 2017). The investment of time and expertise in psychological test measurement, psychometrics, and stakeholder input is unavoidable when it comes to developing, testing, and validating high-quality assessments of these competencies. Past investments have yielded progress in assessing teamwork, a competency greatly valued by employers. Because formative assessment is a critical component of instruction that supports deeper learning, continued investment in assessment development would support deeper learning of transferable teamwork competencies. As noted earlier in this chapter, formative assessment provides ongoing feedback that instructors can use to improve their teaching approaches and students can use to improve their learning strategies.

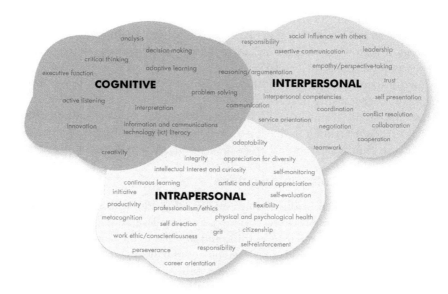

"21st Century Skills" Grouped into 3 Broad Domains.

Although refocusing education on transfer can begin to strengthen students' workforce readiness, graduates entering the workplace will require ongoing training to ensure transfer of their knowledge and skills to the unique teams and tasks they will encounter over time. As employers develop and implement such training, they can draw on the scientifically established principles of instructional design for deeper learning listed above, as well as on the body of research on team effectiveness. By investing in training in a strategic manner informed by research, employers will support development and transfer of teamwork competencies, along with other cognitive, intrapersonal, and interpersonal competencies learned in K–12 and higher education.

Notes

1 Margaret Hilton was formerly on the staff of the National Academies of Sciences, Engineering, and Medicine (the Academies) and served as project director for the three consensus study reports discussed in this article. However, the analysis and opinions are solely those of the author and do not represent the Academies or the three committees.

2 The National Research Council (NRC) was the predecessor to today's National Academies of Sciences, Engineering, and Medicine.

3 Formative assessment regularly monitors student learning for the purpose of providing feedback that instructors can use to improve their teaching and students can use to improve their learning strategies. In contrast, summative assessment generally measures student learning at the end of a unit of instruction for the purpose of evaluating what each student has learned.

4 Due to the lack of research evidence noted above, no purely interpersonal competencies were identified as showing a relationship to college success.

References

Aggarwal, P., & O'Brien, C. L. (2008). Social loafing on group projects structural antecedents and effect on student satisfaction. *Journal of Marketing Education, 30,* 255–264.

American Educational Research Association, American Psychological Association, and National Council of Measurement in Education. (2014). *Standards for educational and psychological testing.* Washington, DC: American Psychological Association.

Autor, D., Levy, F., & Murnane, R. (2003). The skill content of recent technological change: An empirical exploration. *Quarterly Journal of Economics, 118,* 1279–1333.

Barrow, L., & Rouse, C. (2005). Do returns to schooling differ by race and ethnicity? *American Economic Review, 95,* 83–87.

Bass, B. M., & Vaughan, J. A. (1966). *Training in industry: The management of learning.* Wadsworth, OH: Belmont.

Borrego, M., Karlin, J., McNair, L. D., & Beddoes, K. (2013). Team effectiveness theory from industrial and organizational psychology applied to engineering student project teams—A review. *Journal of Engineering Education, 102,* 472–512.

Britton, E., Simper, N., Leger, A., & Stephenson, J. (2015). Assessing teamwork in undergraduate education: A measurement tool to evaluate individual teamwork skills. *Assessment and Evaluation in Higher Education, 42,* 378–397.

Cannon-Bowers, J. A., Salas, E., & Converse, S. A. (1993). Shared mental models in expert team decision making. In N. J. Castellan (Ed.), *Individual and group decision making: Current issues* (pp. 221–246). Hillsdale, NJ: LEA.

Cannon-Bowers, J. A., Tannenbaum, S. I., Salas, E., & Volpe, C. E. (1995). Defining team competencies and establishing team training requirements. In R. Guzzo & E. Salas (Eds.), *Team effectiveness and decision making in organizations* (pp. 333–380). San Francisco, CA: Jossey-Bass.

Casner-Lotto, J., & Barrington, L. (2006). *Are they really ready to work?* Washington, DC: Conference Board, Partnership for 21st Century Skills, Corporate Voices for Working Families, and Society for Human Resource Management. Retrieved from http://files.eric.ed.gov/fulltext/ED519465.pdf [August 2016].

Cervetti, G. N., Barber, J., Dorph, R., Pearson, P. D., & Goldschmidt, P. G. (2012). The impact of an integrated approach to science and literacy in elementary school classrooms. *Journal of Research in Science Teaching, 49*, 631–658.

Chapman, K. J., & van Auken, S. (2001). Creating positive group project experiences: An examination of the role of the instructor on students' perceptions of group projects. *Journal of Marketing Education, 23*, 117–127.

DeChurch, L. A., & Mesmer-Magnus, J. R. (2010). The cognitive underpinnings of effective teamwork: A meta-analysis. *Journal of Applied Psychology, 95*, 32–53.

de Groot, A. D. (1965). *Thought and choice in chess.* The Hague, Netherlands: Mouton.

Delise, L. A., Gorman, C. A., & Brooks, A. M. (2010). The effects of team training on team outcomes: A meta-analysis. *Performance Improvement Quarterly, 22*, 53–80.

Deming, D. (2015). *The growing importance of social skills in the labor market.* NBER Working Paper 21473. Retrieved from http://www.nber.org/papers/w21473 [January 2016].

Duncan, T. C., & McKeachie, W. J. (2005). The making of the motivated strategies for learning questionnaire. *Educational Psychologist, 40*(2), 117–128.

Erez, A., LePine, J. A., & Elms, H. (2002). Effects of rotated leadership and peer evaluation on the functioning and effectiveness of self-managed teams: A quasi-experiment. *Personnel Psychology, 55*, 929–948.

Ericsson, K. A., Charness, N., Feltovich, P. J., & Hoffman, R. R. (Eds.) (2006). *The Cambridge handbook of expertise and expert performance.* New York, NY: Cambridge University Press.

Freeman, M., & McKenzie, J. (2002). SPARK: A confidential web-based template for self and peer assessment of student teamwork: Benefits of evaluating across different subjects. *British Journal of Educational Technology, 33*, 551–569.

Graesser, A. C., Cai, Z., Hu, X., Foltz, P. W., et al., (2016). Assessment of collaborative problem-solving. In R. Scottilare, A. C. Graesser, X. Hu & G. Goodwin. *Design recommendations for intelligent tutoring systems* (Vol. 5, pp. 274–285). Adelphi, MD: Army Research Laboratory.

Harackiewicz, J. M., Canning, E. A., Tibbetts, Y., Priniski, S. J., & Hyde, J. S. (2015). Closing achievement gaps with a utility-value intervention: Disentangling race and social class. *Journal of Personality and Social Psychology, 111*, 745–765.

Harackiewicz, J. M., Rozek, C. S., Hulleman, C. S., & Hyde, J. S. (2012). Helping parents to motivate adolescents in mathematics and science: An experimental test of a utility-value intervention. *Psychological Science, 23*, 899–906.

Hart Research Associates. (2010). *Raising the bar: Employers' views on college learning in the wake of the economic downturn. A survey among employers Conducted on behalf of the American Association of Colleges and Universities.* Washington, DC: American Association of Colleges and Universities. Retrieved from https://www.aacu.org/sites/default/files/files/LEAP/2009_EmployerSurvey.pdf [August 2016].

Hart Research Associates. (2015). *Falling short? College learning and career success.* Washington, DC: American Association of Colleges and Universities. Retrieved from http://www.aacu.org/sites/default/files/files/LEAP/2015employerstudentsurvey.pdf [May 2016].

Haynes, M. C., & Heilman, M. E. (2013). It had to be you (not me)! Women's attributional rationalization of their contribution to successful joint work outcomes. *Personality and Social Psychology Bulletin, 39,* 956–969.

Hughes, R. L., & Jones, S. K. (2011). Developing and assessing college student teamwork skills. *New Directions for Institutional Research, 2011,* 53–64.

Kozlowski, S. W. J., & Klein, K. J. (2000). A multilevel approach to theory and research in organizations: Contextual, temporal, and emergent processes. In K. J. Klein & S. W. J. Kozlowski (Eds.), *Multilevel theory, research and methods in organizations: Foundations, extensions, and new directions* (pp. 3–90). San Francisco, CA: Jossey-Bass.

Kulterel-Konak, S., Konak, A., Kremer, G. E. O., Esparragoza, I., & Yoder, G. (2014). Peer Evaluation and Assessment Resource (PEAR) to assess students' professional skills. In Y. Guan & H. Liao (Eds.), *Proceedings of the 2014 industrial and systems engineering research conference,* Montréal, QC.

Lewis, K., Lange, D., & Gillis, L. (2005). Transactive memory systems, learning, and learning transfer. *Organization Science, 16,* 581–598.

National Academies of Sciences, Engineering, and Medicine. (2017). *Supporting students' college success: The role of assessment of intrapersonal and interpersonal competencies.* Washington, D.C.: The National Academies Press.

National Association of Colleges and Employers. (2017). *The key attributes employers seek on students' resumes.* Retrieved from https://www.naceweb.org/about-us/press/2017/the-key-attributes-employers-seek-on-students-resumes/ [Accessed January, 2018].

National Research Council. (2012a). *Discipline-based education research: Understanding and improving undergraduate learning in undergraduate science and engineering.* S. R. Singer, N. R. Nielsen & H. A. Schweingruber (Eds.), Committee on the Status, Contributions, and Future Directions of Discipline-Based Education Research; Board on Science Education; Division of Behavioral and Social Sciences and Education. Washington, DC: The National Academies Press.

National Research Council. (2012b). *Education for life and work: Developing transferable knowledge and skills in the 21st century.* Committee on Defining Deeper Learning and 21st Century Skills, J. W. Pellegrino & M. L. Hilton, Editors. Board on Testing and Assessment and Board on Science Education, Division of Behavioral and Social Sciences and Education. Washington, DC: The National Academies Press.

National Research Council. (2015). *Enhancing the effectiveness of team science.* N. J. Cooke & M. L. Hilton (Eds.), Board on Behavioral, Cognitive, and Sensory Sciences; Division of Behavioral and Social Sciences and Education. Washington, DC: The National Academies Press.

Ohland, M. W., Loughry, M. S., Woehr, D. J., Bullard, L. G., Felder, R. M., Finelli, C. J., … Schmucker, D. G. (2012). The comprehensive assessment of team member effectiveness: Development of a behaviorally anchored rating scale for self- and peer-evaluation. *Academy of Management Learning and Education, 11,* 609–630.

Organization for Economic Cooperation and Development. (2013). *Skilled for life? Key findings from the survey of adult skills.* Paris, France: Organization for Economic Cooperation and Development. Retrieved from http://www.oecd.org/site/piaac/SkillsOutlook_2013_ebook.pdf [May 2016].

Organization for Economic Cooperation and Development. (2017a). *PISA 2015 assessment and analytical framework.* Retrieved from http://www.oecd-ilibrary.org/education/

pisa-2015-assessment-and-analytical-framework/pisa-2015-collaborative-problem-solving-framework_9789264281820-8-en [February, 2018].

Organization for Economic Cooperation and Development. (2017b). *PISA 2015 results (Volume 5): Collaborative problem-solving.* Paris, France: Organization for Economic Cooperation and Development. Retrieved from http://www.oecd-ilibrary.org/education/pisa-2015-results-volume-v_9789264285521-en [February, 2018].

Pintrich, P. R., Smith, D. A. F., García, T., & McKeachie, W. J. (1991). *A manual for the use of the Motivated Strategies for Learning Questionnaire (MSLQ).* Ann Arbor: University of Michigan, National Center for Research to Improve Postsecondary Teaching and Learning. Retrieved from http://files.eric.ed.gov/fulltext/ED338122.pdf [November 2016].

Pintrich, P. R., Smith, D. A. F., García, T., & McKeachie, W. J. (1993). Reliability and predictive validity of the Motivated Strategies for Learning Questionnaire (MSLQ). *Educational and Psychological Measurement, 53,* 801–813.

Royer, J. M. (1979). Theories of the transfer of learning. *Educational Psychologist, 14,* 53–69.

Salas, E., Cooke, N. J., & Rosen, M. A. (2008). On teams, teamwork, and team performance: Discoveries and developments. *Human Factors: The Journal of the Human Factors and Ergonomics Society, 50,* 540–547.

Sisk, V. F., Burgoyne, A. P., Sun, J., Butler, J. L., & Macnamara, B. N. (2018). To what extent and under which circumstances are growth mindsets important to academic achievement? Two meta-analyses. *Psychological Science, 29,* 549–571.

Thorndike, E. L. (1923). The effect of 1st year Latin upon knowledge of English words of Latin derivations. *School and Society, 18,* 260–270.

Thorndike, E. L., & Woodworth, R. S. (1901). The influence of improvement in one mental function upon the efficiency of other functions. *Psychological Review, 8,* 247–267.

Wegner, D. M., Giuliano, T., & Hertel, P. (1985). Cognitive interdependence in close relationships. In W. J. Ickes (Ed.), *Compatible and incompatible relationships* (pp. 253–276). New York, NY: Springer-Verlag.

Walton, G. M., & Cohen, G. L. (2011). A brief social-belonging intervention improves academic and health outcomes of minority students. *Science, 221,* 1447–1451.

Walton, G. M., Peach, J. M., Logel, C., Spencer, S. J., & Zanna, M. P. (2015). Two brief interventions to mitigate a "chilly climate" transform women's experience, relationships, and achievement in engineering. *Journal of Educational Psychology, 107,* 468–485.

Weinberger, C. J. (2014). The increasing complementarity between cognitive and social skills. *The Review of Economics and Statistics, 96,* 849–861.

12

APPRENTICESHIPS

John S. Gaal

Introduction

In 1978, I started my journey down a career path in carpentry and cabinet-making. Who would have thought 40 years later I would be asked to contribute to a book on workforce development issues? (Hint: Certainly not my Bishop DuBourg High School teachers.) As one can imagine, people who dedicate their lives to becoming top-notch professionals in any field, takes a lot of commitment ... not to mention a good support system (e.g., family, friends, coworkers, mentors, peers). To this end, my time served as an apprentice carpenter (1979–1982) provided a foundation to create and leverage both practical and academic educational experiences for the betterment of others within the construction industry for decades to come.

Having served on a variety of local, state, regional, national, and international workforce development-related boards and committees presented opportunities to research vocational/professional education and training systems that encompassed more than 12 countries on four continents. Nonetheless, I will always cherish the fact that while serving as a labor representative on the U.S. Secretary of Labor's Advisory Committee on Apprenticeship (2003–2010), our efforts launched the most significant update to the Fitzgerald Act of 1937 in November 2008. This major rework of 29CFR29 would eventually allow for the Obama Administration to inject over $200 million into the U.S. Department of Labor's Office of Apprenticeship's (USDOL's OA) efforts to expand registered apprenticeship programs (RAPs). Eventually, this led to two personal invitations to share best practices at The White House in 2015.

It would be remiss on my behalf to pretend that I have all the answers in the area of apprenticeship. Therefore, for this chapter, I selected a unique format by reaching out to a number of trusted contacts within my apprenticeship and international workforce development networks whom I have met along the aforementioned four-decade journey and invoked their assistance in tackling a dozen pertinent topics related to 21st-century apprenticeships across the globe. The following advice should be viewed as contextual input from experts rather than perfect prescriptive answers. I wish to thank each one of them for their insights.

Switzerland

The Gold Standard

John:
With nearly 70% of Swiss secondary students participating in some form of Vocational & Educational Training (VET) program, the Swiss apprenticeship system has been held up as the world's gold standard. Briefly share a few major reasons why this system works so well. And, as the US apprenticeship system attempts to re-invent itself, provide advice on areas you feel educators should focus on as well as pitfalls they need to avoid.

Dr. Ursula Renold:
Director of the Center on the Economics and Management of Education and Training Systems (CEMETS) at ETH Zurich, Switzerland, and previously served as the country's Secretary of the Federal Office for Professional Education and Technology.

The success of Swiss Vocational Education and Training (VET) is based on a well-established ecosystem in which industrial associations, companies, states and their schools, teachers, and federal authorities work closely together throughout the Curriculum Value Chain, or all educational processes, including curriculum design, curriculum application or program delivery, and curriculum updating. We can measure the intensity of this structural coupling in a given program, and Switzerland is one of the leading countries, along with Austria and Denmark.

Swiss apprenticeships start at ages 15–16 as an alternative to academic high school. This is especially important in adolescence, because many teenagers have no desire for more full-time schooling. They want to become adults, so learning in the workplace is particularly successful and satisfying for them for that reason. They can develop self-confidence and professional identities while simultaneously acquiring necessary transferable and theoretical knowledge at school.

Permeability is one of several key features of the Swiss education system. "No educational qualification without a route to further education" is the mantra in Switzerland. When adolescence is over, and young adults are more self-confident, they are often hungry for more knowledge and want to pursue academic or advanced professional programs. It is, therefore, essential that apprenticeships (or any VET program) are part of an education *system* that offers both access to further options and opportunities for professional and academic progression. This means the apprenticeship itself must provide enough academic skills to enable progress along an academic pathway.

The American apprenticeship system is fundamentally different from that in Switzerland. RAs are not part of the education system. They are regulated by the DOL, and educators do not always recognize their certificates. Participants do not have systematically assured admission to higher education programs or institutions. On average, American apprentices are much older—around 27 and climbing—which makes it difficult for companies to see them as "learners" and almost impossible for companies training benefits to outweigh their costs, which would be an incentive for companies to invest in high-quality training.

My most important recommendation is to link American apprenticeships to career and technical education (CTE) and make them part of the education system so that educational authorities recognize them. In developing such programs, educators should avoid gearing them too specifically to the needs of individual companies. This would not help young people face the challenges of rapid technological change and would make it harder for them to move to a different company or region. Instead, designing curricula for *occupations* that span multiple companies makes apprentices innovation-ready and increases portability.

To make this possible, representatives and actors from the education and employment systems need to work together and share power over key decisions. If either side has too much power, the resulting program will be too general (a weak vocational school program) or too specific (a company-oriented training program without enough general content for permeability and progression). Close cooperation can develop the next generation of well-trained experts with bright and diverse futures.

Germany

The Codetermination Model

John:

In your decade-plus research of the German apprenticeship system, please identify several aspects of this system that often makes it the envy of other countries' career and technical education systems. More specifically, since the US system tends to focus on the post-secondary sector, will this system ever be able to attain Germany's level of delivery? If so, why? If not, why not?

Dr. Joe Wise III:

Former Secretary Treasurer of the Greater Louisville Building & Construction Trades Council. He co-established an apprenticeship exchange seminar with industry, educational institutions, craft guilds and labor unions in Germany.

In comparing the apprenticeship training systems between Germany and the United States, one cannot do that by looking at the mechanics of the two systems alone. One must view them in the context of the culture and financial support received from the respective societies. The Germans live by a creed that they must adhere to rules, norms, and regulations and the government has implemented policies to support education financially. This can be seen in the way that their educational system is structured, of which, the Dual System of Apprentice Training plays an important role.

When viewing the apprenticeship systems of Germany and the United States, one has to look at the systems within the context of the overall educational system and the cultural norms and regulations of the respective countries. In the Federal Republic of Germany, the apprenticeship system has evolved over the years from a cultural aspect that the trade should be transmitted from one generation to another. This can be seen in Germany through the transference of knowledge from the journey-worker to the master level, as demonstrated within the craft guilds in Germany. Another component that makes the apprenticeship system so successful is that they operate in a cooperative manner between government, labor, and business. This notion is known as co-determination or "Mitbestimmung."

The entire German society has bought into the system. Businesses have decided that apprenticeship training is the primary method to recruit future workers. This is the reason there are over 300 occupations in Germany today that utilize apprenticeship training. Businesses are committed when they advertise that they have openings for apprentices, and they "seal the deal" when they offer a contract to the apprentice for the duration for the apprenticeship. The government is committed through its financial support of the system, working with business to develop curriculum and by participating in the testing of the apprentice. Labor also participates with the two aforementioned groups via curriculum development and testing.

All these aspects are done before the apprentice reaches the postsecondary level. Upon graduation, the apprentice is a contributing member of society and has a foundation for the direction for his or her respective career. This is not to say that their education is over. The apprentice can go on to achieve master level or even attend a Fachoberschule and earn the equivalent of a college degree.

The American system, by contrast, is mainly geared to directing all students to a college degree through a typical university setting. Many of our students have no direction as to their future career opportunities and oftentimes spend too many years pursuing a career that they either have no interest in or, frankly, for which they do not have the capabilities. The K-12 educational system in the United States has been criticized over the years as "teaching to the test." The testing, however, has been focused in the wrong areas. It needs to identify those areas where the student has talent. Then teaching can be tailored to the student to bring out those talents. Finally, not until the United States truly becomes serious about financing the postsecondary needs for all students will our system attain the level of delivery that we see in Germany.

United Kingdom

A New Way Forward

John:

The deindustrialization of the UK and US from the 1980s forward seemingly had a negative impact on both countries' systems of apprenticeship. However, in the past 10 or so years, the UK has developed and implemented a strategy that has put their apprenticeship system back on the map. Please briefly provide an overview of how the UK is harnessing the power of apprenticeship, and conclude with a few insights that may assist US policymakers grow their once-robust apprenticeship system.

Tom Bewick:

An international expert on active labor market policies and apprenticeships. He graduated from the University of Bath in 1995 with a master's degree in European Public Policy, majoring on comparative labor market economics. Tom was a senior policy and political adviser to the Labour Government, 1997–2003; and he contributed to many of the reforms that resulted in the UK's rapid expansion of apprenticeship. Currently, he is president of the Transatlantic Apprenticeship Exchange Forum (TAEF) and co-founder of Franklin Apprenticeships based in the United States.

By the end of the 1980s, Britain had lost more than one million manufacturing jobs—about one-third of its manufacturing output. Youth unemployment remained stubbornly high during the period, with one in five young people not in education or employment by the start of the 1990s. Like other advanced economies adjusting to a postindustrial future, the United Kingdom faced a stark choice about what to do to tackle growing levels of jobless households and a skills shortage, particularly as the economy eventually improved.

By 1997, apprenticeships in the United Kingdom had all but died out. There were less than 75,000 apprenticeship starts per year. These were mainly in traditional fields, such as engineering and construction. A newly elected Labour Government set about the task of introducing a raft of active labor market policies, including a *New Deal for Young People*, a government initiative to help unemployed youth aged 18–24 be more employable and thus reengage in the workforce.

Apprenticeships were given fresh impetus via the creation of industry-led sector skills councils, which were tasked with writing new apprenticeship programs and rolling them out across an expansive range of sectors, including information technology (IT), public sector, and the creative industries. At the same time, the government took the lead in promoting the apprenticeship brand, encouraging employers to take on apprentices. Public investment in subsidizing the off-job-training element of apprenticeships was doubled with bipartisan support, which led to the rapid expansion of the market.

Traditionally in the United Kingdom, further education colleges had provided the technical training for apprentices, but from the early 2000s onward, a new breed of apprenticeship service provider began to take hold. Today, 75% of the apprenticeship market—around half a million starts per year—is supported by independent "intermediary" training providers. Higher education is increasingly getting involved by delivering new degree apprenticeships. These advanced apprenticeships, in areas as diverse as cybersecurity and management and leadership, are helping to create a learn-and-earn route from high school completion right up to the level of bachelor and master's degree apprenticeships and even beyond.

The apprenticeship system in England is undergoing a further wave of reform. Over 300 new apprenticeship standards have been introduced, designed by employer groups. Investment in the model has doubled again with the introduction of an apprenticeship levy on large employer who must now contribute 0.5% of their payroll (currently an annual cumulative amount of over $5 million), which they can get back if they take on apprentices. It is still early days for these policies, which are experiencing some significant teething problems as they get established, and industry adjusts to the new regime. Currently, apprenticeship starts have fallen by over one third since the reforms kicked in. The government expects the decline to be only temporary as levy-paying employers in particular get used to the scheme.

There are three insights that U.S. policymakers can learn from the UK model:

1. *Build the coalition of support via targeted legislative action:* It is essential to secure ongoing bipartisan commitment to the apprenticeship expansion, including the early buy-in of business and trades union interests. This includes putting in place the right legislative and funding frameworks that can help better incentivize employers to take on apprentices.
2. *Empower the key stakeholders:* Employers and unions (where applicable) need be empowered to come together in sector groupings to develop the industry training standards required to help systematically scale up the apprenticeship expansion effort. This should include a focus on quality systems that can ensure the apprentices qualify with portable credentials that contribute to higher skill levels and improved productivity and performance.
3. *Grow and incentivize the marketplace:* This can be done by encouraging intermediary organizations to set up Apprenticeship Service Providers that can help support firms to take on apprentices. This is particularly relevant in

nontraditional occupational sectors such as IT and professional services oc-cupations, where a major challenge is to successfully market and organize the "apprenticeship offer." In short, the whole posture of the apprentice-ship model has to move from "this is the way we have always done things" to "how can we innovate in apprenticeship and do things differently."

Australia

Dispelling the Apprenticeship Myths

John:

Too often, businesses seeking to engage the apprenticeship system in the USA tend to shy away because of lingering misconceptions, e.g.: 1) Apprenticeships only apply to the construction industry; and/or 2) Apprenticeships only work within a union environment. Briefly explain which emerging industries in Australia are experiencing success and why. And, then share a few promising traits within those areas that might easily be applied to the US system.

Nicholas Wyman:

CEO for the Institute for Workplace Skills & Innovation (IWSI), which works with more than 700 apprentices and trainees within a network of 300+ employer partners across industries throughout the world. He also runs WPC Apprenticeships America, which consults on workforce solutions to govern-ments and businesses in the US.

You could be forgiven for not realizing the range of job vacancies that you could fill in your business with apprentices.

With some sleuthing, I found a list of 1,400 occupations for which appren-ticeships can and have worked in the United States. Sure, you'll find traditional sectors represented, such as construction and manufacturing, but emerging sectors like energy and health care are there, too—plus more. Check out to whether you could solve your hard-to-fill vacancy with an apprenticeship at https://doleta.gov/OA/occupations.cfm.

U.S. Labor Secretary R. Alexander Acosta says, "Apprenticeships hold great promise in helping American workers acquire the skills they need to get good jobs while ensuring companies can attract the talent required to succeed in this fast-moving global economy."

You might be surprised to hear that 91% of apprentices who complete an apprenticeship are still employed nine months later, according to the DOL. However, U.S. businesses seeking to engage with the apprenticeship system too often tend to shy away because of lingering misconceptions. Labor hire com-pany Adecco lists myths such as time-consuming paperwork, lack of control over the program, and not being able to employ minors in manufacturing or trade roles. Other misconceptions include that apprentices did poorly at school, only do manual trades, are low quality, or can only work in unionized workplaces. These are wrong on all accounts!

As a *Washington Post* report said last December, "apprenticeships are increasingly training people in technology roles including internal tech support or software programming ... human resources analysts, insurance customer support agents, account managers and more." This makes sense, because at the core of apprenticeships is on-the-job training combined with study. That's a nuanced "earn-while-they-learn" approach focused on specific skill development. In short, it's a viable solution to the skills gap U.S. employers are increasingly experiencing. I've seen apprenticeships help fill the skills gap in Australia, where I was based for 30 years until recently. That country has had solid success with its apprenticeship and traineeship system to equip young people in particular, who are keen to forge a career pathway.

Apprenticeships can be a remarkable fit, especially for emerging industries. Speed of change is the theme here. Consider this: Of the 10 industry subgroups with the largest projected jobs growth by 2020, nonuniversity courses offer training today fit the bill. And often that training can be completed in a couple of years.

These emerging growth areas include health professionals, careers and aides, administrators, chefs, and electricians. That was one of the findings in a report of one of my organizations, the Skilling Australia Foundation (SAF), which worked on with McCrindle researchers and with funding from the Citi Foundation. The report, *Perceptions*, is not reality: Busting apart the myths of vocational education & training (http://saf.org.au/perceptionsarenotreality/) was released in May of last year. SAF works with Citi and other organizations to run free job-readiness courses for young people experiencing disadvantage and long-term unemployment. In just three weeks, they pick up relevant soft skills, knowledge, and industry work experience with many finding their path to further training or employment such as through an apprenticeship soon after.

Apprenticeships are more than just a rung to equip the emerging workforce—it's the foundation in America's future economic prosperity.

Canada

Private Industry Investment = Skill + Portability

John:
Briefly explain how private sector union-affiliated apprenticeship programs in Canada operate. In the US, various industry recognized credentials (IRC) are quickly becoming the "coin of realm" when it comes to the portability of a worker's skillset. Along these lines, what is the importance of the "Red Seal" program?

Cristina Selva:

Executive Director of the College of Carpenters and Allied Trades Inc. (CCAT). CCAT is the largest Training Delivery Agent (TDA) of Carpentry Apprenticeship in Ontario, and she was recently honored with the inaugural Chair's Award of Excellence by the Ontario College of Trades.

Union-affiliated pre-apprenticeship, apprenticeship, and continuing education programs are models of private industry investment in the recruitment, education, and upgrading of unionized workers across Canada. For every hour worked by union members in construction sector trades as well as others, private industry (i.e., the employers and workers) contributes a set rate into a Training Trust Fund (TTF). TTF contributions—which are made mandatory through negotiated collective agreements—are used to subsidize the costs of different types of training, including apprenticeship training.

TTF contributions enable the unionized industry to provide enhanced educational opportunities to its workers within "real-world" (site-simulated) conditions and frequently on full-scale projects. This level of investment into a comprehensive educational model—that spans pre-apprenticeship training through to lifelong continuing education programs—is unparalleled in the nonunion world. It works in the best interest of tradesmen and women seeking to obtain journey-level certification and beyond in their trade areas.

In Canada, provinces and territories are responsible for apprenticeship training and certification within their respective jurisdictions. However, national certification may also be obtained through the Interprovincial Standards Red Seal Program. The Red Seal Program was originally created by the federal government in partnership with the provinces and territories in order to facilitate greater mobility of apprentices and tradespeople across the country, thereby helping to address the changing needs of local economies. The program establishes consistent standards against which the skills of tradespeople are assessed through standardized Red Seal examinations. The Canadian Council of Directors of Apprenticeship (CCDA) is the body responsible for the administration of the Red Seal Program and consists of representatives from all provinces and territories, as well as the federal government.

There are currently 56 trades—across all industries—in Canada that have officially been recognized as Red Seal Trades. Tradespeople who challenge and pass the Red Seal Examination, receive a Red Seal endorsement on their provincial or territorial certificates of qualification. This Red Seal designation allows skilled workers with greater flexibility and opportunities to seek out employment anywhere in Canada. The program also benefits employers and unions, who can rely upon an invaluable consistency of mastered skills across provincial/territorial borders.

Private industry plays a vital role in the Red Seal Program, especially with respect to establishing the national standard for each trade. Because of their proactive involvement, demonstrated expertise, and significant investment in training, representatives from the unionized industry are frequently invited by the CCDA to participate in the review and revision of national trade standards and in the development of test questions for Red Seal Examinations.

Attaining a Red Seal endorsement is not easy and often involves multiple attempts at the challenging examination. As a result of the TTF investment model that can be leveraged to provide for enhanced/augmented apprenticeship programs, and for continuing education courses such as Red Seal Examination Preparation Courses, unionized apprentices are well supported in their pursuit of the ultimate Red Seal designation as compared with their nonunion counterparts (see http://www.red-seal.ca/about/pr.4gr.1m-eng.html).

United States

Words from Wisdom

John:
You are often referred to as the "Godfather" of the US apprenticeship system. Having nearly five decades of experiences within this system, what is the most significant development you have seen to date? Which aspects of 29CFR29 (Revised 2008) and 29CFR30 (Revised 2017) do you feel will assist and/or hinder growing the US system? And, briefly explain why?

Dr. Robert "Bob" Lerman:
Institute fellow in the Center on Labor, Human Services, and Population at the Urban Institute as well as Professor Emeritus of Economics at American University and a research fellow at IZA in Bonn, Germany.

The most significant development in recent years is that apprenticeship expansion has become a major bipartisan goal, endorsed and acted upon by President Trump at the beginning of his term and President Obama toward the end of his two terms. The Obama administration allocated $175 million to 46 apprenticeship initiatives by nonprofits and community colleges. With the Congress adding another $90 million for apprenticeship, the USDOL allocated about $60 million for state apprenticeship expansion grants, and intermediaries focusing on specific industries or specific populations received another $20 million. In June 2017, President Trump called for expanding apprenticeship at a White House ceremony, and he signed an executive order titled "Expanding Apprenticeship in America" that proposed nearly doubling the funding for apprenticeships, to $200 million per year. Recognizing the need for fundamental reforms in the nation's apprenticeship system, the executive order established a task force to examine other administrative and legislative reforms, strategies for creating industry-recognized apprenticeships, and the best ways to encourage the private sector to create apprenticeships. The task force recently issued white papers—based on their deliberations—calling for the development of industry-recognized apprenticeship programs (IRAPs) overseen by a variety of accrediting bodies.

Meanwhile, states have become more active in pursuing apprenticeship initiatives. Although it is too early to say whether state apprenticeship expansion grants will stimulate significant apprenticeship initiatives, several states are certainly trying to move forward. For instance, Colorado is pursuing a major, long-term effort to create a youth apprenticeship system under a public/private venture. South Carolina is continuing to scale apprenticeship, adding youth apprenticeship and mentor training to their portfolio. Kentucky's Secretary of Labor is making apprenticeship expansion his primary goal, with initiatives to help intermediaries sell and organize apprenticeships and to make state human resource systems more receptive to apprenticeships. Forums on apprenticeship in Washington, DC, with hundreds of attendees attest to the newly found enthusiasm for apprenticeship. Policymakers are increasingly recognizing the success of overseas apprenticeship programs in extending their reach into nearly all major occupations and into apprenticeships linked with BA degrees. Another trend is the increasing tendency of community colleges and other nonprofits to become apprenticeship sponsors (intermediaries), thereby reducing the paperwork required of individual firms.

Regulations 29CFR29 (Revised 2008) and 29CFR30 (Revised 2017) have updated the organization and equal opportunity components of RAPs. A key feature of 29CFR29 clarified the acceptability of competency-based occupational frameworks for apprenticeship, in addition to the traditional time-based frameworks. Although the regulation apparently did not significantly shift registrations toward competency-based criteria, one can at least see movement toward competency-based frameworks, especially as apprenticeships extend into health, IT, and other nonconstruction occupations. The EEO provisions in 29CFR30 probably are having little effect as well. But there is a danger that adding more formal requirements to RAs might cause a decline in registrations. Overall, without additional research, it is difficult to know the impacts of these regulations.

Why the Labor-Management Model Works

John:
Your career has spanned several decades and, in turn, exposed you to a number of apprenticeship systems from coast to coast. Please provide a few insights as to which industry sectors and programs in the US are operating first-rate apprenticeship programs. In your opinion, will current efforts to encourage community colleges to become "intermediaries" help significantly grow the US system? If so, why? If not, why not?

Andy Wermes:
Consultant for Skilled and Technical Sciences with the Iowa Department of Education. He served an apprenticeship as a Carpenter. Prior to coming to work at the Department of Education 11 years ago, he ran the Building Trades Program for 11 years at North Iowa Area Community College.

Having seen apprenticeship programs throughout the nation, the organizations operating first-rate RAPs in the United States, without a doubt, would clearly be those offered through joint labor-management efforts supported through collective bargaining contributions. The partnership between labor and management is the firm foundation of the structure these programs are built upon.

Building trades unions and contractors have been supporting skilled trades RAPs for over 100 years. The same is true in manufacturing areas, such as Joint Apprenticeship Training Committee (JATC) machinist programs. Such programs have planted and cultivated the tree of apprenticeship in the United States by helping to foster and support federal regulations that govern the establishment and operation of RAPs (29 CFR Parts 29 and 30) because they are committed to the foundational purpose of those regulations: To ensure the welfare and training of the apprentice.

The commitment that joint labor-management apprenticeship programs make provides for superior training facilities, highly qualified instructors, results in no student loans for apprentices, uses little or no public funding, and produces journey-workers who possess industry recognized/portable credentials. Historically, labor-management partnership JATC system programs train nearly three quarters of construction apprentices, and almost two thirds of all U.S. registered apprentices. The JATC system has also worked hard to foster pre-apprenticeship programs that recruit, prepare, and support underserved populations to enter and succeed in RAPs.

I believe the current growth of our tree of apprenticeship is in jeopardy because of efforts to graft branches that may affect the health of the existing RA system. Current efforts have the potential to destroy the RA system down to its original roots if we're not careful. The president's recent executive order citing overburdening apprenticeship regulations, and creating a parallel un-RA system, is an ill-thought-out growth strategy because it could remove what currently safeguards the welfare and training of the apprentice. Likewise, efforts to encourage the community colleges to become apprenticeship intermediaries must be carefully planned around structured guidance consistent with RA regulations, or we risk outcomes which could also negatively impact RA.

U.S. Department of Labor, Employment and Training Administration, Office of Apprenticeship (OA) Bulletin 2016–2026 defines intermediaries in the apprenticeship system as:

> A workforce intermediary is an organization that can help broker local, regional, and national workforce solutions by, among other things, helping job seekers find jobs and employers find workers; convening employers and community partners to determine workforce trends; and assisting in blending customized services and seed funding to grow the demand for new apprenticeship programs.

JATC system programs are right on target in aligning with the intermediary definition within OA Bulletin 2016–2026. JATC systems have actively involved labor-management members that manage the development and allocate the funding of training that provides apprentices with progressive attainment of manual, mechanical, or technical skills and knowledge which is in accordance with industry-wide standards, and results in a completion of apprenticeship certificate and credentials in an apprenticeable occupation that are portable and have meaning to employers nationwide. By comparison, community colleges compete for public funding appropriations as well as federal and state grants to offer programs that mainly award completion of programs of study: associate degrees (typically two years) diploma (typically one year), and certificates (six months +). Understand that this is different from industry-based certifications, although industry-based certifications may be included in programs of study, and for purposes of being a community college intermediary, must be so. And most community colleges struggle to maintain active advisory committees, delivering programs in the same front-loaded instructional format as they have for the past 40 years, by promoting the two-year AAS degree.

Apprenticeship was always meant to be a combination of on-the-job training, accompanied by periodic related technical instruction. This combination is intended to result in best-practice, relevant, industry-driven teaching and learning. Most current community college programs don't include a mandatory paid internship experience for students, and they should. Graduates of JATC system programs do not have student loan debt, whereas graduates from community colleges have an average debt of $5,000—not counting what students missed in lost earnings while enrolled in the community college program. Providing paid industry experience while also funding student cost for community college apprenticeships should also be an essential intermediary goal.

JATC system programs hire teachers who have the broad-based skill set, industry experience, and have attained established industry-based certification that qualifies that person to teach and prepare apprentices to industry standards. Community colleges do not always hire at that level, but if they are to become apprenticeship intermediaries, they must have teachers qualified to offer broad-based programs that qualify as apprenticeable, through the RA Partners Information Data System. Further, they must be required to provide a framework that meets federal RA regulations...*for the welfare and training of the apprentice!*

Tweaking the Traditional Model

John:
The (union) construction sector in the US economy is often credited with the 50+ years of success tied to the traditional US apprenticeship system. In recent years, the US Department of Labor has sought to grow the apprenticeship system, such as by courting emerging

technology sectors. When looking outside the US for new ideas, one must consider the focus of the leading global systems (i.e., Swiss and German) on secondary students, versus the relatively myopic US focus on post-secondary students. In your opinion, what have some of the more progressive US registered apprenticeship programs done to address the need to "cast a wider net" in order to address future (real or imagined) skilled worker shortages?

Dr. Tom Kriger:
Director of Research at North America's Building Trades Unions in Washington, DC. From 2008 to 2012 he was Professor of Labor Studies and Provost and Vice President for Academics at the National Labor College.

One of the best models in the United States for addressing the career awareness gap in construction and for integrating secondary CTE programs with RA is found in Minnesota. This model, which was developed by the Minnesota, Minneapolis, and Saint Paul Building Trades Councils, in cooperation with local CTE teachers, policymakers, and contractors, sets what we see as a national standard for aligning secondary education with RA. Known as the Construction Careers Pathways (CCP) program, this model is designed to educate and inform future Building Trades members. The program is divided into three categories: Career Exposure, Career Exploration, and Career Choice.

The first challenge addressed in Minnesota is this: With the decline of shop classes in secondary schools, young men and women could go their entire academic career without ever learning about construction or the building trades. To expose students to construction careers, the state and local Building Trades Councils in the Twin Cities implemented a new career awareness fair that provided area high school students with hands-on demonstrations of the various building and construction trades. Funded in part by the Minnesota Department of Labor and Industry, the Construct Tomorrow career fairs focused on providing secondary school students with realistic depictions of the types of training students would receive in Building Trades' RAPs. These events give students a chance to interact with apprenticeship coordinators and learn what a day in the life of an apprentice really looks like. Over the past five years, the Building Trades in Minnesota have pitched middle-class construction careers to over 60,000 high school students.

In the Career Exploration phase of the CCP program, the Building Trades and their educator partners focus on the next set of challenges: Engaging high school students with construction education and allowing them to explore the ins and outs of work in the Trades. This part of the program is further broken up onto two categories to best make use of the academic school year and the summer break. During the academic year, interested students enroll in the high school construction programs. This is done through the Multi-Craft

Core Curriculum and Alliance Partners. During their summer break, students are placed into internships at Building Trades training centers through the Minnesota Trades Academy. In these internships, students directly experience the type of work they would do in construction and how to best prepare for apprenticeship. Importantly, students also have access to mentors who provide career navigation and other forms of support.

During the final phase, Career Choice, prospective apprenticeship candidates are either hired into joint labor-management RAPs or placed on a two- or four-year educational track. Involving students early and making them aware of the opportunities in construction can eliminate the career gap that many young people face. It also helps to ensure that young people, if they choose to pursue these opportunities, have access to construction jobs with good pay and benefits, including health insurance and pensions.

The Minnesota Building Trades and their employer, policymaker, and educator partners have devised what we believe is a system that attracts their graduates to the industry, provides them with an in-depth view of the careers available in the industry, and helps them to make an informed career choice in the Building Trades RA system.

Emerging Sectors: Health Care & Early Childhood Education

John:

The Health Care sector is an emerging sector that is playing an important role in growing the US apprenticeship system and the work you are doing on the East Coast is garnering positive attention. To this end, briefly share a few pointers on how your union's approach helped build these early-success stories. What do you see as a key to sustainability?

Cheryl Feldman:

Executive Director of the District 1199C Training & Upgrading Fund, a labor-management educational trust fund founded in 1974 by the National Union of Hospital and Health Care Employees AFSCME that now includes 50 contributing healthcare employers.

Since its creation in 1974, District 1199C Training & Upgrading Fund (Training Fund) has always focused on connecting low-income residents to career pathways in Healthcare and Human Services. However, training programs historically have not been tied to a guaranteed job for the participant upon completion. RA has flipped this traditional training model; in RA, the participant first has a paid job and then is trained to the specifications of the employer. It is truly a game changer for the healthcare and human services industry. And, we are proud to have supported 94 apprentices employed by 29 employers since 2014.

The Training Fund is a labor-management partnership that has always been driven by a strategic industry approach to workforce development and education. In approaching apprenticeship as a workforce opportunity, the first step—as with any workforce program—is to understand where the real pain points exist for employers. Some examples include high turnover of certain occupations, lack of qualified staff to fill open positions, and lack of a career path and advancement opportunities. Once the need is identified, we meet with different employers to gauge their interest in building an apprenticeship model together. We do the groundwork in engaging employers and unions in identifying the on-the-job learning competencies and aligned classroom instruction, along with opportunities for college credit and industry recognized credentials in partnership with postsecondary providers. Thus, we have been successful in establishing multiemployer apprenticeship partnerships that we can standardize for the industry and also customize for individual employers.

Another big selling point for our partners is that the Training Fund has served as the workforce intermediary for the apprenticeship programming. We support the development of the standards; we interact with the state Apprenticeship and Training Council in developing the standards in accordance with state and federal requirements; we take responsibility for collecting and tracking documentation of hours of work and attainment of competencies; we provide mentor training and support; and we help to organize apprenticeship committee meetings. The Training Fund's support ensures that the employer and union can focus on-the-job learning implementation and not have to worry about whether the apprenticeship requirements are being met. We also play a leading role in raising public and philanthropic funding to help alleviate some of the costs associated with apprenticeship implementation. Furthermore, in our role as intermediary, we help employers increase the return of investment of apprenticeship, given that we can take on much of the behind the scenes work required, and they end up with loyal, well-trained employees.

Sustainability and capacity building are essential if we are going to maintain and grow RAPs. In early childhood education, we are working on the development of a model that enables replication outside our region in response to great interest at national and state levels. We are designing a replication toolkit and determining how we can best support implementation beyond our geographic location. Interested employers and unions can benefit greatly from support in going through the steps we went through to determine the workforce need, map career pathway opportunities along with the potential postsecondary partners, identify funding sources, and determine what organization can serve as an intermediary to facilitate the development and implementation process. Key to sustainability is a well thought-out apprenticeship model that can be customized to specific employers and that provides for open communication and input from all partners.

Emerging Sector: Transportation

John:

The transportation sector is key to the success of any market-based economy. What caused your union to embrace the registered apprenticeship model? And, how do you anticipate technology will impact the future work of your members?

Tia Brown-Johnson:
Served as the Program Manager for the Transit Coach Operator Apprenticeship at the Transportation Learning Center in Silver Spring, MD.

As an industry intermediary, the Board of the International Transportation Learning Center (Center) has been key to the success of our apprenticeship development within public transportation. Having key stakeholders from both management and international unions promoting apprenticeship has made it possible for the Center to reach out to agencies and work with them on apprenticeship development.

Once the agencies and international unions embraced apprenticeship, it wasn't that hard to get buy-in from local unions at public transportation agencies. For unions, RAPs allow them to have a stake in the training of their union members. In public transportation, the transportation agencies are generally responsible for the training of the workforce with little to no input from the union. Having an RAP requires the transportation agency to collaborate with union members and have an open discussion regarding the needs of the frontline workforce. This is truly valuable to the unions as they represent the frontline workforce and are typically the first line of communication for issues regarding training.

An important benefit for unions observed from our Transit Coach Operator apprenticeship program is that RAP development and implementation can lead to a joint problem-solving approach. At VTA in San Jose, CA, they have developed a mentoring program for operators that includes quarterly meetings with mentors and management representatives to discuss problems that new operators are having during the first year of the program. These meetings allow the mentors and management representatives to sit around the table and collectively discuss problem-solving approaches to issues such as safety, accidents, work-life balance, to name a few. This collective problem-solving approach has also led to a reduction in grievances and an improved relationship between the agency and the union.

As technology changes and the industry starts to move toward autonomous vehicles, the role of the Transit Coach Operator will likely begin to change. This will be a learning curve for agencies, where they will have to experiment with training and transit coach operator roles until they find a fit for the community, the agency, and the union. Hopefully, the goal is not to replace the transit coach operators. Transit Coach Operators connect people to jobs, school, and opportunities. They build relationships with their customers and ensure that passengers get to their destinations safely. Having this connection with the community that they serve should be an important goal for the transit agency.

For maintenance occupations, the autonomous vehicle will bring a different set of training challenges. The agencies will need to continuously retrain and upgrade the training of their technician workforce to ensure that their technicians are receiving the necessary skills to perform their jobs.

As the older workers with years of transit industry knowledge leave and technology changes, RA becomes an even more valuable tool for workforce training. Apprenticeship allows an agency to "grow their own" while also providing a structured model for consistent training for quality workers.

A Nontraditional Approach

John:
South Carolina has played an important role in growing the US apprenticeship system and is often promoted as a model to emulate. Right or wrong, apprenticeship is almost always linked to unionized industry sectors and regions. To this end, briefly share a few noteworthy tips as to how your state's approach quickly moved it to the top of the pile. And, if you had to do it over again, what would you do differently? Why?

Brad Neese:
Associate Vice President of the Division of Economic Development with the South Carolina Technical College System. He has responsibilities for two nationally recognized programs readySC and Apprenticeship Carolina.

We began operations for Apprenticeship Carolina in 2007. At that time, South Carolina had only 90 companies with RAPs and only 777 apprentices. Today, there are nearly 1,000 companies with RAPs, and we have served nearly 29,000 apprentices in South Carolina since 2007. There is no one root cause to this growth; rather, there have been several important factors that have contributed:

1. Apprenticeship Carolina was strategically placed from the outset within the South Carolina Technical College System. This placement benefitted from the 16 Technical Colleges that have already established relationships with business in local markets. Apprenticeship Carolina was given instant credibility because of the stature of the colleges in the State.
2. Apprenticeship Carolina embraced an intermediary approach to apprenticeship development that makes the process easy for employers. Apprenticeship consultants walk employers through the apprenticeship development

and registration process at no charge to the company, regardless of the size of the employer.

3. Apprenticeship Carolina targeted industry sectors that are considered non-traditional for apprenticeships. Today, health care, hospitality and tourism, IT, and advanced manufacturing are among the top industries participating in apprenticeship in South Carolina.

4. Apprenticeship Carolina has a strong relationship with the USDOL. Together, Apprenticeship Carolina and USDOL have streamlined processes and made the registration of apprenticeship programs easy. Additionally, Apprenticeship Carolina has benefitted from nearly $7 million in USDOL grant money that has been used primarily to offset the education costs for apprentices in advanced manufacturing, IT, professional services, and health care.

5. South Carolina made a commitment in 2007 to be "all in" on apprenticeships. To aid in this, a unique tax credit was created to incentivize apprenticeships in a way that had not been done throughout the country at the time. The tax credit is $1,000 per apprentice for up to four years. This tax credit remains in place today.

6. Low unemployment rates have forced employers to become increasingly creative with how they will maintain a pipeline of talent coming into their operations. To assist in this, Apprenticeship Carolina is now encouraging South Carolina employers to consider sponsoring youth apprentices. The youth apprentices are generally juniors or seniors in high school and are dually enrolled in one of the 16 technical colleges. Upon completion, apprentices have a high school diploma, a credential from the USDOL, and often as much as 27 hours toward an associate's degree. To date, nearly 200 South Carolina employers have active youth apprenticeship programs.

A lesson that we have learned over the years with Apprenticeship Carolina is that the needs of the employer or apprentice are not complete upon program registration. Employers also require assistance navigating various aspects of the apprenticeship, workforce, and education system that can be time-consuming and present roadblocks. Thus, it is imperative to allocate as many resources to providing ongoing technical assistance as has been allocated for program development. Technical assistance allows employers to explore expansion opportunities for apprenticeships, thereby allowing more opportunities for future apprentices.

A Case that Challenges the "Tracking" Myth

John:
You have gone from serving an apprenticeship in the (non-union) shipbuilding arena to earning a doctorate. Please explain how the "earn while you learn" model played a role in your ascent through the company ranks.

Dr. J. Scott Christman:

An apprentice graduate himself, Scott has more than 30 years of experience in apprenticeship. He currently serves as the vice president of the American Apprenticeship Round Table, a national organization that helps companies meet their requirements for an ample number of technically informed and skilled employees through apprenticeship.

The "earn while you learn" model played a significant role in my personal and professional success. Although my experience included an apprenticeship, it really began when I became employed with a larger company and ultimately became a legitimate member of that community. For most, learning—real learning—occurs situationally. It happens when individuals join a legitimate community and have to perform legitimately in situations. When this happens, learning becomes constructive and personal discoveries motivate the learner to seek additional knowledge to become more legitimate within the community. And that's what happened to me.

Upon graduating from high school, for one reason or another, I did not fall victim to the "college-only" trap. I entered a program that provided a dual system, one that provided formal education along with specialized training toward an occupation, and one that legitimately hired me to contribute to an organization through full-time employment. Here, I earned an associate's degree in a relevant field and gained the work experience that gave me an advantage over many of my peers entering the workforce. To do this, I joined a large employer that offered an apprenticeship program. It was while being an apprentice and working in a real community, and being provided legitimate feedback, that my motivation and understanding accelerated. For instance, after installing a component or adding value to a product in some way, when that job passed inspection, I was proud. Conversely, if the job failed, I was not happy, and I did all I could to learn from those mistakes so that it didn't happen again. As I learned and grew within the community, I gained self-worth and a sense of legitimacy, ultimately affecting my self-efficacy and the desire to advance even further into the community. Every time I gained a higher level of knowledge (i.e., a bachelor's or master's degree) or increased my level of skills, I gained a higher status of legitimacy within the community and ultimately more enthusiasm. Here, my learning had purpose.

Additionally, apprenticeship allowed me to become gently introduced to the community and not trusted upon it the ways so many are today. Simply being labeled as an apprentice, in many respects, signaled to others that I was a learner-worker, and thus, allowed me to become acquainted with the tasks, vocabulary, and organizing principles of the community at a reasonable pace. The most influential figure overseeing and controlling my experiences and participation in the workplace community was my supervisor. Because I was an apprentice, my supervisor ensured that I received high-quality opportunities to discover solutions to situations that normally occur at the job site. With an emphasis on discovery, I was allowed to receive a deeper understanding of the business, as I was given the opportunity to reflect and articulate the information I was learning in my college classes to the job at hand. Applying trigonometric functions on the job while taking a college trigonometry class provides connectivity that is far superior to the make-believe scenarios and strategies that most schools create for their students.

Conclusion

The Good

As a supporter of the RA system for more than 30 years, this author would be the first to endorse evidence-based strategies to growing RAPs across the country, both horizontally and vertically. Being creative and having willing partners makes a world of difference. However, to suggest that the current system is too difficult to manage or navigate is seemingly nothing more than an excuse to not try and/or to burden the taxpayers with training obligations once considered the responsibility of businesses. A great example of growing an industry sector vertically is Apprenticeship 2000 in Charlotte, NC. The advanced manufacturing employers in this area stepped up to design, development, and implement a solution to meet their needs with the assistance of the DOL, area high school, and community college. When asked why his firm was involved with RAP versus an "in-house" apprenticeship, Walter Siegenhaler, from Max Daetwyler Corporation, said, "Firms need to look beyond what is merely just good for them and consider the impact of the community. Journey-worker status signifies recognition as a professional and offers portability" (Gaal & Johnson, 2016, p. 41).

Food for thought: Should firms—large or small—view training as an investment versus a cost when strategically planning workforce development?

The Bad

In this author's opinion, when it comes to putting "apprenticeship" on the map, the publishing of the Harvard Graduate School of Education's "Pathways to Prosperity" in 2011 opened the minds of government officials and school administrators across a broad spectrum. Furthermore, a report from such a prestigious institution allowed groups such as the National Governors Association, National Skills Coalition, and Association for Career and Technical Education (ACTE), to place "apprenticeship" squarely on their agenda. Unfortunately, this often came at a price. That price was the cost of watering down a system known for its rigor and high-quality. Soon, terms like apprenticeship (purposely not using the proper terminology of RA), work-based learning, and internships started to enter the space of USDOL's OA. One can only speculate that forces behind the scenes were pushing to soften the age-old and misinformed stigma of RAPs. In fact, after the delegates at the 2016 ACTE Convention fully endorsed both "paid and unpaid" internships under the guise of work-based learning, this author resigned from its national election process for the position of president. In general, to suggest that unpaid internships are for the benefit of the intern is a bit naïve and somewhat unethical, at least in the for-profit arena. Accordingly, Morrison (2018) notes,

> Internships have become increasingly popular...But the fact that so many are unpaid means many are a viable option only to those with the financial backing to support themselves for several months at a time, and without the imperative to earn money...This, in turn, puts another obstacle in the way of social mobility, preventing young people from breaking out of a cycle of disadvantage.
>
> *(para 3, 5, and 11)*

Food for thought: Should cheap labor serve as a major objective for creating a parallel system to one that has decades of success stories?

The Ugly

On one hand, this author cautions readers when analyzing the early outcomes of some of the programs more recently placed under the "glamour" spotlight. Most notably, the United Kingdom. In fact, McGurk and Allen (2014) proclaim, "...apprenticeship training in England has been resurrected from near-extinction in the 1980s, but continual reforms since then have resulted in a fragmented, mismanaged, poorly coordinated and under-resourced system" (p. 27). On the other hand, this author finds it ironic that the Trump administration often holds up the Swiss and German systems of apprenticeship as the world's gold standard when promoting the value of the apprenticeship concept to U.S. employers, but fails to acknowledge a key element of their tripartite success: the government's role, as in third-party unbiased oversight (the other two being labor and management)! Along these lines, *The Final Report* from the Task Force on Apprenticeship Expansion (TFAE, 2018) supports the notion that a parallel system to RAP is to be created, to be known as industry-recognized apprenticeship programs (IRAPs). Herein, industry associations and community-based organizations (functioning as intermediaries) will create, manage, and certify the IRAPs. Consequently, McCarthy, Parton, Tesfai, and Prebil (2018) warn that if IRAPs are allowed to outsource quality assurance and accountability measures, the system may be prone to conflicts of interest.

Equally disturbing is the Trump Administration's misguided focus on business as the major benefactor, while seemingly treating the apprentice as an afterthought. Wermes (2018) asserts that apprenticeship is, "[f]or the welfare and training of the apprentice." Yet the TFAE (2018) claims, "Many employers, especially small businesses, are concerned about the return on investment for developing apprenticeship programs" (p. 19). Interestingly, the TFAE goes on to further contradict itself when it posits, "Apprenticeships fill employers' skill needs while reducing unemployment and providing a debt-free career path for young people" (p. 14). Meanwhile, less than 15 pages later, the TFAE promotes the use of "income sharing agreement models" (p. 27). This appears to shift the training cost burden to the apprentice, versus the firm. As a result, one would need to question the following U.S. business axiom: "People are our most cherished assets." Not to mention, RAPs require and ensure apprentices receive wage increases upon successful completion of each term. Under the TFAE's proposal, IRAPs "are not required to follow specific wage progression rules" (p. 11).

Food for thought: Is bending the rules for the sake of scaling up apprenticeships nationwide worth the cost of potentially devaluing the very system the TFAE intends to improve/expand?

In Closing

Much of the activity surrounding the recent upsurge of interests in apprenticeship programs has to do with the perceived shortage of skilled workers. Both this author and Wharton School of Business Professor Peter Cappelli (2014) have on more than one occasion suggested that businesses need to move beyond this myopic view as few have considered the issue of the wage gap … until recent 2018 unemployment numbers hit the 3% range. From a tangential standpoint, the editorial board at the St. Louis Post-Dispatch (2018) further magnifies how misguided policies, at the state level, in Missouri, have legislators following the lead of the Chamber of Commerce, in essence exacerbating the current dilemma:

> The miscommunication between the two sides is glaringly obvious. When the business community calls for improvements to schools, the Legislature responds with tax breaks for business without a corresponding investment in workforce development. The lax attention to education then results in more complaints from business. The Legislature responds with more business tax cuts.
>
> *(para 4)*

This author wishes to make clear that growing apprenticeships in the United States can be a good thing—but not at all costs or for bogus reasons. Too often, small employers indicate that the current system overseen by the USDOL's OA is too burdensome. In St. Louis, the Carpenters' Union and its partner, the St. Louis Chapter of the Homes Builders Association, still build approximately 80% of the new homes within a 75-mile radius of downtown. Most of these residential builders are small firms (<25 employees)—and yet these builders, since the 1950s, have relied upon an RAP—known as the St. Louis Carpenters Joint Apprenticeship Program—to supply them with skilled entry-level carpenters. This system is self-funded—not asking for a government subsidy for training as a vital aspect of a successful business. When both labor and management have skin in the game, then together they tend to make decisions in the best interest of the apprentice on behalf of the industry. Make no mistake, the OA has been nothing short of helpful but never meddlesome—always ensuring that neither labor *or* management take advantage of the apprentice! To this end, it is disingenuous to continue the anecdotal mantra that today's RA system is broken and/or in serious need of repair. Therefore, in this author's opinion, the United States may be headed for a myriad of unintended consequences not unlike in the United Kingdom, unless and until unbiased empirical research is performed to support the full launch of the proposed parallel IRAP system.

References

Cappelli, P. (2014). *Skill gaps, skill shortages and skill mismatches: Evidence for the US.* Retrieved from http://www.nber.org/papers/w20382.pdf

Editorial Board - St. Louis Post-Dispatch. (2018, May 28). *Missouri falls behind as employers complain of a skills gap schools are not filling.* Retrieved from http://www.stltoday.com/opinion/editorial/editorial-missouri-falls-behind-as-employers-complain-of-a-skills/article_28afb05b-4e81-56f7-810d-44a3f0bca24b.html?mode

Gaal, J., & Johnson III, H. (2016, March). *The renaissance of registered apprenticeship programs.* Retrieved from https://www.acteonline.org/wp-content/uploads/2018/05/Techniques-March2016-RenaissanceRegisteredApprenticeship.pdf

McCarthy, M. A., Parton, B., Tesfai, L., & Prebil, M. (2018, May 11). *CESNA's first reactions to recommendations from the president's task force on apprenticeship expansion.* Retrieved from https://www.newamerica.org/education-policy/edcentral/first-reactions-apprenticeship-task-force/

McGurk, P., & Allen, M. (2014). *Apprenticeships in England: Impoverished but laddered.* Retrieved from http://iceres.org/wp-content/uploads/2014/10/Apprenticeships-in-England.pdf

Morrison, N. (2018, January 30). *Unpaid internships are pricing young people out of the best jobs.* Retrieved from https://www.forbes.com/sites/nickmorrison/2018/01/30/unpaid-internships-are-pricing-young-people-out-of-the-best-jobs/#4fb25ef77864

Task Force on Apprenticeship Expansion (TFAE). (2018, May 10). *Final report to: The President of the United States*. Retrieved from https://www.dol.gov/apprenticeship/docs/task-force-apprenticeship-expansion-report.pdf

Wermes, A. (2018, May 21). Pre-apprenticeship into registered apprenticeship. Webinar presentation to Iowa Department of Education.

13

CREDENTIALING IN THE 21ST CENTURY

Looking Beyond the Event Horizon

James Keevy, Volker Rein, Borhene Chakroun, and Lori L. Foster

Introduction

The recognition of learning through the award of work- and occupation-related qualifications is steeply entrenched into the history of education and training globally. In recent years, notably since the 1990s, qualifications frameworks have emerged as a new policy instrument that has attempted to improve the recognition of different forms of learning, the transferability of such recognition, and, ultimately, the mobility of individuals as global citizens (Keevy & Chakroun, 2015). At least three generations of qualifications frameworks have evolved since then, expanding with sectoral, national, and also regional coverage, and with wide international acceptance, although there has also been some criticism regarding their relevance and impacts (International Labour Organisation [ILO], 2017). Concerns have been raised about the promises of qualifications frameworks, while "very little has been documented about the effectiveness of [qualifications frameworks] in bringing about change in skills development systems or about their actual use by employers, workers, and training providers" (ILO, 2009, p. v).

In more recent research, it is acknowledged that there is "some evidence of impact, including possible indirect effects" (ILO, 2017). The fact that extensive policy borrowing has taken place is also a key theme in the research (see ILO, 2009 and also Chakroun, 2010). The view is also expressed that National Qualification Frameworks (NQFs) are not quick fixes, and caution should be taken before embarking on development and implementation when other parts of the education and training system may be weak and in need of funding and support. For many reasons, these and other findings are important for the current study on the role of skills development and skills recognition for supporting and extending the impact of a regional system of regulated labor mobility. A regional system must take into account that employers need to trust the qualifications that are being offered. Also, and importantly, the possession of qualifications is increasingly vital to gain access to labor markets (ILO, 2017, p. 55):

> And what has worked in the past may not carry on working. As diplomas and certificates become more and more necessary to gain access to labour markets, their possession also becomes less and less sufficient. For example, in France, a combination of qualification inflation, growing youth unemployment, and the growth of short-term contracts, may counteract embedded agreements about training levels and occupational levels.

The "upward drift of TVET" (Ibid.) is another important factor as employers are not always able to express what they require in skills development, resulting in unrealistic expectations and ultimately in a lack of trust in and employability of the qualifications holder. The ILO places strong emphasis on the building of institutions and strong relationships with social partners. We are in strong agreement with this point and it forms a central theme of this contribution. Another point to keep in mind is that a fixation with an NQF in the form implemented by some early starter countries should be cautioned against. NQFs take many forms and quite often require minimal adjustment to function effectively, without the need to radically transform the existing system:

> The incremental development of qualifications frameworks, building on existing systems, and not making unnecessary changes where there is trust in and understanding of systems and qualifications, are also important. Perhaps most importantly, the study clearly demonstrates the importance of the holistic approaches to the reform of work and of TVET systems, which the ILO has supported in principle for many years.
>
> *(ILO, 2017, p. 4)*

International qualifications are also important to mention here. This is a growing trend (see Cedefop, 2012) and fits rather uncomfortably with more established qualifications systems that are tightly managed by state agencies and are arguably also slower to adapt to new trends. Qualifications being offered across borders can play an important role in regions where there is extensive migration and national systems are underdeveloped.

Over the past five years, a fourth generation of qualifications frameworks has started to emerge, with a strong focus on credentials and the inclusion of 21st-century skills (also see Casillas, 2018). This most recent generation of qualifications frameworks has embraced new developments, including the digitization of credentials (Lumina, 2016), a closer alignment with credential evaluation methodologies (Dutch Organisation for Internationalisation in Education NUFFIC, 2012), and international recognition and agreements. On this last point, examples include the Lisbon Recognition Convention of 1997 in

Europe; the Revised Convention on the Recognition of Studies, Certificates, Diplomas, Degrees and Other Academic Qualifications in Higher Education in African States of 2014; and the Asia-Pacific Regional Convention on the Recognition of Qualifications in Higher Education of 2011.

In 2012, the UN Educational, Scientific and Cultural Organization (UNESCO) convened the Third International Congress on Technical and Vocational Education and Training (TVET) in Shanghai to debate current trends and future drivers for the development of education and training. This global dialogue culminated in the Shanghai Consensus, which recommended, among other things, the development of international guidelines by UNESCO on quality assurance for the recognition of qualifications based on learning outcomes. This included the proposal that a set of world reference levels (WRLs) be considered to facilitate the international recognition of TVET qualifications and implicitly other credentials as well. Looking beyond the reach of the existing qualifications frameworks, UNESCO convened a working group of international experts to contemplate a set of WRLs in 2013. In essence, the WRLs were conceived as a translation device that would be able, in the future, to act as a neutral reference point for the recognition of learning across countries, regions, and education sectors as well. A range of reviews, analysis, and developments have been conducted, including (i) publication on the use of level descriptors (Keevy & Chakroun, 2015); (ii) analysis of quality assurance arrangements in Asia-Pacific (Bateman & Coles, 2017); (iii) draft proposal for WRLs (Chakroun, 2016); (iv) referencing guidelines (Booker, 2016); and (V) a review of level descriptors internationally (Hart, 2017). More recently, the *Global inventory of regional and national qualifications frameworks* published by the European Centre for the Development of Vocational Training (Cedefop), the UNESCO Institute for Lifelong Learning (UIL), and the European Training Foundation (ETF) (Cedefop, UIL & ETF, 2017), while work by Keevy and Chakroun (2018) have further contributed to the process.

The Case of the Credentials Framework for the United States

Facing ongoing changes and increasing labor market and societal requirements, many countries worldwide promote transparency, comparability, connectivity as well as quality development of credentials in terms of competencies and learning outcomes achieved in any formal or nonformal way. In 2015, the *Lumina Foundation for Education* released a Credentials Framework (CF) for U.S. postsecondary education to address these targets. This instrument is intended to promote the strategic objective, that 60% of U.S. adults should obtain a high-quality postsecondary credential by 2025. The framework, therefore, addresses both degrees and all kind of nondegree credentials, such as certificates, industry certifications, licenses, apprenticeships, and badges. The Foundation proposed the development of new systems of quality credentials and credits, defined by learning outcomes and competencies rather than by time-to-completion, and which would offer clear and transparent pathways to students, assure high-quality learning, and address workforce requirements (Lumina Foundation, 2015).

Preceding Developments: Labor Market, Politics, and Education

To clarify the educational, economic, and political context of credentialing, this section analyzes, firstly, the framing conditions, drivers, and preceding developments on the labor market and in the education system and how they are politically addressed. As in other highly industrialized countries, the globalized knowledge-based economy in the United States requires a postsecondary education system that contributes significantly to the development of knowledge and skills to address the dynamic developments in not only technology and work organizations but in society as a whole. According to labor market and education projections, about two-thirds of job openings in the United States require at least some postsecondary education and training by 2018 (Carnevale, Smith, & Strohl, 2010). This includes an increasing number in the middle-skill occupations covered by workers with an associate's degree or an occupational certificate.

Nationwide standards for the quality and transferability of academic degrees do not exist in U.S. higher education. The credentialing process and the portability of noncredit bearing occupational learning are weakly regulated. As long ago as in 2005, the U.S. Government Commission on Education concluded that students must have clearer pathways between education levels, and institutions and colleges have to remove barriers to student mobility and promote new learning paradigms (U.S. Department of Education, 2005) and motivate students in persisting in programs progressing toward credentials. The political debate on postsecondary education focused on measures to promote institution and program accountability and to increase the completion of degree and non-degree credentials in order to address the relevant labor market demands for an advanced skilled workforce (cf. Birtwistle & McKiernan, 2010).

In 2010, the Lumina Foundation initiated the development of a Degree Qualifications Profile (DQP) framework for academic U.S. higher education to define educational quality in terms of student learning. More labor market-oriented initiatives were developed, including skills classification instruments. The CLASP report *Give credit where credit is due* (Bird, Ganzglass, & Prince, 2011) demanded the creation of a nationwide comprehensive and competency-oriented qualifications framework for all postsecondary education and training credentials to meet these targets.

Construction Characteristics and Challenges

The development of the CF is embedded in a worldwide trend in education and training systems to develop and implement qualifications frameworks in order to promote transparency, comparability, transferability, quality assurance, and quality development of credentials.

As in previously developed comprehensive qualifications frameworks for lifelong learning (cf. EU, 2008), the CF focuses on learning outcomes to address required competencies as common reference points in terms of what the learner knows and is able to do in colleges, with training providers, or in other contexts. The required learning outcomes are described in *knowledge* and *skills* subdivided in *specialized, personal, and social skills*. In the CF, *knowledge* and *skills* are regarded as learning domains of *competency*, which is classified as the overarching key term of the instrument. The competencies for each domain are described independently, but they have to be understood and used in combination with one another, as different credentials represent different patterns of competency attainment across domains. The eight levels categorize competencies and learning outcomes based on an increasing degree of complexity, depth, and breadth of knowledge and skills. The descriptors permit a scoring judgment for learning outcomes represented by a credential. The levels are designed in a credential-neutral manner, but a credential-specific profile can be addressed by different levels for each domain. The eight levels relate to de facto existing major levels of credentials in the U.S. education and training landscape; for example, a Ph.D. degree relates to level 8 and an associate's degree relates to level 5.

Conceptually critical is the inconsistency of definitions of key terms such as *competency*. The framework defines *competency* as a characteristic or as a capability of an individual, which contradicts the holistic and complementary approach of the learning domains in the framework. The instrument tries to facilitate lifelong learning, career pathways, and credentialing across education and training subsystems. However, referring to both study and work situations, the instrument does not describe requirements in a synthesized and comprehensive way.

Compatibility and Connectivity Toward Other Qualifications Frameworks

A specific challenge for the CF implementation is the compatibility and connectivity toward other capability-oriented frameworks in the field of education and work. For this purpose, the CF is compared with the sectoral DQP for U.S. higher education, with the Occupation Network (O*NET) and the European Qualifications Framework (EQF) for lifelong learning.

Degree Qualifications Profile

The comprehensive CF and the sectoral DQP frameworks share the same major objectives to promote transparency, comparability, portability, quality assurance, and quality development of credentials in terms of learning outcomes. All credentials addressed offer pathways or options, both sequential and non-sequential, for lifelong learning. Consistently, both frameworks promote the recognition of prior learning via the learning outcomes orientation.

The DQP approach is firmly set in the context of higher academic education, providing learning domains as reference points for what students should know and be able to do to address the requirements of associate's, bachelor's, and master's degrees across all fields of study. The DQP is focused on *proficiency* as the instrument's guiding key term, understood as a label for a set of demonstrations of knowledge, understanding, and skills that satisfy the levels of mastery sufficient to justify the award of an associate's, bachelor's, or master's degree in five learning domains: *specialized knowledge, broad and integrative knowledge, intellectual skills, applied and collaborative learning,* and *civic and global learning.*

In contrast with the DQP, CF is a broader overarching, comprehensive framework relevant not only to educators, but to lifelong learners, employers, and those responsible for measurement and assessment. The CF outlines the levels, types of competencies, and learning outcomes represented by diverse types of credentials, including degrees, industry certifications, and certificates. The CF and the DQP both focus on the domains *knowledge* and *skills*, with intersections and differences due to the aforementioned approaches of the frameworks, whereas the DQP only provides this overarching descriptor approach for the associate learning outcomes (Rein, 2016).

Occupation Network

As described in Dierdorff and Ellington (this volume), the U.S. O*NET reflects characteristics of relevant occupations and the workforce. The 2018 O*NET database contains numerous standardized occupation-specific descriptors on 974 occupations implemented in the public and private sector of the U.S. labor market. The database is continually updated from data provided by job analysts and job incumbents.

Every occupation is described by a competency mix of knowledge, skills, and abilities, performed in a variety of activities and tasks. They are characterized by a standardized, measurable set of 277 O*NET Content Model descriptors in six domains, describing the key attributes and characteristics of occupation-specific information and job requirements, worker requirements, and workforce characteristics and projections. Additionally, they provide occupational information to be applied across jobs, sectors, or industries (U.S. Department of Labor, 2018).

In spite of the different conceptual and functional approach of the CF and O★NET, the instrumental intersections and the alignment potential to support transparency, comparison, and connectivity of credentials is evident. Both instruments refer to a broad scope of different types of credentials such as degrees, certifications, and apprenticeship certificates. Furthermore, they use as well competency categories like knowledge and skills and in addition abilities to describe characteristics and requirements of occupations, jobs and the workforce.

European Qualifications Framework for Lifelong Learning

Following a joint comparative study of UNESCO, ETF, and Cedefop (2015), it is evident that qualifications frameworks internationally differ by their conceptual and structural organization concerning domains, descriptors, key terms, as well as by their regional national, regional, or sector orientation. Furthermore, they might include nonformal and informal learning, a credit transfer system, and they might provide a regulatory approach like the Scottish framework (SCQFP, 2001) or just provide a voluntary approach like the German framework (Federal Ministry of Education, 2011) for orientation purposes for specific education and training systems.

The EQF is an international example of a comprehensive meta-framework for lifelong learning (EU, 2008). The EQF was relevant for the CF development in the U.S. context as it had been designed as a meta-reference instrument for the different qualifications frameworks and systems of the European Union (EU) member states. Like the CF, the EQF tries to promote transparency, comparability, and the quality purposes and share the same voluntary orientation function to promote the shift to learning outcomes in specific education and training systems. The EQF concept and language had been developed broadly enough to be inclusive of the differences between states, industries, occupations, and education systems. But at the same time, it is specific enough to successfully define levels, learning outcomes, and performance measures (Rein, 2016).

As with the CF, the EQF covers eight levels of requirements and competencies. Furthermore, the experience in the connectivity of the EQF inside the EU and toward other countries and regions is relevant for the international compatibility of the CF as well. Both frameworks use the domains of *knowledge* and *skills*. The key terms of both instruments differ as follows. Based on a political compromise of EU member states and education sectors, the term *competence* in the EQF is very broadly defined as the proven ability to use knowledge, skills, and personal, social, and methodological abilities in work or study situations and in professional and personal development (EU, 2008). The CF document, by contrast, defines competency as learnable, measurable, role-relevant, and behavior-based characteristic or capability of an individual, which uses both constructivist and behavioristic approaches. In contrast to the EQF, the CF introduces in addition to the description of the required knowledge and skills, a domain-overarching level description based on competencies and requirements to address both academic and occupational requirements and competencies, respectively, all different types of quality-assured and certified credentials (Rein, 2016).

Implementation Challenges and Perspectives

In the CF vision, boundaries between occupational and academic orientations and between formal and nonformal become less important, trumped by the demand for the representation of all the learning an individual can acquire throughout life, and the recognition of this learning through credentials that are portable, validated, and valued in labor markets and more broadly, in the U.S. society.

In discussing these developments, the following questions are critical in terms of a sustainable acceptance and applicability of the CF across disciplines as well as education, occupational, and other areas of the society:

1. How and to which extent the CF in the United States will promote the implementation of the shift to competency-oriented learning outcomes and appropriate developments of curricula, didactic, and assessment approaches?
2. How will the CF facilitate cross-walking between credit and noncredit learning to assess prior learning, for example, between academic associate degrees and apprenticeship programs in terms of the benefit for educational institutions and learners as well as employers and employees?
3. Will the CF facilitate to improve licenses in terms of transparency, quality, and connectivity toward other credentials? And will it support the access to jobs and other formats to earn a living? Occupational licensing in the United States constantly increased during the past years (Carpenter, Knepper, Erickson, & Ross, 2012). This is embedded in the general trend to quality standards in education and training.
4. How will the sector overarching CF approach contribute to clarify the traditional concepts of *degree* or *certificate*, that is, the concept of connectible credentials (and associated competencies) that doesn't blur the essential characteristics of specific educational systems? The current guide to use the CF as a universal credentials translator recommends comparing competencies described by credentials via an atomized approach (Lumina, 2016). That said, connecting the atoms is essential in terms of a jobseeker having a marketable portfolio of credentials (even if it is not called a degree or certificate), or for any lifelong learner to understand and take advantage of pathways of micro-credentials.
5. How will the conceptual reference of the CF to study and work situations can be synthesized and can be extended to requirements situations of the broader society in terms of credentialing?

The success of the CF will not only be determined by the most appropriate construction and design, but critically by the way in which the stakeholders in the education and business sectors as well as in government organizations are being continuously involved and engaged in the development and implementation process right from the beginning. To increase acceptance, the Lumina Foundation started a national dialog including major stakeholders with an ongoing nationwide response how to create a more seamless and comprehensive system of credentials. The intention is to create a U.S. version of a zone of mutual trust between stakeholders (Coles & Oates, 2005) in terms of transparency and portability of achieved learning outcomes.

Since the CF had been implemented in 2016, roundtable discussions on the regional and national levels are taking place with increasing interest of educators, employers, and political bodies in order to improve the construction of the instrument and to promote the acceptance by U.S. postsecondary education. In 2017 *Connecting Credentials*, the Foundation's framing initiative started a number of programs to empower learners to navigate the credentialing ecosystem, to develop common language centered on competencies, and to foster shared understanding of credential quality and reciprocity among quality assurance processes. It promotes field-based development of new credentialing tools, policies, and practices and creates an interoperable data and technology infrastructure. *Connecting Credentials* pursues a public policy that advances equity in the credentialing ecosystem. Finally, a pilot alignment of credentials of all forms and types had been started to test the validity and applicability of the descriptors, levels, and domains (Lumina Foundation, 2016).

Developments in Europe, Africa, Asia-Pacific, and Australasia

The global trends in reforming qualifications systems is well captured by the third edition of the *Global inventory of regional and national qualifications frameworks* (Cedefop, ETF & UNESCO, 2017), which provides an up-to-date account of recent developments in different parts of the world. In Europe, the revised EQF (adopted 22 May 2017) is expected to play a key role in taking forward EU skills and lifelong learning strategies, with particular attention to transparency and portability of qualifications for better and larger mobility of learners and workers within Europe. The Global Inventory also reports on progress in developing other regional qualifications frameworks. For example, the Association of Southeast Asian Nations qualifications reference framework (AQRF) attained an operational status in 2017 and some countries such as Malaysia are preparing to reference their national frameworks to the AQRF. The Caribbean region is moving from regional vocational qualifications focusing on TVET qualifications to an overarching lifelong learning regional qualifications framework.

Initiatives in the South African Development Community (SADC) also illustrate this tendency where a network for credential verifications was recently established (JET Education Services, 2017).

At national level, the inventory indicates that more than 150 countries worldwide are at different stages of developing and implementing national qualifications frameworks. Most of these countries see learning outcomes-based and quality-assured qualifications as instruments for improving transparency and relevance of qualifications, and as a way to open opportunities to wider access to learning opportunities and certification of learning taking place in different settings.

Although, in the past, economic drivers clearly dominated the pressures for creating an NQF, qualifications frameworks are becoming increasingly shaped by broader developments objectives. This perspective is highlighted by Chakroun (2017) exploring the role of qualifications frameworks in addressing the 2030 Sustainable Development Agenda adopted by the United Nations in 2015. Chakroun (Ibid.) argues that NQFs cannot be defined according to a narrow set of economic objectives but need to be understood as a tool facing a multifaceted reality and contributing to objectives of economic growth, social equity, and sustainability.

The thinking on WRLs, as well as the development of qualifications systems and recognition of qualifications at national, regional, and international levels, has increasingly been impacted by the move toward the digitization of credentials. Recent developments that are engaging directly with the digitization of credentials include the Groningen Declaration Network (GDN), the Post-Secondary Electronic Standards Council, and the Common Student System in Norway—these all point to the importance to map the landscape, identify key actors, and chart with partners the future developments that lie at this critical event horizon.

Conventional degrees continue to serve an important purpose signaling to employers that a graduate is employable. Increasingly, however, there is dissatisfaction with the qualification (and the accompanying academic record) as a proxy for employability (Oliver, 2016). Alternatives are being mooted and, in some instances, already implemented, such as a digital passport, e-qualification (Chen-Wilson & Argles, 2010), "3D CV" (Oliver, 2016), and the seminal work by Bjornavold and Coles (2008) on "representation" that went by largely unnoticed. Representation is a concept that attempts to improve transparency by providing more information related to learning and learning outcomes, such as the changing value of qualifications in certain settings, occupational standards on which the qualification is based, the extent to which social partners contribute to the design and assessment of the qualification, the extent to which nonformal and informal learning is recognized, the quality of the providing institution, and also the extent to which learning has advanced since the award of the qualification. More broadly, these new developments should be considered in the context of Open Education (Bates, 2015; Wiley, 2014), where in addition to open credentials, massive open online courses (MOOCs) and open access to courses, open educational resources, open data, and other dimensions are impacting the way people learn and have their learning outcomes recognized and valued. In our view, the world stage is set for greater disruption in the world of learning and training the workforce. The challenge to policymakers is whether and how they embrace digital intermediation and look beyond the current event horizon.

Today, the ability of digital technology to create data management structures where users have increased ownership and control over their own data and where any kinds of certificates or learning achievements issued by organizations or firms can be permanently and reliably secured opens new horizons for the recognition of skills and qualifications within and across borders.

A key actor steering the development of the global digital credential ecosystem is the GDN. The GDN started in 2012, and by 2017 involved some 1,150 role-players. These include digital student data repositories, the education sector, international membership organizations, national and international public bodies, policy influencers and consultancies, the IT industry, evaluation and recognition bodies, and employment and professional licensing boards (Keevy and Chakroun, 2018).

We also see many rapidly evolving, potentially transformative technologies on the horizon. For example, a recent European Commission report (2017) exploring the introduction of blockchain in education finds that several areas of education and training will be impacted by the adoption of blockchain technology, including (a) the acceleration of the end of paper-based system for certificates, (b) reinforcement of users' ability to automatically verify the validity of certificates without the need to contact the organization that originally issued them, and (c) creation of data management structures, where users have increased ownership and control over their data and as consequence reduction of organizations' data management costs.

As countries, regional economic communities, and the international community struggle to develop a unified strategy to ensure better and fair recognition of skills and certification across-boarders, Keevy and Chakroun (2018) identified at least seven key implications for the recognition of learning: (1) ubiquity and interoperability should be based on agreed standards; (2) there is need to protect the learner (user); (3) digital technologies can lead to more transparent recognition of skills and qualifications required by employers, including transversal skills; (4) there is an inherent risk associated with open degrees and micro-credentials that the "whole will not be greater than the sum of the parts"—stated differently, that the stacking to form a macro-credential will not be conceptually sound and, as a result, be unrecognizable by employers; (5) quality assurance and governance systems need to be more responsive to the changing landscape; (6) digital credentials have the potential to enable the recognition of prior learning; and (7) government support and multistakeholder cooperation need to be effective. As a result, international cooperation should be directed toward (i) gathering and making accessible at scale credentialing information from all types of sources; (ii) developing methodologies for comparing credentials; (iii) addressing the multilingual challenges involved in processing credentialing data at international levels; and (iv) creating and promoting an international label for "open learning records."

A New Vision for Credentialing

Digitalization is changing the status quo, offering new ways for learners to acquire expertise and demonstrate what they know and can do (see Blivin, 2018). These opportunities are not usually geographically bound, and many are often low cost or free of charge. As such, they have the potential to transcend geography, socioeconomic status, and other borders. As discussed below, these emerging opportunities raise questions and generate concerns that need to be taken into account as the acquisition, demonstration, and recognition of learning and expertise becomes increasingly digital.

Several technological and digitization trends are happening, bot independently and in concert, to enable new pathways for developing and demonstrating knowledge, skills, and competencies. These include increased accessibility and affordability of mobile broadband as well as information and communication technologies, MOOCs, digital badges, gamification, the collection and analysis of big data, and artificial intelligence.

Information and communication technologies have become increasingly accessible worldwide, while Internet connectivity is also speeding up. According to the International Telecommunications Union (ITU, 2017), the growth of mobile broadband subscriptions has exceeded 20% annually in the past five years, with more than four billion subscriptions globally by the end of 2017. In addition, the price of mobile broadband has dropped an average of 50% over the past three years (ITU, 2017).

Increasing access to high-speed Internet worldwide improves access to education and training. MOOCs represent an important development in online learning. The term MOOC was first introduced in 2008, with the aim of providing free university-level education to as many students as possible. Stefanovic and Milosevic (2017) point out two key features of MOOCs: (a) open access such that anyone can participate in the course for free and (b) scalability such that courses are meant to support an indefinite number of students. An early example of an MOOC was an online course on artificial intelligence offered in 2011 by Sebastian Thrun, a Professor of Computer Science at Stanford University, and Peter Norvig, Director of Research at Google. The course was met with enthusiasm, with 160,000 registrants. Although no official credit was offered for course completion, students who finished the course were issued a Statement of Accomplishment (Downes, 2017). Today, MOOCs are offered by a variety of providers around the world, on a wide range of topics, such as operations management, philosophy, computer programming, data analysis, poetry, financial accounting, circuits, and electronics, to name a few examples. Three well-known MOOC platforms are Coursera, edX, and Udacity. MOOCs are largely free, though certification of the knowledge and competence acquired in an MOOC may require a fee (Keevy & Chakroun, 2018).

Many MOOCs and other online course offerings include assessments, which help the learner gauge and demonstrate mastery. Upon course completion, learners may be awarded course credit, certificates, or even digital badges. Digital badges are logos or icons that learners can collect and display to peers, prospective employers, and other relevant stakeholders online through personal websites and social media platforms such as LinkedIn. They are digital representations of learning outcomes that can be used to represent credentials, certifications, competencies, technical skills, "soft skills," achievements, and dispositions (Ford, Izumi, Lottes, & Richardson, 2015; Janzow, 2014). They can be used to signify the completion of a course, a qualification like problem-solving, or the accomplishment of any number of objectives such as creating a product, reading a book, participating on a team, publishing an article, teaching a seminar, or rebuilding a car engine (Ellis, Nunn, & Avella, 2016). Digital badges can be collected and "stacked," allowing learners to display a wide combination of skills and qualifications.

Digital badges are often associated with gamification, though the two trends are distinguishable (West & Randall, 2016). Badges can become gamification elements alongside points and leaderboards to motivate engagement by providing feedback toward goal attainment, and sometimes allowing learners to compete with themselves or others in an educational environment (Gibson, Ostashewski, Flintoff, Grant, & Knight, 2015).

Outside the educational context, games have become a popular mechanism for allowing people to test themselves and demonstrate their competence in a range of areas. A variety of platforms exist, including apps that serve as gamified psychological tests measuring characteristics such as empathy, integrity, intellectual curiosity, creativity, persistence, and prioritization (Economist, 2017; Peck, 2013). Playing these games for a mere 20 minutes generates megabytes of behavioral data, including how long players hesitate before taking an action, the sequence of actions chosen, how problems are solved, and so forth (Peck, 2013). Such apps may or may not be part of a learning platform. Some are primarily built to assess players' attributes, allowing employers to use them to identify desired characteristics in their applicant pools. As with MOOCs, there is the potential for knowledge, skills, and competencies demonstrated in these games to be represented in the form of digital badges and certificates, which can be shared online.

Advances in big data analytics and artificial intelligence coincide with the trends described above. New opportunities to understand people's behavior and underlying characteristics emerge as our working lives and our nonworking lives become increasingly digitized. Data are produced with each option that a mobile phone or computer user chooses and clicks, however seemingly insignificant. Such data quickly add up, resulting in reams of "big data," if such information is electronically captured and stored. Advances in data science, machine learning, and artificial intelligence can help make sense of such data, potentially revealing behavioral patterns and underlying characteristics such as skills and competencies. This can occur (a) via platforms that are built with the intention of measuring or surveying key attributes, and (b) by analyzing data captured more or less incidentally as people engage in everyday behaviors. First, as suggested earlier, behaviors and underlying characteristics can be discerned through deliberate actions taken in online learning, gaming, and assessment platforms. For example, learners' scores and time spent on practice exercises in an MOOC may provide information about their mastery of the subject matter at hand. Second, information about people's attributes can also be gleaned by "scraping" existing data—online searches, web browsing, credit card purchases, banking behavior, social media activity, and other information transmitted from mobile phones and wearable devices, which are capable of detecting physical activity such as footsteps and movement from one geographic location to the next. Already, analyses of the things people opt to "like" on Facebook have been shown to reveal their personality characteristics (Youyou, Kosinski, & Stillwell, 2015). This suggests a future in which it will be increasingly possible to identify potential if not key knowledge, skills, and competencies by examining the digital footprints that people leave behind in their work lives as well as their personal lives. The recent case of Cambridge Analytica, and the extent to which such data can be abused, is an important rider to consider in this new digital world.

Micro-credentials: Opportunities and Challenges

The preceding trends lead to a potentially disruptive pivot from macro-credentials (i.e., conventional qualifications) to micro-credentials (i.e., new credentials based on digital technologies). Micro-credentials help overcome limitations and invite additional lifelong learning and career-based opportunities. Clearly, they also create new educational, professional, and legal challenges with respect to coordination, quality control, and privacy.

From the perspective of the learner and the employer, micro-credentials offer the possibility of both granularity and flexibility. Rather than relying on traditional university degrees as a proxy for employability, micro-credentials allow employers to determine, in more precise detail, whether candidates have demonstrated specific knowledge, skills, and competencies of interest. As employers' needs evolve, micro-credentialing opportunities can as well, in a relatively rapid manner. Unlike the traditional academic pedigree, the low cost with which many micro-credentials can be acquired also potentially opens new doors for individuals from lower income households and from wider regions of the world. This presumes, however, adequate connectivity, equipment, and digital skills. Heightened reliance on technology in micro-credentialing creates a real risk that those lacking access to the digital revolution will fall further behind as workforce readiness and credentialing become increasingly digital. Smartphone-based credentialing is certainly an important alternative avenue to consider for less developed countries and context (Internal Labour Organisation, 2018).

There are also issues of quality control. There need to be systems in place to help learners and employers readily understand which digital learning opportunities and micro-credentials are valid. Learners need to be able to distinguish a high-quality educational opportunity from one that is not based on sound learning principles and content. Employers and other decision makers need assurance that the attributes represented by digital badges and other representations of micro-credentials have evidence for their quality and validity. Mechanisms that prevent cheating in obtaining micro-credentials are also essential. In short, verification—that is, checking the source and authenticity of a micro-credential—is a fundamental aspect of ensuring trust in novel forms of credentials and assessments based on big data (Keevy & Chakroun, 2018).

Learner control is a hallmark of micro-credentials. But this is a double-edged sword. Learner control gives students the freedom to pursue their own interests and paths. However, learners may not always be in the best position to make such choices. Lacking an expert mental model, they may not have the capacity to effectively sequence courses and learning experience to ensure the kind of scaffolding often needed for learning to occur. There is a risk that learning and expertise may become too fragmented, failing to result in a unified, meaningful whole. Even when learning does occur, another risk is a fragmented set of well-defined skills that are difficult to make sense of in combination. It is an open question whether and how frameworks for qualifications or credentials can address this demand. The American CF and the EQF have not yet offered appropriate solutions to align outcomes of learning beyond existing formats for credentials and qualifications.

Finally, issues pertaining to the interoperability of systems is a technical detail that can prove problematic if not attended to. Interoperability implies seamless exchanges between products such as badges from different vendors, or even between past and future revisions of the same product (Keevy & Chakroun, 2018). To trust in the process, learners need to be confident that their micro-credentials will be portable across platforms and over time. There must be some assurance that a hard-earned badge will not be forever lost, for example, to a technology upgrade or a system that becomes obsolete.

Concluding Comments

Education and training systems have always had both external and internal pressures and that will continue into the future. First, they will have to respond to the external demand for skills from the digital society and facilitate the transition to the new world of work. Second like other sectors, education and training systems will have to embrace digital transformation in all its guises. The ultimate aim of such transformation must be to deliver successful skills development policy outcomes in the context of the Sustainable Development Goal (SDG) 4, and specifically SDG 4.4: "to ensure inclusive and equitable quality education and promote lifelong learning opportunities for all, in particular to substantially increase the number of youth and adults with relevant skills for employment, decent jobs and entrepreneurship."

In sum, a number of technological and digitization trends are working together to provide new and innovative means to make credentials more transparent, portable, and stackable. In this vision, boundaries between countries and regions, between vocational and academic orientations, and between formal and nonformal become less important, trumped by a more accessible and flexible knowledge supply and structure for the learning an individual can acquire throughout life, and the recognition of this learning through credentials that are internationally portable, validated and accepted by the labor market, and by society in general. Digitization, note Keevy and Chakroun (2018), "will raise a number of important policy challenges including privacy, security, consumer protection, competition, taxation, new skills, cross-border and international delivery of education and training, new forms of credentialing, to name but a few." Its borderless nature renders international dialogue on credentialing more important than ever.

References

Bateman, A., & Coles, M. (2017). *Towards quality assurance of technical and vocational education and training.* Retrieved from http://unesdoc.unesco.org/images/0025/002592/259282e.pdf

Bates, T. (2015). *Teaching in a digital age.* BCCampus, Canada. Retrieved from https://www.tonybates.ca/teaching-in-a-digital-age/

Bird, K., Ganzglass, E., & Prince, H. (2011). *Giving credit where credit is due: Credentialing and the role of post-secondary non-credit workforce learning.* Washington, DC: Center for Postsecondary and Economic Success.

Birtwistle, T., & McKiernan, H. H. (2010). Making the implicit explicit: Demonstrating the value added of higher education by a qualifications framework. *The Journal of College and University Law, 36*(2), 512–564.

Bjornavold, J., & Coles, M. (2008). Governing education and training; the case of qualifications frameworks. *European Journal of Vocational Training, 42–43*, 203–235.

Booker, D. (2016). Global referencing processes: a comparative study. Input to the Fourth Experts Meeting on World Reference Levels, 21 May 2016. Unpublished.

Blivin, J. (2018). Competency based learning and employment. In F. Oswald, T. S. Behrend, & L. L. Foster (Eds.), *Workforce readiness.* Accompanying chapter in WFR Book.

Carnevale, A., Smith, N., & Strohl, J. (2010). *Help wanted, projections of jobs and education requirements through 2018.* Washington, DC: Center on Education and the Workforce, Georgetown University.

Carpenter, D. M., Knepper, L., Erickson, A. C., & Ross, J. K. (2012). *License to work. A national study of burdens of occupational licensing.* Arlington, VA: Institute for Justice.

Casillas, A., Kyllonen, P., & Way, J. (2018). *Preparing students for the future of work: A formative assessment approach.* Accompanying chapter in WFR Book.

Cedefop, UIL & ETF. (2017). *Global inventory of regional and national qualifications frameworks 2017. Volume I: Thematic chapters.* Thessalonica, Greece: Cedefop.

Chakroun, B. (2016). World Reference Levels of Learning Outcomes. Fourth Experts Meeting 21 May 2016, Cape Town, South Africa. Summary Report. Unpublished.

Chakroun, B. (2017). *Qualifications Frameworks in a sustainable development context.* Global Inventory of Regional and National Qualifications Frameworks, Vol. 1. Retrieved from http://unesdoc.unesco.org/images/0026/002603/260363e

Chen-Wilson, L., & Argles, D. (2010). Towards a framework of a secure e-qualification certificate system. *2010 Second International Conference on Computer Modeling and Simulation,* January 2010, Sanya, China.

Coles, M. & Oates, T. (2005). European reference levels for education and training. Promoting credit transfer and mutual trust. Study commissioned to the Qualifications and Curriculum Authority, England. Thessalonica, Greece: Cedefop.

Dierdorff, E., & Ellington, J. K. (2018). O*NET and the nature of work. In F. Oswald, T. S. Behrend, & L. L. Foster (Eds.), *Workforce readiness.* Accompanying chapter in WFR Book.

Downes, S. (2017). New models of open and distributed learning. In M. Jemni, K. Kinshuk, & M. K. Khribi (Eds.), *Open education: From OERs to MOOCs* (pp. 1–22). Berlin, Germany: Springer-Verlag.

Economist. (2017, January). Cognitive switch: The role of employers. *The Economist, 422* (9023), 7.

Ellis, L. E., Nunn, S. G., & Avella, J. T. (2016). Digital badges and micro-credentials: Historical overview, motivational aspects, issues, and challenges. In D. Ifenthaler, N. Bellin-Mularski, & D. Mah (Eds.), *Foundation of digital badges and micro-credentials: Demonstrating and recognizing knowledge and competencies* (pp. 3–21). Geneva, Switzerland: Springer International Publishing.

European Parliament and the Council. (2008). Recommendation of the European Parliament and of the Council on the establishment of the European Qualifications Framework for lifelong learning (2008/C 111/01). *Official Journal of the European Union.*

Federal Ministry of Education. (2011). *German qualifications framework for lifelong learning.* Berlin, 23.03.2011. Retrieved from http://www.dqr.de

Ford, E., Izumi, B., Lottes, J., & Richardson, D. (2015). Badge it! A collaborative learning outcomes based approach to integrating information literacy badges within disciplinary curriculum. *Reference Services Review, 43,* 31–44.

Gibson, D., Ostashewski, N., Flintoff, K., Grant, S., & Knight, E. (2015). Digital badges in education. *Education and Information Technologies, 20,* 403–410.

Hart, J. (2017). World Reference Levels Expert Group—6th meeting. Paper one: draft rationale. Unpublished.

Holzer, J. (2018). *Technology and workforce readiness: Implications for skills training and the economy.* Accompanying chapter in WFR Book.

ILO. (2009). *Researching NQFs: Some conceptual issues.* Stephanie Allais, David Raffe, Michael Young. Employment Sector Employment Working Paper No. 44 2009.

ILO. (2017). *Labour market impact of National Qualification Frameworks in six countries.* Geneva, Switzerland: ILO.

ILO. (2018). The potential of skills development and recognition for regulated labour mobility in the IGAD region. A scoping study covering Djibouti, Ethiopia, Kenya, Uganda and Sudan. James Keevy, Andrew Paterson and Kedibone Boka. Forthcoming.

International Telecommunications Union. (2017). *ICT facts and figures 2017.* Retrieved from https://www.itu.int/en/ITU-D/Statistics/Documents/facts/ICTFactsFigures2017.pdf

Janzow, P. (2014). Connecting learning to jobs through digital badges. *The Catalyst, 42*(2), 9–11.

JET Education Services. (2017). Southern African Development Community Regional Qualifications Framework: Analytical Review of Level Descriptors. Research report prepared for the SADC Secretariat. Unpublished.

Keevy, J., & Chakroun, B. (2015). *Level-setting and recognition of learning outcomes. The use of level descriptors in the twenty-first century.* Paris, France: UNESCO.

Keevy, J., & Chakroun, B. (2018). *Digitalisation of credentialing: Implications for the recognition of learning across borders.* Paris, France: UNESCO.

Lumina Foundation. (2015). *Connecting credentials.* A beta credentials framework. Indianapolis, IN: Lumina Foundation.

Lumina Foundation. (2016). *Connecting credentials. Lessons from the National Summit on credentialing and the next steps in the national dialogue.* Indianapolis, IN.

NUFFIC. (2012). *European area of recognition manual. Practical guidelines for fair recognition of qualifications.* The Hague, The Netherlands: Nuffic.

Oliver, B. (2016). *Better 21C credentials. Evaluating the promise, perils and disruptive potential of digital credentials.* Geelong, VIC: Deakin University.

Peck, D. (2013). They're watching you at work. *The Atlantic, 312*(5), 72–82, 84.

Rein, V. (2016). *Making an American Credentials Framework. Intentions, Construction, Challenges and Perspectives.* Retrieved from https://bibb.academia.edu/VolkerRein

Scottish Credit and Qualifications Framework Partnership. (2001). *Scottish Credit and Qualifications Framework.* Retrieved from http://www.scqf.org.uk/

Stefanovic, N., & Milosevic, D. (2017). Innovative OER model for technology-enhanced academic and entrepreneurial learning. In M. Jemni & M. K. Khribi (Eds.), *Open education: From OERs to MOOCs* (pp. 337–359). Berlin, Germany: Springer-Verlag.

UNESCO, ETF, & Cedefop. (2015). *Global inventory of regional and national qualifications frameworks.* Vol. I/II. Thessalonica, Greece: Cedefop.

US Department of Education. (2005). *Education in the United States.* Washington, DC: US DOE.

US Department of Labor. (2018). *Occupation Network.* Retrieved from https://www.onetcenter.org/

West, R. E., & Randall, D. L. (2016). The case for rigor in open badges. In L. Y. Muilenburg & Z. L. Berge (Eds.), *Digital badges in education: Trends, issues, and cases* (pp. 21–29). New York, NY: Routledge.

Wiley, D. (2014). *The Open Education Infrastructure, and why we must build it.* Retrieved from https://opencontent.org/blog/archives/3410

Youyou, W., Kosinski, M., & Stillwell, D. (2015). Computer-based personality judgments are more accurate than those made by humans. *Proceedings of the National Academy of Sciences of the United States of America, 112*, 1036–1040.

PROSPECTS AND PITFALLS IN BUILDING THE FUTURE WORKFORCE

Ruth Kanfer and Jamai Blivin

The chapters in this volume reflect one of the most consequential issues of the day—namely, how advances in technology and automation will affect the nature of working and employment in the 21st century. Obviously, this is an ongoing process and there is no definitive answer, but there is growing agreement among scholars and practitioners that recent advances in technology and automation herald the early stage of another "revolution" with respect to the organization, execution, and human experience of work. For some people in the workforce, technology and automation has already led to job displacement and major life changes. For young people preparing to enter the workforce, advances in technology and automation speak directly to the question of workforce development and readiness. What knowledge, skills, abilities, and other attributes will be most valued in the 21st century? What knowledge and skills should be prioritized in education? How should education be delivered to improve employability for all segments of the population, not just immediately after graduation but throughout a working life that may last five or more decades? For organizations, advances in technology and automation offer both opportunities and challenges. Innovations in the organization and production of work, brought about by new technologies and automation, are creating a sea change in organizational thinking about the attributes that make for a desirable employee, the costs and benefits of new generation training strategies, and how to effectively manage an increasingly diverse (and robotic) workforce. For public policymakers and societies, the transformation taking place has spurred discussion and implementation of new policies and programs to help people cope with the myriad consequences associated with job loss, occupational transitions, and reskilling. As the chapters in this volume attest, understanding the effects of technology and automation on the future of work and identifying the needs for workforce development to meet that future is a complex, wicked, and urgent problem.

In spring 2018, the editors convened a workshop at the Stanford Center for Advanced Study in the Behavioral Sciences aimed at fostering exchange among scientists, educators, organizational leaders, and policymakers on the challenges associated with addressing the intertwined questions about the future of work and improving workforce readiness in the 21st century. Workshop discussion was informed in part by the 2018 National Academies of Science report documenting the current and anticipated impact of information technology on work and its implications for research, educational practice, organizational practices, and public policy. With this report as background, three broad conference themes emerged. The first theme pertained to how automation and technological advances compel a more nuanced conceptualization of the nature of work and work activities, the impact of automation and technology on the distribution of employment opportunities, and the implications of these developments on patterns of employment and worker well-being. A second, related conference theme focused on workforce readiness, including identification of critical person attributes, educational challenges, and exemplar policies and programs that promote workforce development of key attributes. The third theme addressed the numerous ways that public policy and research findings can help to shape the development of workforce readiness for future work. Consistent with these themes, the present volume organizes and expands on these issues in four major sections: education, employment, technology, and policy.

Understanding Work. How policymakers conceive the future of work critically shapes the goals and methods used to advance workforce readiness. Two valid points of view exist. The first, practical point of view derives from a consideration of how technology and automation are changing the work and employment landscape, and the human skill sets that will be most highly valued by employers in this new landscape. Building on recent trends and developments, Dierdorff and Ellington, and Guzzo describe how automation and technology can be expected to change what employee resources will be needed in the future. For example, technology has already begun to significantly influence the organization of work. The growing use of teams and multiteam systems, in which employees are not co-located and/or perform tasks in asynchronous manner, has focused employer attention on inter- and intrapersonal skills that facilitate collaboration and underlie complex competencies such as leadership. Other chapter authors envision a future of work in which automation and robots will take over many repetitive tasks, leaving humans to perform tasks and work that requires strong cognitive competencies in areas such as critical thinking, problem-solving, and creativity. Still others describe how automation and new technologies encourages employers to place greater value on individuals who possess high levels of digital literacy and content knowledge in STEM areas. Taken together, these authors emphasize a world of employment opportunities and work experiences that require a different portfolio of knowledge and skills than emphasized in the past—a portfolio that emphasizes not just knowledge but also process competencies for learning, problem-solving, working with others, and effective self-management of motivation and emotion.

A second, person-oriented point of view on the future of work highlights the experiences and consequences of automation and technology in work for human well-being. In the opening chapter, Douglas et al. (2018) address this issue in terms of the ramifications of technology and automation for the opportunity and experience of decent work. Building on the definition of decent work by the International Labor Organization (ILO, 2008, 2012), Douglas and his colleagues describe the psychological as well as the economic benefits of work that contribute to worker well-being, and in turn society. They argue that workforce development programs must go beyond existing vocational models of person-job fit to understand how the broader context in which individuals live critically affects opportunities and constraints in the pursuit of decent work. Perhaps most importantly for the topic of workforce readiness, Douglas et al. note four person and societal attributes that moderate the negative effects of less privileged life circumstances: proactivity, critical consciousness, social support, and public policies that promote employment and training. These themes, running throughout the volume, imply that the future of work is not univocally determined by technology and automation, but rather by their interaction with societal, organizational, and individual factors as they enable the satisfaction of basic human motives and needs.

A final issue in understanding the future of work pertains to the current and anticipated changes that automation and technology have for employment biographies. Through much of the 20th century, individuals entered an occupation or career with the expectation of employment in that field until retirement. Economic and technological changes have challenged that view. Although individuals continue to prepare for entry into a particular occupational cluster, there is growing evidence that employment biographies in the future will be increasingly characterized by periods of unemployment, reskilling, and periodic engagement in gig work. For many new entrants, employment represents a less permanent state of affairs and a stronger commitment to developing social networks and skills to sustain job search and learning.

Work in the Future. Developing an effective workforce readiness policy critically depends on understanding the tasks and roles individuals will perform and their associated attributes. In this domain, there appears to be general agreement on two points: (1) advances in automation and technology will increase marketplace demand for digital literacy and foundational knowledge in STEM areas, and (2) there will be strong demand for individuals who possess high levels of socioemotional and nonability skills that currently lie beyond the capabilities of deep learning agents, such as critical thinking, complex problem-solving, effective communication, leadership, proactivity, and self-management of motivation and emotions. Nonetheless, as Holzer notes, the implementation of technologies will likely be uneven over time and industry. In addition to the creation of new jobs that do not exist currently, there will remain a market for jobs (e.g., service sector jobs) that do not place high value on STEM knowledge and/or proactivity for some time.

This conceptualization of the future of work has direct implications for workforce development. For example, as Schneider and Young explain, all other things equal, changing market demands brought about by technology and automation advantages individuals with higher levels of digital literacy and sufficient resources to complete higher levels of formal education, particularly in STEM areas, and so has the potential for further exacerbating income and minority inequality absent the development of mitigating public policies and educational efforts. As a consequence, a critical aspect of workforce readiness pertains to developing content knowledge in these areas. This is particularly the case for aging societies with a shrinking young adult workforce.

Workforce Readiness: Knowledge and Skills

As Hilton notes, the 2012 National Research Council tasked with identifying 21st-century skills to be developed in K-12 or higher education organized knowledge and skills into three distinct but related competency areas: cognitive, interpersonal, and intrapersonal.

Several chapters (e.g., Renninger & Hidi, Castillas et al., Schneider & Young) focus on the development of socioemotional workforce readiness during K-12 education. A common theme running through these chapters is the emphasis on developing socioemotional skill sets that enable the effective self-management of motivation, behavior, and emotion. In contrast to procedural skills needed to operate machines and robots, or content knowledge necessary for innovation, socioemotional skill sets pertain to the development of proficiency in modulating self-processes for these activities. It is important to note that self-management skills are typically developed in the context of a purposive activity, such as solving a difficult math problem or designing a new program. As such, these skills are typically developed *in the context of learning or problem-solving* and can be developed in a variety of knowledge domains where learning is largely under the control of the learner. Although the immediate rationale for developing socioemotional skills typically focuses on findings that indicate employers are placing an increasing premium on these skills, it is also the case that these skills provide students with critical tools for lifelong learning. For example, in their chapter on the development of interest, Renninger and Hidi discuss the notion of interest. In their description of the development of interest, they point out that interest serves to help individuals find personal meaning in work and learning activities. In the context of education, interest is a key component of educational interventions to develop STEM area competencies.

The call for socioemotional skill development during the individual's first two decades of life is not new, but advances in technology and automation are spurring the development of educational/curricular programs aimed at explicitly developing these skills. The work presented in this volume suggests three reasons that the development of such skills may benefit students in the 21st century. First, socioemotional skills reflect the development of personal attributes that provide the foundation for learning. When developed early in the life span, having such skills can be expected to confer some resilience with respect to skill obsolescence in later adulthood. That is, the development of these skills in early education provides individuals with the psychological tools for extending and developing new bodies of knowledge across the life span and beyond the traditional structure provided in formal educational settings. Second, the development of socioemotional skills often occurs within but differs from the development of domain-based knowledge. Whereas some domain-based knowledge may become obsolete, socioemotional skills are represented in the individual's psychological makeup and can be expected to deepen and be applicable across the life span. The development of competencies and confidence for problem-solving, persistence, and performance alone and in teams during education provides a scaffold for meeting the many challenges that occur in the workplace. Third, the development of socioemotional skills has positive implications for adult development and worker well-being over the life span. In a work world characterized by uncertainty, such skills provide individuals with tools for remastering occupational identity and coping more effectively with periods of unemployment.

Another personal attribute often cited as highly desirable by employers and supported by empirical research is proactivity. Individuals high in proactivity are characterized as future-focused and more likely to self-initiate action than those low in this attribute. Although proactivity is often considered more trait-like, there is growing evidence that culture and methods of instruction can play a major role in the development of a more active and engaged orientation toward learning, work, and the pursuit of employment.

Workforce Readiness: Programs

Several chapters in this volume describe educational programs and policies aimed at developing socioemotional skills. As Casillas and his colleagues note, since socioemotional skill development focuses on self-related processes rather than achievement per se, programs to build these skills require different methods for assessing and monitoring action than is typically used in educational settings. Casillas et al. describe a principled, action-based approach, while Schneider and Young describe the contextual features of such programs (e.g., social support) that are particularly important for skill building among low-income and minority youth.

Although most workforce readiness programs focus on skill development in the K-12 setting, Gaal and Ainspan et al. describe a readiness program in use by the military to aid adults in the transition to civilian employment. Unlike the readiness programs for adolescents, the military program focuses provides structural guides to assist exiting military personnel in identifying viable occupational options and developing the social skills associated with work and nonwork challenges encountered during job pursuit.

As several authors note, the scale and diversity of workforce development programs to develop socioemotional skills makes their efficacy difficult to properly evaluate. All too often, the success of these programs is evaluated by the attainment of performance or work objectives. The development of common tools for age- and content-relevant strengths and deficits with respect to self-management and working with others is a critical need.

Workforce Readiness: Policies

The adoption of new technology, expansion of data integration, and expansion of new work and learn strategies pose particular challenges to both businesses and policymakers. While automation will surly increase productivity for the U.S. economy, companies will need to adopt new technologies rapidly, which leaves policy implications complex. How will policies catch up accordingly to the rapid technological environment we are living in? With policies representing a lagging indicator, this poses policy challenges for businesses and government and ultimately impacts the worker and learner in big ways.

Questions addressed throughout this book challenge how economies and companies will be able to leverage these new technological advances while assuring workers adapt to the changing environment of workforce. Retooling becomes even more critical as automation reduces job positions. And, understanding what automation *produces* in new jobs is also a critical policy driver. Throughout the globe, "future of work" summits are occurring. Companies like Amazon, JP Morgan, McKinsey, and Google are speaking about the future of work.

Key policy discussions are evolving around topics such as:

- Benefits—How can we assure benefits are available via technology and more modern infrastructures?
- How can we infuse the workforce system with more transferable skills and training resources?
- How does O★NET become more vibrant as jobs and their KSABs (knowledge, skills, abilities, behaviors) change with the technological economy?
- How do we merge the landscape of working and learning, as 80% of learners must work while they learn?

- How do funding formulas change across states (from both DOL and DoEd federal funding) to create more flexibility for lifelong learning?
- How do Eligible Training Provider lists approved by states become more flexible and open to learners, employers, and workers?
- How do we assure resources are made available broadly to all learners and that there are supporting systems to assure low-income and entry-level learners have the resources they need to move to middle-skill jobs?
- How will the future of work change—with companies such as Task Rabbit and more contracting work becoming the theme of the future?

> We do recognize the inability to predict what will happen in the future. But, the trends are already being shown and data shows that the "nation is upside down" when it comes to access for most U.S. citizens. (Blivin/Mayo/Jassal http://innovate-educate.org/a_nation_ upside_down/). Policy will be a critical driver for the future of workforce success. And, it must not lag too much, or the entire system is at risk for failure in providing successful strategies to citizens.

Using Technology as a Workforce Readiness Tool

Multiple chapters in this book address data and technology and the use of technology in expanding workforce readiness. Having a deeper understanding of workforce readiness requires a transformation in both the use of data and how the technology reaches the end-user (both employer and candidate). Philanthropy has funded experiments in this space, as highlighted in the chapter on Impact Hiring. However, the author notes that although well designed, these experiments were more exploration around solutions and best viewed as early indicators of new ways to hire nondegreed higher risk candidates.

In a recent article in the *Wall Street Journal,* see https://www.wsj.com/ articles/employers-eager-to-hire-try-a-new-policy-no-experience-necessary-1532862000. Companies are beginning to look at data in new ways, realizing that the degree and experience requirements are preventing them from finding competitive talent. But, the capturing of data is difficult, and companies remain very cautious is sharing incumbent data, retention, and outcomes from new ways to hire. As the authors note, individual employers have a great deal to gain from the application of talent analytics. In addition, technology must catch up to reach the consumer (i.e., the learner/job candidate). Harry Holzer in his chapter notes the need to begin creating "lifelong learning" systems to help workers more easily retrain under future of work circumstances. Currently, job platforms are very disconnected between job search, lifelong learning, retraining, and support services. Job and workforce learning platforms must be more inclusive to reach hard-to-serve populations, and workforce resources must include services including transportation, childcare, and other critical services that are proven to impact workforce success. Technology advancements must be made in connecting workforce and workforce indicators to assure workforce success. This work around data and technology is still in its infancy stage in many ways and more powerful piloting and research must continue to assure a transformative workforce for the future of working and learning.

Final Comments

This volume describes the promising possibilities by which to improve workforce readiness in the 21st century. As with each "revolution," the changing nature of work associated with automation and technology entails job loss and job gain. Whether (as feared by many) job losses ultimately outweigh job gains, and the nature of future jobs for promoting a healthy citizenry, remains an important but empirical question. At a more manageable level, however, is the question of how to prepare the current and future workforce for coming changes. The chapters in this volume provide a wealth of evidence for what changes to expect, how these changes can be implemented in practice, and the critical educational and public policy changes that need to take place in order to equip citizenry with the tools and resources to adapt and remain part of the future workforce. Toward this goal, we highlight an issue that we view to be critically important in this endeavor.

Although demographics is not destiny, it has powerful implications for the task of building a ready workforce and lessening the disruptions of technology-driven transitions in the workplace. As Ainspan et al. note, we cannot be focused solely on educational reformation efforts for future entrants. Advancing workforce readiness also involves broader sociopolitical support for the transition of working-age adults and older workers in public and private sector firms. Findings in the workforce aging literature, for example, show a rapid decline in job search success among individuals over the age of 50 (Wanberg, Kanfer, et al., 2015). Public and corporate support is needed to develop more effective HR practices (e.g., job crafting), employee development programs, and adaptive job design interventions that allow these persons to continue to participate and contribute to organizational objectives.

In summary, the editors and contributors to this volume have done an excellent job delineating the issues and the way forward in confronting the challenge of technology and automation for human work. We can only hope that this marks the beginning of a wider initiative that provides all citizens a place in the future of work.

References

Blivin & Mayo (2018). *A nation upside down: A new vision for the future of learning.* Santa Fe, NM: Innovate+Educate.

Gee, K. (2018, July 2018). *Employers eager to hire try a new policy: 'No experience necessary'.* The Wall Street Journal. Retrieved from https://www.wsj.com/articles/employers-eager-to-hire-try-a-new-policy-no-experience-necessary-1532862000.

International Labour Organization (2008). *Measurement of decent work: Discussion paper for the Tripartite Meeting of Experts on the measurement of decent work.* Geneva: International Labour Organization.

International Labour Organization (2008). *World of work report 2008: Income inequalities in the age of financial globalization.* Geneva: International Labour Organization.

International Labour Organzation (2012). *Decent work indicators: Concepts and definitions.* Geneva: International Labour Organization.

National Academies of Sciences, Engineering, and Medicine (2017). *Information technology and the U.S. workforce: Where are we and where do we go from here?* Washington, DC: The National Academies Press.

National Research Council (2012). *Education for life and work: Developing transferable knowledge and skills in the 21st century.* Washington, DC: The National Academies Press.

Wanberg, C. R., Kanfer, R., Hamann, D. J., & Zhang, Z. (2016). Age and reemployment success after job loss: An integrative model and meta-analysis. *Psychological Bulletin, 142*(4), 400–426.

INDEX

Note: Page numbers followed by "n" denote endnotes

Lightning Source UK Ltd.
Milton Keynes UK
UKHW020038260322
400650UK00021B/500